The Secret Revelation

4-29-01

To Irminio

Enjoy the truths
within
Stella Riego

The Secret Revelation

Unveiling the Mystery of the Book of Revelation

Stella Religa

with **Byron Belitsos**

Origin Press/Celestia
Novato, CA.

Origin Press/Celestia

1122 Grant Ave, Suite CA. Novato, CA 94945
888/267-4446 • ikosmos.com/Celestia

Publisher's Cataloging-in-Publication
(Provided by Quality Books, Inc.)

Religa, Stella,
    The Secret Revelation: unveiling the mystery of
the book of revelation / Stella Religa with Byron
Belitsos.—1st ed.
        p. cm.
        LCCN: 00-111955
        ISBN: 1-931254-07-9

    1. Bible N.T. Revelation—Criticism, interpretation,
etc. 2. Urantia Book—Criticism, interpretation, etc.
I. Belitsos, Byron, 1953—11. Title.

BS2825.52.R45 2001   228.06
                               QB101-700044

Printed in the United States of America
10 9 8 7 6 5 4 3 2 1

Table of Contents

When in temporary exile on Patmos, John wrote the Book of Revelation, which you now have in greatly abridged and distorted form. This Book of Revelation contains the surviving fragments of a great revelation, large portions of which were lost, other portions of which were removed, subsequent to John's writing. It is preserved in fragmentary and adulterated form.

—*The Urantia Book,* p.1555

Jesus Speaks with the Apostle Nathaniel

"The Scriptures contain much that is true, very much, but in the light of your present teaching, you know that these writings also contain much that is misrepresentative of the Father in heaven, the loving God I have come to reveal to all the worlds.

"...The thing most deplorable is not merely this erroneous idea of the absolute perfection of the Scripture record and the infallibility of its teachings, but rather the confusing misinterpretation of these sacred writings by the tradition-enslaved scribes and Pharisees at Jerusalem. And now will they employ both the doctrine of the inspiration of the Scriptures and their misinterpretations thereof in their determined effort to withstand these newer teachings of the gospel of the kingdom. Nathaniel, never forget, the Father does not limit the revelation of truth to any one generation or to any one people. Many earnest seekers after the truth have been, and will continue to be, confused and disheartened by these doctrines of the perfection of the Scriptures.

"The authority of truth is the very spirit that indwells its living manifestations, and not the dead words of the less illuminated and supposedly inspired men of another generation. And even if these holy men of old lived inspired and spirit-filled lives, that does not mean that their words were similarly spiritually inspired...

"Mark you well my words, Nathaniel, nothing which human nature has touched can be regarded as infallible. Through the mind of man divine truth may indeed shine forth, but always of relative purity and partial divinity. The creature may crave infallibility, but only the Creators possess it."

—from *The Urantia Book,* pp.1767-8

Acknowledgements

My heartfelt gratitude goes to my many unseen friends, including Christ Michael (Jesus Christ), Corelli, Solonia, Aflana, Meister Eckhart, and to the Apostle John (John Zebedee) for his permission to correct his work, as imperfect as this attempt may be. Without their guidance and help, this book would have been impossible.

My thanks also to my editor and publisher Byron Belitsos for accepting and publishing this controversial work. Also I want to thank Norman Ingram for his support and encouragement; my son James Religa and Bob Lawson for their computer expertise; my daughter Sharilyn Religa for her practical, no-nonsense approach to life; and to my other son Robert Religa who opened a new vista of thought by his gift of *The Urantia Book*.

A special thanks is also due to Duane L. Faw, whose reference work *The Paramony* was essential in directing me to those passages in *The Urantia Book* which most closely correlated with the Book of Revelation.

Another reference of inestimable importance was Clyde Bedell's *Concordex of The Urantia Book*. This devoted man spent almost a lifetime, long before computers were available, lovingly indexing every topic, name, sentence of this vast text, and all of Jesus travels and teachings—almost an encyclopedia in itself. His admonition was: "Why are you so slothful in going about our Father's business?"

I thank all of you for the privilege of being able to serve and to go about my Father's business. I hope I have not been slothful.

— Stella Religa

Preface

Armageddon, the Rapture, the Antichrist, the end-times...Such scary terms are once again on the minds of millions of Christians—as they usually have been in times of crisis over the last two millennia. But are such cataclysmic events really imminent? Are the end-times almost upon us? Even as I write this, the *Left Behind* series of novels are the best-selling religious books in the country. Its authors use literal interpretations of ancient biblical prophecies as a basis for a contemporary drama involving the physical disappearance of true believers (the so-called Rapture), the seizure of world power by the Antichrist, the rebuilding of the temple in Jerusalem, mad travails for the "left behind" nonbelievers, and much more. But are such images really a part of the divine plan for our planet or are they merely a false sword of Damocles hanging over the heads of believers and nonbelievers alike?

The Secret Revelation shows that, despite the sincerity of generations of Christian believers, there is in reality no prophetic or factual basis for such ideas. The Christian myth of the end-times arises from the unfortunate fact that much of what we call the Book of Revelation is a fabrication that departs drastically from the original vision of John. The corruption of the original text—by scribes and priests who followed after John's death—has led many an honest Christian down a dangerous road toward a tragic misinterpretation of biblical prophecy.

While reinterpreting the Book of Revelation with celestial help, I have been fortunate enough to be presented with the original meanings that John of Patmos tried to convey, using as my reference a contemporary revelation called *The Urantia Book*, which is cited often throughout this book. The actual work of reconstruction of John's original message was accomplished with the direct guidance of a group of dedicated celestial beings who are introduced below. These unseen helpers did the actual reinterpretation of the text over a period of years, in response to my questions about each verse.

Thanks to the amazing Urantia Book, with its revealed biography of Jesus and so much more, I have come to a whole new appreciation of the Bible. The Urantia Revelation has also has led me to love Jesus all the more and to humbly appreciate his amazing love for us as shown in his incarnation on our planet; I believe it will do the same for you too. But of course this Jesus is a different person than the glorious Christ of the New Testament. The picture of Jesus that is newly revealed to us in the 700 pages of Part IV of *The Urantia Book* is even more glorious and vivid than the biblical Jesus.

What you will learn from *The Secret Revelation* is the startling reality that John's original message was one of great hope and love, a prophecy containing firm yet gentle warnings—rather than dire end-times prophecies. The sad truth is that most of the original vision of John was lost to the world a few centuries after his death.

Rather than a grim forecast of events based on the literal interpretations of a fabricated document, there is rather a spiritual renaissance that is occurring throughout the world. I say this in the face of all the wars, poverty, illiteracy, and disease that we read about. Our Father-brother Jesus, and the Apostle John, greatly desire to convey to us that despite the great challenges and difficulties ahead, this world is on the threshold of a golden age, an age of light and life. The coming new epoch will include the return of Christ, as well as other exalted celestial teachers, and will demonstrate that God's love for us is greater than we had ever imagined.

—S.R., with B.B.

Foreword

On February 27, 1996, my journey into the mystery of John's revelation began. I could never have imagined before that evening that casual televison browsing would eventually lead to my writing a book on of all subjects, the Book of Revelation, dictated by John of Patmos, the Apostle John, who is sometimes called St. John the Revelator, St. John the Divine, and other names. The odd truth is that the idea of revising the Book of Revelation came to me in a most ordinary way—through something that caught my eye one day when I was flipping televison stations with my remote control. But the actual writing of this book happened in a most extraordinary way.

As I changed stations that night, I was momentarily caught by the word "Armageddon" on a Christian station. Mumbling something to myself about depressing predictions for the future, I continued flipping.

On a hunch, I decided to return to the religious station to learn what they had to say. They were talking about Armageddon, the Rapture, the Antichrist's imminent appearance, other drastic scenarios of the end-times that were about to be fulfilled. The talk-show host and guests even seemed elated at the prospect of these things. My curiosity was piqued like never before.

Suddenly, I was hooked. From that day foreward, my search for the truth about these things began in earnest. In my research, I became very intrigued by a paragraph that I found in *The Urantia Book*, which is also quoted with the frontispiece for this book. This is what it had to say about the Book of Revelation:

> When in temporary exile on Patmos, John wrote the Book of Revelation, which you now have in greatly abridged and distorted form. This Book of Revelation

contains the surviving fragments of a great revelation, large portions of which were lost, other portions of which were removed, subsequent to John's writing. It is preserved in fragmentary and adulterated form. (1555)

As I read this passage I wondered just what parts of this great revelation were deleted or distorted? What were the true meanings of the many strange symbols John used that so profoundly affected the lives of Christians for 2,000 years? Could it be updated in the light of the teachings of *The Urantia Book*? If so, how could this be done? Were there other writings, other messages—even from the beyond—which could shed light on these hidden meanings? After all, much of the Bible was inspired through dreams, visions, even supposed conversations directly with God. Hadn't God spoken to Adam and Eve, to Abraham, and to the many prophets in the Old Testament? John of Patmos had also received a divine revelation. Maybe *The Urantia Book,* I thought, or the dramatic new celestial contacts then occurring in the Urantia community, could be of some help.

And then one day as I meditated something extraordinary happened. I began to see the most glorious visions. First to appear were jewel-like figures that changed into all sorts of colors, shapes and designs. Next I saw flowers of the most beautiful hues—and then buildings. Something very important was happening. I timidly mentioned this to the celestial teacher transmission group I was attending, but very briefly. [Details about how I came to join this group, and more general background, can be found in the section "More about the Author" at the end of this book.]

Now this was odd. In fact it was kind of scary. Was I being prepared for something? There was no way I could conjure these visions, as they came upon me involuntarily. But even with this experience, I would not allow myself to transmit a celestial being.

Finally one Sunday, after over a year of witnessing others transmit celestial teachers, I decided to try receiving. Suddenly I heard the words, "This is Corelli." Now, I thought she said "Corolla." Of all things, why am I thinking about a Toyota Corolla? No, I had misunderstood. It was indeed an ascended mortal named Corelli! She said she was my assigned teacher, and she had been eager to contact me. Later I learned that there were many other teachers who are anxious to contact mortals; in fact there is nothing special about being a transmitter/receiver, as it is called. Anyone anywhere may receive a personal teacher if they so choose. [See the sections on the new celestial teachers later in "The Appendex".]

Corelli later confirmed what I had heard from others. Something called the Teaching Mission had been planned long ago in association with the Urantia Revelation, and was now being put into practice. And these contacts were authorized by Michael of Nebadon [see glossary], known on our world as Jesus Christ. She also confirmed that our world is in urgent need of spiritual upliftment.

And so slowly, and informally at first, I began to ask my many questions about the Book of Revelation. I sought constant reassurance that what I was doing was approved by John and Jesus. Each time I was told to go ahead with the work, which they would support as much as they could. With my teachers' permission, I proceeded to ask questions almost line by line about the Book of Revelation. What an adventure this has proved to be!

In closing, I apologize if I have erred in what I heard from my celestial teachers and compiled in this book. Perhaps there are others who can and will do a better job of updating the Book of Revelation. However, if this information is correct, I hope it will be a source of inspiration and will add to your understanding of John's original vision. I also designed this book, with my editor's help, as an introduction to key teachings of *The Urantia Book*.

But the main purpose of this book is my attempt to bring John's glorious vision back to the world, with his permission. May it be as rewarding for you as it has been for me.

—Stella Religa
Whittier, California
March, 2001

Background on Translations and Biblical Traditions

As I pursued my project, I also wondered how the Bible was compiled. How did so many apparent mistranslations or changes occur?

Some of the problem can be attributed to the way the King James version was handled. In 1604 King James of England authorized forty-seven learned men to revise the translation of the Bible then in use. They had only eight manuscripts from which to translate, none of which were earlier than the tenth century. These eight were mostly based on John Wycliffe's 1367 verbatim translation directly from the Latin Bible; none of these manuscripts had been translated from the original Greek. Today there are at least 700 manuscripts in existence, many of which are quite ancient. In creating this book, I have used—as a reference against which to check the King James version—the so-called *Diaglott* or Greek translation that was made directly from many of these texts. It is widely considered by theologians to be the best at the present time.

The problem is this: It is said that there are at least 20,000 errors in the King James' version. Many of the King James translators complained that they could not follow their own judgments but were restrained by "reasons of the crown." They were instructed to follow the Bishop's Bible (one of the eight manuscripts) as the basis of the new version and not to make too many changes. I nonetheless decided to use the King James trranslation as my key source, as it remains so popular among Christians everywhere.

Biblical traditions, as well as translations, are a therefore a key factor. My research also revealed, for example, that from about 600 B.C. to 100 A.D., the so-called Apocalyptic writers flourished among Jews and Christians. (The term "apocalypse" derives from the Greek word meaning "to reveal.") Arising out of the extreme oppression of the Jews at the hands of their conquerers, these writings offered a mystical escape from the Jew's racial despondency, promising an eternal Messianic kingdom as well as the resurrection of the dead.

But in those times clear speaking often brought a death sentence. The apocalyptic authors were forced to protect themselves from persecution by developing a secret set of symbols, unearthly images, bizarre beasts with horns, etc., and numeralogical juggling. There arose many cryptic and strange predictions that were used by alarmists to foretell all kinds of events, including the end of the world.

This type of writing is particularly characteristic of the Book of Daniel, Ezekiel, as well as the Book of Revelation. Noting these similarities, I asked my celestial teacher Corelli whether John deployed the same symbologies as Daniel. She replied that he did. And what about Ezekiel? Some of his passages almost match word-for-word John's revelation, even though they are 500 to 600 years apart. Was Ezekiel aware of the true meaning of these symbols? Her answer again was yes, for Ezekiel had access to the Chaldean tablets that told the stories of the Lucifer Rebellion and of Adam and Eve [please see the glossary definitions of these terms]. Of course, this arcane information was beyond the comprehension of the people in those times. When the Apostle John through his assistant Nathan came to write the Revelation much later, they resorted to the symbols of old. Like his apocalyptical forebears, John had to be careful about what he wrote—at pain of death. To add to the difficulty of my task, you will see as you read this book that scribes and priests who lived after John distorted his great revelation for their own purposes, fabricating whole sections and even chapters, and deploying apocalyptical images in new ways that John never contemplated. This distortion and misuse has continued right on down to the writers of today's *Left Behind* series.

Editor's Preface

This book is the result of Stella Religa's uncompromising search for the secret revelation that lies buried within the Book of Revelation. I believe that she and her celestial helpers have succeeded in unveiling many, though certainly not all, of the Apostle John's secrets that have been lost to the Christian world for two millennia. As you will see, the message provided in *The Secret Revelation* is positive and hopeful.

Ms. Religa's chief discovery is that there will be no Armageddon, no Antichrist, no Rapture and no end-time as some conservative Christians have conceived it. If there is any sort of ending, this book marks the end of the mythic picture of our planet's fate rooted in ancient Mediterannean apocalypticism and early biblical Christianity. It points to the beginning of a new understanding of our destiny based on common sense, celestial assistance, and the futuristic revelations of *The Urantia Book*.

THE AUTHOR'S METHOD OF RESEARCH

This work is the result of Stella Religa's perserverance as a seeker of the facts and the truth about John's vision. Stella is not a scholar; though I can assure you that she has the mind of one. Nor is she an estericist, although she has certainly deployed unusual methods in her research. She is not a Bible expert; she was not even a student of the Bible when she began in 1996. But she brought to the project ingredients that have resulted in a helpful, plausible, and I believe revolutionary new discovery of John's original vision. And it is not insignificant that Stella is a woman and a long-time feminist, one of the few to my knowledge who has attempted a new interpretation of this decidedly patriarchal document.

Stella's method of celestial contact, combined with her

layperson status, sets her far apart from other major interpreters of the Apostle's revelation. But as her editor and publisher I believe that the approach she and her celestial helpers have taken has been efficacious. The problem is that so much of John's revelation has been lost—so much of his great work has been hidden away beyond any possibility of human discovery—that the assistance of superhuman revelators was, it would appear, critical to this endeavor. As you will see, a key part of that celestial assistance is Stella's liberal use of the revealed Urantia text as her reference; it is in fact the chief reference used by her own celestial advisors.

Although in certain respects it may have been an advantage for a Biblical scholar to have been the contactee, there is an advantage in bringing the fresh eyes of a layperson to this work. The overriding purpose of *The Secret Revelation* is a fervent appeal that is not directed to specialists but to the millions of laypeople like Stella herself, who are led to question the fearful messages about our planet's future based on Biblical prophecy. This appeal comes from a group of our unseen celestial friends who grace our planet led by Corelli (Stella's personal celestial teacher) as well as other beings named Solonia, Aflana, Meister Eckhart—and John himself.

ABOUT OUR CELESTIAL INTERLOCUTORS

The following special plea comes directly to us from the Apostle John. He relayed the following message to Stella through her teacher Corelli:

> John's overriding desire, and that of his other celestial cohorts, is that we must grow up and turn a sharp corner in our understanding of the destiny of our planet. We must also have a new presentation of the heavenly places that John visited in his vision—where we too will sojourn in the afterlife. For these are, like John's generation, times of great revelation.

John's main point is that much new information, even revelation, is available today; we need not rest on the arcane and fear-based teachings of the past. As evidence for this, the celestial interlocutors who were there for Stella are also available to you too, dear reader. Enter into a still place and ask for the protection of the Father; in this sacred space you may ask for the presence of a celestial teacher of your own.

In asking questions about old beliefs we must build on them, and not wholly forsake the past. Out of her respect for the original text of the Book of Revelation—and out of her regard for the millions of Christians who rely on it—Stella has gone so far as to accomplish a line-by-line reinterpretation. She was not content to publish yet another channeled "new age" broadside with little reference to the concrete details of Christian tradition and belief. This was not her charge, nor is it the charge of her helpers. Rather, she and her celestial cohorts are attempting to build bridges from the past, carrying forth what is worth preserving in the Christian tradition that has arisen out of the Book of Revelation.

Further, Stella's teachers were even willing to answer questions about those sections of John's text that they had outright declared to be fabrications by later writers. Providing interpretations of these fraudulent passages was a practice with which I strongly disagreed at first. Their response to my objections was that these forged verses, for example almost the entirety of chapter 3—though not written by John—have meant much to Christians and should be interpreted on their behalf.

At the same time, readers should not construe that this work is in itself a "revelation" from Stella's teachers. This celestially-guided exegesis is filtered through the mind of one person, and is given only in response to her particular questions and concerns. Different questions would have evoked shades of difference in the celestial responses. Even as her editor I glimpsed numerous lines of inquiry that I regret Stella has missed. But the questions she did manage to ask were nonetheless most fruitful in my opinion. The answers also gave Stella (and myself) occasion to add commentary and introductory materials on *The Urantia Book* where amplification was needed.

Yet another intention of Stella's celestial guides, as I understand it, has been to show just how responsive the celestial world has now become to our needs and our questions. Indeed, Stella's celestial teachers worked hard to make this book possible, as did she. They stayed near her and answered hundreds of painstaking and even quibbling questions, for almost four years, from 1996 to 2000. They richly supported her and me through this process, and I daresay they will support others in building upon Stella's achievement or even correcting the errors that others may chance to find in this book.

THE ROLE OF *THE URANTIA BOOK*

The Secret Revelation is just one species of the new teachings now available as part of the so-called Correcting Time. (Other texts in this series are listed in the back of this book.) The Correcting Time is a new phase of planetary uplift initiated by Jesus Christ himself in these "late-times." A key aspect of the Correcting Time is the Teaching Mission, which involves "live" and interactive celestial teachings specifically using *The Urantia Book* as a supporting textbook or reference text. (For more information, see the Appendix.)

Both Stella and I come to this work as Teaching Mission participants. This specialized mission exists to apply the Urantia teachings to problems of all kinds from the expanded revelatory point of view of *The Urantia Book*. The need for an update of John's revelation in the light of the Urantia teachings is just one project among many.

The Urantia Book (or "*UB*") is crucial as a bedrock, reliable reference source in such work. It is especially useful in guarding one against the inevitability that personal biases will enter the picture. In the case of *The Secret Revelation*, we will admit to our Urantia Book friends that some of the responses herein do not always perfectly harmonize with the Urantia Revelation—and we are not sure why. But these are rare exceptions to the rule. Stella checked her celestial input against the *UB* very frequently, and at times was aggressive in making sure the *UB* was not contradicted by what she thought she heard from her teachers. I too checked her writings against the *UB* as best as I could, though I am sure there are gaps and mistakes that will be discovered by others.

At the same time, *The Secret Revelation* contains many amplifications of facts provided in *The Urantia Book*. This book extends its teachings into the arcane area of Bible interpretation; by necessity, Stella had to evoke new and heretofore unheard-of information from her celestial helpers. Almost every one of the 22 chapters in this book contains such information.

—Byron Belitsos

A Special Note to Christians

Stella and I are well aware that tradition-minded Christians will be sorely taxed by the claims presented in this book. Our best hope in the face of your skepticism is to appeal to Jesus himself. Jesus was not an "esotericist" in his teaching and preaching. He was not given to obscure, fear-mongering, and arcane pronouncements such as those that frequently appear in the Book of Revelation. He revealed the plain truth in the clear light of day, in all its practical and spiritual consequences. He was the living truth—and he declared that this truth "shall make you free". He encouraged fearless truth-seeking. Jesus sought a radical overcoming of those Hebrew traditions that had become a useless burden to the souls of his people. And he died rather than foresake his prophetic opposition to these oppressive beliefs that supported a social system that was eclipsing the access of his children to the love of our Father.

We created this book in that prophetic spirit. For is it not time to similarly reject the outworn images in the Book of Revelation—even while embracing its enduring truths? At present, liberal Christians simply ignore this key source of Biblical prophecy. But millions of Christians take seriously its statements about Satan's influence, the coming rise of the Antichrist, the delivery of believers in the Rapture, and the destruction of the earth that could result from man's disobedience. We take these images seriously as well. That's why our stance is not to ignore the Book of Revelation as hopelessly outdated, but rather that it is time to return to the text itself and to respectfully update it. Many of the images and the characters in the Book of Revelation that some consider mere metaphors, are, according to our sources, real—but wrongly presented or distorted.

We also believe that Jesus would not approve of the picture of a wrathful, vengeful God and angels as it is presented throughout the Book of Revelation. He stood for and died for a God of love, undivided in his nature. The essence of his teachings are the victory of love over fear, of hope over despair, and these teachings are richly represented in the Gospel of John. But this very same Apostle John, in his Book of Revelation, appears to depart in many ways from the best of Jesus' teachings. Christians throughout the centuries have intuited that it is a special case, and that perhaps the text has been corrupted by others who came after John.

The celestial teachers who speak in *The Secret Revelation* take the stand that the original text was indeed corrupted, and much of it lost. And even that which is authentic with John also needs decoding and extensive updating. Stella and I believe what the Urantia Revelation says on this subject, as amplified by her celestial teachers. We ask that you muster the courage to consider its possible truth.

We invite you to also use *The Secret Revelation* as a helpful introduction to *The Urantia Book*, which is a gift of Jesus to Christians as well as all sincere people. You will see that we have in fact designed the book as a stand-alone introduction to the Urantia Revelation.

Finally, in supplying portions of the lost vision of John, we realize that we are contradicting much that Christians take as cardinal beliefs. We only ask that you approach the text with an open mind and in the truthful spirit of He who is the sponsor of our faith.

—Byron Belitsos

The First Transmissions

Apostle John communicated to me the following message about the Book of Revelation just as I began working on this book. It is, to say the least, overwhelming and humbling. I repeat it here verbatim:

> Thank you, Stella, for attempting to correct centuries of misinterpretation. You are wise to question. I wrote this through Nathan knowing my remaining years were few. Nathan did a wonderful job, although subsequent translators left out the heart of my message: to do God's will, to love God, to be of service to everyone, and above all to believe in eternal life.
>
> It is glorious here and well worth the struggle in life to finally arrive. We are watching your efforts with great interest. Be of good cheer. Your efforts will be well rewarded, and generations to come will thank you for your attempt to correct much misinformation. I must go now, and thank you very much.
>
> — Apostle John

This message from John was inspiring and encouraging. Yet I wondered how I was to carry out such a massive, controversial project as to rewrite the Apostle's revelation! My initial questions grew out of my curiosity about a subject of which I knew almost nothing. But would I dare to actually publish it? That was another story.

I knew I would be subject to criticism and skepticism. That's why I many times asked my celestial teacher Corelli how best to write this book. The following reply was crucial in getting me started:

> Corelli: Stella, we are happy to aid you in your re-translation. Begin with this introduction:

John was on the island of Patmos in the year of our Lord 97A.D. John had been banished to Patmos by Herod the Second because he was accused of heresy by Herod's court due to his activities with the Christians.

John was a true and loyal servant of Jesus Christ. His sorrow over the death of Jesus was unending. He was somewhat comforted by the news of Jesus' resurrection, but, nevertheless, his sorrow was acute and ever-present. He came to Patmos heavy-hearted, but once there, he had many dreams and visions. He was given the privilege of seeing heavenly worlds, including Salvington and Jerusem.

As he chronicled these visions, he grew increasingly happy to realize that what he was seeing was a foretaste of what God's loving souls would experience once they entered the afterlife. He was told: "Write what you have seen so that ages to come will be comforted." He proceeded to do just that.

Because his message was so kind and loving, he became a threat to the established order, and his writings had to be stopped. After his death in 103A.D. his works were confiscated and almost destroyed, but a few copies were saved by scholars. But subsequent generations could or would not let this hopeful message reach the population. They destroyed certain passages, added others and greatly distorted the message. We will work with you, if you will, and attempt to reconstruct the message as accurately as possible.

As we have attempted this reconstruction of John's message, Corelli and my celestial friends have shown the patience of saints with my endless and repetitive questions. (Of course, they are not actually saints, but beings sent to uplift the human race spiritually. See "Teaching Mission" in the glossary.) My initial questions regarding John's writings were almost perfunctory. From February through October 1996, I asked questions on points that happened to interest me at the moment, without really understanding what I heard in reply. But for several years after these initial queries, I continued to press for more details and clarification on every line in John's revelation.

My first formal transmission is just below. I am providing it verbatim to show you how my work has evolved over time.

MY FIRST QUESTIONS

Stella: What is the real meaning of chapter 1, Corelli?

Corelli: The first three verses of chapter 1 should remain substantially correct except for the archaic language. [Below she gives brief answers on each verse.]

1:4 - Correct as written.

1:5 - Remove "and the first begotten of the dead" and "Unto him that loved us, and washed us from our sins in his own blood."

1:6 - This should read: "And he hath made us kings..."

1:7, 8, 9, 10, 11 are OK as written.

Q: What do the seven candlesticks mean at 1:12?

A: Seven superuniverses. [This term is explained in chapter 1 in the interpretation of 1:12.]

1:13,14 and 15 are OK as written.

Q: What is the meaning of the "seven stars" at 1:16?

A: Seven capital cities.

Q: Two-edged sword?

A: This symbol represents the option to choose either evil or good.

1:17 - This one is OK.

1:18 - "Keys of hell and death" should instead read "hope and despair."

1:19 - Correct as written.

1:20 - [I neglected to ask about verse 20 in the first transmission. See below for further information.]

This was hardly an auspicious beginning. I was beginning to realize that I would have to ask more searching questions and wait for more detailed answers. I also knew I had better do some research on my own to compare Corelli's answers with what is already known in this field.

An element of doubt lingered in my mind throughout this process. I knew I had to check and recheck and corroborate all this new information, because what was forthcoming from Corelli and the others was totally unfamiliar to me.

MY SECOND ATTEMPT

In my next reading of chapter 1, a whole new set of questions came to mind. Would Corelli answer them? Below is a verbatim list of these questions and my notes to myself. It shows what I was thinking about in these early days of my decoding:

1:4 - Who are the seven spirits?

1:5 - Why did Corelli say to remove this sentence: "Unto him that loved us, and washed us from our sins in his own blood"? (I did not ask about "the first begotten" then.)

1:12 - What are the seven candlesticks?

1:16 - What is the meaning of seven stars? Two-edged sword?

1:18 - If "keys of hell and death" should read "hope and despair," what does the original Greek say?

1:20 - This verse states that the seven stars are the angels of the seven churches, and the seven candlesticks are the seven churches. However, Corelli said that the seven stars are capital cities. Which is correct? She also states that the seven golden candlesticks are seven superuniverses. What and where are they?

Shifting from my initial stance of idle curiosity, I was becoming drawn further and further into the mystery of John's revelation. For example, I decided to check the original Bible translations directly from the Greek against the King James version of chapter 1. In this case, the differences between the two are negligible. Verses 1, 2, 3, 6, 7, 9, 10, 13, 14, 15, 17 and 19 needed no particular inquiry, but the other verses raised important questions.

I soon came to realize that different translations can influence theological thought and can even affect generations of human beliefs. As a result, I decided to compare quotations from the original Greek with the *Diaglott* translation from the Greek, and in turn to compare these to the King James version. I share these comparisons through this book.

But Corelli's initial comments were sketchy. As she later explained to me, the celestial beings who were watching wondered what I would do with the brief information first given in February 1996. Would I pick up on what I was told or would I drop it and lose interest? She said, "We all watched with great interest. What would this human do?"

The results of my four years of research are now in front of you.

How This Book Is Organized

Each chapter (after this one) will start out with a full citation of the chapter from the King James version that we are interpreting.

As we proceed through the revision of each chapter, I always quote one or a few verses from the original King James version first. You'll notice that I have also included the original chapter subheads from the Bible. (The more modern-looking subheads mark off special commentary sections.)

My questions to my celestial helpers almost always come next, and these are always in italics. These are followed by the answers from my unseen friends, after which you will see my commentary or research. Also, each chapter usually includes my introductory comments to get you oriented.

Note that at the end of each chapter are bulleted *Highlights*. If you want to skip over a chapter quickly, you can rely on these bullets to give you the key points that you may have missed.

You will also note that I sometimes include quotations directly from *The Urantia Book* (or *"UB"*) to help clarify definitions of terms and concepts. I will note here again that I am a believer in the revelations of *The Urantia Book*, and you will see as you go that my celestial teachers refer to it very frequently. Throughout this reinterpretation, *The Urantia Book* is our main reference text aside from the Bible itself.

1

King James Translation

1 The Revelation of Jesus Christ, which God gave unto him, to shew unto his servants things which must shortly come to pass; and he sent and signified it by his angel unto his servant John:

2 Who bare record of the word of God, and of the testimony of Jesus Christ, and of all things that he saw.

3 Blessed is he that readeth, and they that hear the words of this prophecy, and keep those things which are written therein: for the time is at hand.

4 John to the seven churches which are in Asia: Grace be unto you, and peace, from him which is, and which was, and which is to come; and from the seven Spirits which are before his throne;

5 And from Jesus Christ, who is the faithful witness, and the first begotten of the dead, and the prince of the kings of the earth. Unto him that loved us, and washed us from our sins in his own blood,

6 And hath made us kings and priests unto God and his Father; to him be glory and dominion for ever and ever. Amen.

7 Behold, he cometh with clouds; and every eye shall see him, and they also which pierced him: and all kindreds of the earth shall wail because of him. Even so, Amen.

8 I am Alpha and Omega, the beginning and the ending, saith the Lord, which is, and which was, and which is to come, the Almighty.

9 I John, who also am your brother, and companion in tribulation, and in the kingdom and patience of Jesus Christ, was in the isle that is called Patmos, for the word of God, and for the testimony of Jesus Christ.

10 I was in the Spirit on the Lord's day, and heard behind me a great voice, as of a trumpet,

11 Saying, I am Alpha and Omega, the first and the last: and, What thou seest, write in a book, and send it unto the seven churches which are in Asia; unto Ephesus, and unto Smyrna, and unto Pergamos, and unto Thyatira, and unto Sardis, and unto Philadelphia, and unto Laodicea.

12 And I turned to see the voice that spake with me. And being turned, I saw seven golden candlesticks;

13 And in the midst of the seven candlesticks one like unto the Son of man, clothed with a garment down to the foot, and girt about the paps with a golden girdle.

14 His head and his hairs were white like wool, as white as snow; and his eyes were as a flame of fire;

15 And his feet like unto fine brass, as if they burned in a furnace; and his voice as the sound of many waters.

16 And he had in his right hand seven stars: and out of his mouth went a sharp two edged sword: and his countenance was as the sun shineth in his strength.

17 And when I saw him, I fell at his feet as dead. And he laid his right hand upon me, saying unto me, Fear not; I am the first and the last:

18 I am he that liveth, and was dead; and, behold, I am alive for evermore, Amen; and have the keys of hell and of death.

19 Write the things which thou hast seen, and the things which are, and the things which shall be hereafter;

20 The mystery of the seven stars which thou sawest in my right hand, and the seven golden candlesticks. The seven stars are the angels of the seven churches: and the seven candlesticks which thou sawest are the seven churches.

revised

Introduction

1:1 - The Revelation of Jesus Christ, which God gave unto him, to shew unto his servants things which must shortly come to pass; and he sent and signified it by his angel unto his servant John:

1:2 - Who bare record of the word of God, and of the testimony of Jesus Christ, and of all things that he saw.

1:3 - Blessed is he that readeth, and they that hear the words of this prophecy, and keep those things which are written therein: for the time is at hand.

Corelli: The messages in verses 1-3 are basically fine.

Salutation to the seven churches in Asia

1:4 - John to the seven churches which are in Asia: Grace be unto you, and peace, from him which is, and which was, and which is to come; and from the Seven Spirits which are before his throne;

Although Corelli indicated that verse four is correct, she did not elaborate on the meanings of the "seven spirits which are before his throne." For help on this I checked with *The Urantia Book*:

> Next to the trinity, Father, Son and Spirit, each of these Seven Spirits supervise the seven superuniverses [see glossary]....It is literally true that these Seven Spirits are the...spiritual presence of the triune Deity, 'the Seven Spirits of God sent forth to all the universes.' (*UB*:186-191)

> 1:5 - And from Jesus Christ, who is the faithful witness, and the first begotten of the dead, and the prince of the kings of the earth. Unto him that loved us, and washed us from our sins in his own blood,

Corelli initially said to simply remove: "Unto him that loved us, and washed us from our sins in his own blood." In a later conversation, she revealed this passage was added long after Nathan's death and was not in John's original revelation. (As I noted earlier, Nathan was John's associate during his exile on Patmos. Nathan also wrote the Gospel of John at John's direction. See *The Urantia Book* 1342 and 1555.)

REGARDING THE ATONEMENT DOCTRINE

According to ancient pagan and Hebraic beliefs, the shedding of blood was necessary to appease the anger of the gods. *The Urantia Book* tells us that Moses tried valiantly to change the belief that "without the shedding of blood there could be no remission of sin." He did manage to forbid human sacrifice by substituting the sacrifice of animals. Unfortunately, the belief that Jesus died for our sins by shedding his blood (the so-called atonement doctrine) was incorporated into Christianity and is still with us today. Jesus never taught such a doctrine according to *The Urantia Book*. I quote this crucial passage at length:

When once you grasp the idea of God as a true and loving Father, the only concept which Jesus ever taught, you must forthwith, in all consistency, utterly abandon all those primitive notions about God as an offended monarch, a stern and all-powerful ruler whose chief delight is to detect his subjects in wrongdoing and to see that they are adequately punished, unless some being almost equal to himself should volunteer to suffer for them, to die as a substitute and in their stead. The whole idea of ransom and atonement is incompatible with the concept of God as it was taught and exemplified by Jesus of Nazareth. The infinite love of God is not secondary to anything in the divine nature. (*UB*:2017)

The barbarous idea of appeasing an angry God, of propitiating an offended Lord, of winning the favor of Deity through sacrifices and penance and even by the shedding of blood, represents a religion wholly puerile and primitive, a philosophy unworthy of an enlightened age of science and truth. Such beliefs are utterly repulsive to the celestial beings and the divine rulers who serve and reign in the universes. It is an affront to God to believe, hold, or teach that innocent blood must be shed in order to win his favor or to divert the fictitious divine wrath. (*UB*:60)

Regarding the phrase in 1:5, "the first begotten of the dead," I belatedly thought to ask Corelli, what does "of the dead" mean?

A: It means all those celestial beings present throughout eternity who are not really dead, but beautifully alive on the other side. Jesus was not the first begotten of the dead. There are many Sons like him throughout the universes.

1:6 - And hath made us kings and priests unto God and his Father; to him be glory and dominion for ever and ever. Amen.

The coming of Christ

1:7 - Behold, he cometh with clouds; and every eye shall see him, and they also which pierced him: and all kindreds of the earth shall wail because of him. Even so, Amen.

Corelli indicated that this paragraph is alright as stated. The only change in the Greek translation is the word "tribes" rather than "kindred."

1:8 - I am Alpha and Omega, the beginning and the ending, saith the Lord, which is, and which was, and which is to come, the Almighty.

Although Corelli initially stated that verse 8 was also okay as written, it occurred to me to ask about "Alpha and Omega." Is this referring to Jesus—or to God the Father?

A NEW CHRISTOLOGY

Christianity has always considered Jesus to be the Son of God, the second person of the Trinity. But in checking *The Urantia Book* (73-90), we learn that the Son in the Trinity is the "Eternal Son," who is not literally Jesus.

The Eternal Son has charge of all spiritual matters throughout the seven superuniverses. But we also read that the Eternal Son acts through his Sons, in our case Jesus Christ, who is a "Son of the Eternal Son." *The Urantia Book*'s revelation of who Jesus really is will delight most Christians: He is a Creator deity to his local universe; he possesses all the attributes of the Father and Eternal Son, and portrays them in perfection to his local creation; and he was also incarnate God on this planet. That's why when Jesus said, "He who has seen me has seen the Father," it is literally true. We will learn much more about Jesus as we go. His "local" creation includes ten million inhabitable planets, for example, and is called "Nebadon." (See 1:12 below and also the entry for "Christ Michael" in the glossary.)

Much later on January 17, 1998, I asked if in 1:8, "I am Alpha and Omega..." refers to the Eternal Son, the second person of the Trinity, or did John have a vision of Jesus who embodies the attributes of the Eternal Son?

> A: Yes, this verse does refer to the Eternal Son. John saw Jesus in a vision in which Jesus shows himself as possessing the wisdom, strength, and love of the Eternal Son who is the second person of the Trinity. The Eternal Son has charge of all spirit values, and you are literally pulled towards Paradise via his spiritual circuits. In some distant time you will eventually stand before this Eternal Son who is distinct from Jesus. But both incorporate the same attributes of the Father who is the First Source and Center. You are wise to try to clarify this.

I did not feel so wise since I had to ponder this and could only hope to grasp what Corelli told me and what I read in *The Urantia Book*.

John's vision on Patmos

> 1:9 - I, John, who also am your brother, and companion in tribulation, and in the kingdom and patience of Jesus Christ, was in the isle that is called Patmos, for the word of God, and for the testimony of Jesus Christ.

This verse is straightforward. John is on Patmos. However, rather than "...for the testimony of Jesus Christ," the Diaglott version reads: "and patient waiting for Jesus."

As one checks other translations of the Bible, the variations in meaning become more apparent. I have found these kinds of discrepancies throughout the Greek version when compared to the rest of John's Book of Revelation. However, I will cite only the most glaring differences in the rest of this book.

> 1:10 - I was in the Spirit on the Lord's day, and heard behind me a great voice, as of a trumpet.

A: As written. John hears the voice of the Eternal Son.

1:11 - Saying, I am Alpha and Omega, the first and the last: and, What thou seest, write in a book, and send it unto the seven churches which are in Asia, unto Ephesus, and unto Smyrna, and unto Pergamos, and unto Thyatira, and unto Sardis, and unto Philadelphia, and unto Laodicea.

1:12 - And I turned to see the voice that spake with me. And being turned, I saw seven golden candlesticks;

THE SEVEN SUPERUNIVERSES

The Urantia Book has no direct explanation of the meanings of the symbols "seven candlesticks" or "seven stars." However, let's assume that Corelli's and John's explanation that the seven candlesticks represent the seven superuniverses is correct. Consider some of the amazing facts that the *The Urantia Book* tells us about the seven superuniverses: Each one is composed of about one trillion inhabited planets, and contains numerous galaxies and other structures. Our superuniverse is called "Orvonton," and within it is our local universe of 10 million inhabited planets, known as "Nebadon" (see just below). The superuniverses rotate in a great ellipse in a counterclockwise course around the so-called eternal central universe which is known as "Havona":

> Your local universe of Nebadon belongs to Orvonton, the seventh superuniverse....(UB:165)

> The vast Milky Way starry system represents the central nucleus of Orvonton.... Gazing through the main body of this realm of maximum density, you are looking toward the residential universe and the center of all things. (UB:167)

> Orvonton is one of the seven evolutionary superuniverses of time and space which circles the never-beginning, never-ending creation of divine perfection—the central universe of *Havona*. At the heart of this eternal and central universe is the stationary Isle of Paradise, the geographic center of infinity and the dwelling place of the eternal God. (UB:1)

Well, we sure have come a long way from "candlesticks," with all this talk of trillions of inhabited planets and an eternal central universe! Let's continue on.

> 1:13 - And in the midst of the seven candlesticks, one like unto the Son of man, clothed with a garment down to the foot, and girt about the paps [breasts] with a golden girdle.

As we have seen, "one like unto the Son of man" refers to the Eternal Son who is in charge of the spiritual energies of all seven superuniverses (i.e., the candlesticks). To learn more about the Eternal Son's spiritual ministry, see page 81ff. in *The Urantia Book.*

> 1:14 - His head and his hairs were white like wool, as white as snow; and his eyes were as a flame of fire;

> 1:15 - And his feet like unto fine brass, as if they burned in a furnace; and his voice as the sound of many waters.

Corelli: This is a description of the Eternal Son radiating spiritual energies.

> 1:16 - And he had in his right hand seven stars: and out of his mouth went a sharp two edged sword: and his countenance was as the sun shineth in his strength.

According to Corelli, the seven stars in 1:16 are in fact the "capital cities" (actually celestial headquarters planets) of the seven candlesticks (seven superuniverses) as indicated in 1:12—over which the Eternal Son presides.

As she explains later in 1:20, it was much easier for the ancients to interpret the stars as angels. The idea of seven superuniverses, each with a capital city, was obviously beyond their comprehension. The "two-edged sword" symbolizes the choice between good and evil.

> 1:17 - And when I saw him, I fell at his feet as dead. And he laid his right hand upon me, saying unto me, Fear not; I am the first and the last:

1:18 - I am he that liveth, and was dead; and, behold, I am alive for evermore, Amen; and have the keys of hell and of death.

Corelli's previous statement that the "keys of hell and of death" should read "hope and despair" poses a number of questions regarding meanings and translations. The Greek translation reads "keys of the death and of the unseen," and the Diaglott translation of the Greek translation reads, "keys of death and of Hades."[1] There are shades of difference among all three meanings. The differences in wording again point out how various influences can affect generations of theologians and the lives of individuals who hear these teachings.

Among these options for 1:18, I believe that Corelli's statement is by far the most hopeful. "Hope" rather than "death" would signify that eternal life is possible if one chooses to do the Father's will. Despair will result if one turns away from living a godly life.

We know that generally we are allotted a certain span of time, but God does not necessarily decide how and when we die. There are accidents in time, diseases, events over which we may have no control that are simply due to nature or to man's own making. Prayer and faith in a loving Father and in an eventually just universe can cushion many of life's blows.

1:19 - Write the things which thou hast seen, and the things which are, and the things which shall be hereafter;

Corelli commented that this verse can stand as written.

1:20 - The mystery of the seven stars which thou sawest in my right hand, and the seven golden candlesticks. The seven stars are the angels of the seven churches: and the seven candlesticks which thou sawest are the seven churches.

The Diaglott translation uses the word "secret" rather than "mystery." The fact that the Greek translation reads "secret" is a clue to me that John knew the hidden meanings of "stars" and "candlesticks." Again, the candlesticks refer to the seven superuniverses and the stars their capital cities.

But I was still unsatisfied with Corelli's explanation of the meaning of the seven candlesticks, so I again questioned her:

> Q: *You told me that seven candlesticks meant the seven superuniverses. Yet in 1:20, the King James version states the seven stars are the angels of the seven churches, and the seven golden candlesticks are the seven churches. Can you clear up these diverse interpretations?*
> A: In the case of 1:20, the seven candlesticks do refer to the seven churches and the seven stars to the seven angels of the churches. We wish we knew why John used the same metaphors in two different ways. We will ask John. Perhaps he can clarify his meaning.

As I waited, they literally asked John!

A few minutes later they came back with the message that the seven churches are a microcosm of the seven superuniverses, the macrocosm. In other words, the problems in the seven churches are also present on the superuniverses. Human nature is pretty much the same throughout the universes. There are savages on planets in many universes, and this message would apply to them as well.

Corelli also indicated that the "angels of the churches" refer to "religious guardians," which are special angels who seek to preserve moral values from one epoch to another. (See *The Urantia Book*:1255 for more about this order of angels.)

Still curious about these symbols, as I sat in the kitchen after dinner on February 8, 1998, I began thinking about the correlation between the candlesticks and the superuniverses. I decided I would ask Corelli again if she knew why John used this metaphor. She had tried to explain, but it made no sense to me. This time I asked her to ask John one more time.

After a pause, she said, "John, Stella wants to know why you used the candlesticks as a symbol for the superuniverses?"

And he replied, "In those times people had only candlesticks as a source of light. A candlestick has the potential of holding many lights, so it was logical to use that symbol."

So I asked, "You mean the candlesticks are really a symbol of the suns of which there are trillions in each superuniverse?"

"Yes, that's right. The stars or suns seem to flicker like a candle flame. The candlesticks were an appropriate symbol. This is one of those hidden meanings you have been searching for."

Stella: "Well, I guess that clarifies that. Thank you."
"You are more than welcome."

What began for me with simple and naïve questions, became a chapter with a wealth of new knowledge. I hope I have done justice to what John tried to do, and I only hope he is pleased.

I actually heard the words: "He is, and thanks you."

FOOTNOTE

[1]*The Urantia Book* states on page 1045: "The concept of judgment in the hereafter for the sins of one's life in the flesh on earth was carried over into Hebrew theology from Egypt. The word judgment appears only once in the entire Book of Hebrew Psalms, and that particular psalm was written by an Egyptian." This notion of judgment in the afterlife was subsequently carried over into Christianity.

Highlights from Chapter 1

- As his vision begins, John is visited by an angel sent by God with a message from Jesus and the "Seven Spirits before the throne" of God (1:4). These Seven Spirits are the personalized presence of the divine Trinity—the supreme directors of the far-flung universe. (*UB*:186).

- The atonement doctrine is a fallacy. Jesus did not "wash us from our sins" (1:5) by the shedding of his blood. This misconception is based on a primitive belief that shedding blood was necessary to appease an angry God. (*UB*:60).

- John hears a great voice, turns and sees a great divine being (1:10). He is in the presence of Jesus, who reveals himself as a "Son" of the Eternal Son (the second person of the Trinity), possessing all of the Eternal Son's atrributes. (*UB*:73) But the voice John hears is actually that of the Eternal Son.

- The Eternal Son/Jesus holds "seven candlesticks" (1:12) that represent the seven superuniverses—the totality of the inhabited creation (see glossary). John used the image of the candlesticks as a symbol because candles flicker as do suns.

- The "seven stars" (1:20) and the seven candlesticks have a double meaning. They refer to the seven churches that John is addressing, whereas the seven stars also symbolize the seven capitals of the seven superuniverse, as well as the churches. The seven churches are like a microcosm of the whole universe, in that human nature is pretty much the same everywhere throughout the universe.

- The idea of hell (see footnote 4) was invented to keep people in a state of subjugation and fear. It was carried over into Hebrew theology from Egypt and subsequently incorporated into Christianity.

2

King James Translation

1 Unto the angel of the church of Ephesus write; These things saith he that holdeth the seven stars in his right hand, who walketh in the midst of the seven golden candlesticks;

2 I know thy works, and thy labour, and thy patience, and how thou canst not bear them which are evil: and thou hast tried them which say they are apostles, and are not, and hast found them liars:

3 And hast borne, and hast patience, and for my name's sake hast laboured, and hast not fainted.

4 Nevertheless I have somewhat against thee, because thou hast left thy first love.

5 Remember therefore from whence thou art fallen, and repent, and do the first works; or else I will come unto thee quickly, and will remove thy candlestick out of his place, except thou repent.

6 But this thou hast, that thou hatest the deeds of the Nicolaitans, which I also hate.

7 He that hath an ear, let him hear what the Spirit saith unto the churches; To him that overcometh will I give to eat of the tree of life, which is in the midst of the paradise of God.

8 And unto the angel of the church in Smyrna write; These things saith the first and the last, which was dead, and is alive;

9 I know thy works, and tribulation, and poverty, (but thou art rich) and I know the blasphemy of them which say they are Jews, and are not, but are the synagogue of Satan.

10 Fear none of those things which thou shalt suffer: behold, the devil shall cast some of you into prison, that ye may be tried; and ye shall have tribulation ten days: be thou faithful unto death, and I will give thee a crown of life.

11 He that hath an ear, let him hear what the Spirit saith unto the churches; He that overcometh shall not be hurt of the second death.

12 And to the angel of the church in Pergamos write; These things saith he which hath the sharp sword with two edges;

13 I know thy works, and where thou dwellest, even where Satan's seat is: and thou holdest fast my name, and hast not denied my faith, even in those days wherein Antipas was my faithful martyr, who was slain among you, where Satan dwelleth.

14 But I have a few things against thee, because thou hast there them that hold the doctrine of Balaam, who taught Balac to cast a stumbling block before the children of Israel, to eat things sacrificed unto idols, and to commit fornication.

15 So hast thou also them that hold the doctrine of the Nicolaitans, which thing I hate.

16 Repent; or else I will come unto thee quickly, and will fight against them with the sword of my mouth.

17 He that hath an ear, let him hear what the Spirit saith unto the churches; To him that overcometh will I give to eat of the hidden manna, and will give him a white stone, and in the stone a new name written, which no man knoweth saving he that receiveth it.

18 And unto the angel of the church in Thyatira write; These things saith the Son of God, who hath his eyes like unto a flame of fire, and his feet are like fine brass;

19 I know thy works, and charity, and service, and faith, and thy patience, and thy works; and the last to be more than the first.

20 Notwithstanding I have a few things against thee, because thou sufferest that woman Jezebel, which calleth herself a prophetess, to teach and to seduce my servants to commit fornication, and to eat things sacrificed unto idols.

21 And I gave her space to repent of her fornication; and she repented not.

22 Behold, I will cast her into a bed, and them that commit adultery with her into great tribulation, except they repent of their deeds.

23 And I will kill her children with death; and all the churches shall know that I am he which searcheth the reins and hearts: and I will give unto every one of you according to your works.

24 But unto you I say, and unto the rest in Thyatira, as many as have not this doctrine, and which have not known the depths of Satan, as they speak; I will put upon you none other burden.

25 But that which ye have already hold fast till I come.

26 And he that overcometh, and keepeth my works unto the end, to him will I give power over the nations:

27 And he shall rule them with a rod of iron; as the vessels of a potter shall they be broken to shivers: even as I received of my Father.

28 And I will give him the morning star.

29 He that hath an ear, let him hear what the Spirit saith unto the churches.

revised

Chapter 2 opens with the voice of the Eternal Son, the second person of the Trinity. We have learned that the Eternal Son reigns spiritually over the seven superuniverses (candlesticks) and that the "seven stars" actually refer to the celestial headquarters worlds of each superuniverse.

In this chapter John is told to convey certain instructions to the churches. While the King James version reads: "Unto the angel of the churches write...," the Diaglott literal translation reads: "By the messenger of the congregation write..." In other words, rather than to an angel, it is John—in his capacity of messenger to the churches—who is given these critical instructions.

John begins by citing the good works of the churches followed by a listing of their deficiencies. The most important teachings in chapter 2 come in verses 7, 11, and 17. Verse 2:7 states that "you will eat of the tree of life." In other words, those who turn to God will be given eternal life in Paradise (see glossary). Verse 2:11 goes on to say he who "overcomes" will have eternal life, and will not have to fear the "second death." (As we will see, the second death refers to final extinction.) Verse 2:17 promises that we will receive God's grace; our life's records will never be effaced; and we will be given a new name in the afterlife. The last verse, 2:29, admonishes all to listen to the prompting of the Spirit.

I started my research on chapter 2 with a series of questions dating from September 19, 1996. Over time I became increasingly curious about this material and the whole enterprise of trying to decode John's revelation. Why did John write to the seven churches in the first place? What could be the meaning of the many new cryptic symbols introduced in this chapter? And what was my role in this work? I continued to ask questions almost verse by verse. The answers were a revelation, to say the least.

Q: Why was John told to write to the seven churches? Is there a key to interpreting the new symbols?
A: Stella, we are here.

Q: Who?
A: Corelli and Aflana, also Meister Eckhart...John was told to contact the churches because the churches were in Asia Minor, a primitive land by all known standards. The people there were backward in their beliefs, in their cultures; they knew little about Jesus Christ, the Son of God. They worshipped pagan gods, squabbled among themselves, were hot-tempered and prone to fight. Their main desire in life was to get the best of their neighbors. They had little conscience and could not comprehend the love of God. Their gods reflected their human characteristics.

John was specifically directed to address these far regions in an attempt to combat their aggressiveness and to instill love and faith in a loving God. They were told to stop their senseless fighting, but they would only listen if a representative of God, any god for that matter, would admonish them to adopt a better way of life.

John's task was difficult. He was in exile on Patmos; he had to be careful what he said. He had to rely on certain individuals in these churches who could preach to the semi-literate savages. We know he succeeded to a degree because his words have been passed down through the ages and have been a comfort to many.

Message to Ephesus

2:1 - Unto the angel of the church of Ephesus write; these things saith he that holdeth the seven stars in his right hand, who walketh in the midst of the seven golden candlesticks.

See 1:1 and 1:2 where Corelli and John explain the dual meanings of the seven candlesticks and seven stars.

2:2 - I know thy works, and thy labour, and thy patience, and how thou canst not bear them which are evil: and thou hast tried them which say they are apostles, and are not, and has found them liars.

2:3 - And hast borne, and hast patience, and for my name's sake hast laboured, and hast not fainted.

Q: To whom are verses 2:2-3 being addressed?

A: These are addressed to a judge who presumably had been trying people who claimed to be Christian apostles in order to avoid being imprisoned. The judge knew they were not apostles and accordingly gave them the proper punishment.

2:4 - Nevertheless I have somewhat against thee, because thou hast left thy first love.

Q: Even though the judge had ruled justly, he had turned away from God?

A: Yes, that is correct. But he subsequently did return to God.

Q: What is the meaning of "thy first love"?

A: The love of God, of course. Humankind's first instinct is to seek God in whatever shape or form he or she can find him. It is for those who turn away from their first love—God—that the danger arises.

2:5 - Remember therefore from whence thou art fallen, and repent, and do the first works; or else I will come unto thee quickly, and will remove thy candlestick out of his place, except thou repent.

Q: Why would he remove a candlestick except he repent? What candlestick would he remove?

A: The candlestick, in this instance, refers to that particular church which would fail if they (the people) did not turn to God.

2:6 - But this thou hast, that thou hates the deeds of the Nicolaitanes, which I also hate.

Q: Who were the Nicolaitanes?

A: The Nicolaitanes were a minor Gnostic sect in Jerusalem. They worshiped Baal, a pagan deity that was abhorrent to the Christians. This passage in the Book of Revelation was addressed to them so that they would cease their worship of a pagan god and turn to Christ who offers eternal life. Sadly, they did not listen, and as do all such groups who fail to recognize a loving God, they faded from the world scene.

Life without a belief in a loving God is futile and can only lead to despair and hopelessness.

2:7 - He that hath an ear, let him hear what the Spirit saith unto the churches; to him that overcometh will I give to eat of the tree of life, which is in the midst of the paradise of God.

THE ROLE OF THE HOLY SPIRIT

For background on the reference to "Spirit" at 2:7, I consulted what *The Urantia Book* says about the the Holy Spirit— the third person of the Trinity—at page 96: "The Infinite Spirit is a universe presence, an eternal action, a cosmic power, a holy influence, and a universal mind....The Spirit exerts a direct and personal influence on created beings." I came to the conclusion that the "Spirit" who is speaking to the churches is the Infinite Spirit, who is "the divine equal of the Universal Father and the Eternal Son."

> *Q: Corelli, is this idea correct according to your understanding?*

A: Yes it is, Stella. This is the divine spirit which ever urges you upward in your spiritualization efforts.

I also wondered about the reference in 2:7 to "him who overcometh."

> *Q: Corelli, wouldn't this passage refer to God's promise of eternal life to those who overcome?*

A: Yes, you are correct. God will grant eternal life as an ascender to Paradise if one turns towards living a Godly life and overcomes the many temptations of secular life.

Message to Smyrna

2:8 - And unto the angel of the church in Smyrna write; These things saith the first and the last, which was dead, and is alive.

The angel (John) is again instructed by Christ, who was dead but is alive, to send a message. This verse seems to be referring to Jesus, whereas 2:1 refers to the Eternal Son. I mentioned this to Corelli, and she indicated that the writer of 2:8 had assumed that 2:1 was also Jesus speaking. (We learned earlier that Jesus shares all of the divine attributes of the Eternal Son.)

2:9 - I know thy works, and tribulation, and poverty, (but thou art rich) and I know the blasphemy of them which say they are Jews, and are not, but are the synagogue of Satan.

Q: What are the synagogues of Satan?

A: Those temples of worship dedicated to Baal, to

pagan beliefs. These were cults which deal not with the spiritual love of God, but rather served as temples to the "devil" in whom many fervently believed.

Note that the Greek translation reads "assembly of the adversary" rather than "synagogues of Satan."

2:10 - Fear none of those things which thou shalt suffer: behold, the devil shall cast some of you into prison, that ye may be tried; and ye shall have tribulation ten days: be thou faithful unto death, and I will give thee a crown of life.

Q: *Corelli, who is the devil or enemy who will "cast some of you unto prison"?*

A: The devil in this case symbolizes your own worst enemy—yourself. You choose evil or good based on your own impulses, and you will cast yourself into a self-imposed prison if you choose evil. The point is that people are responsible for how they live. People were very fond, and still are, of blaming others for their misdeeds. In this verse, the devil is you. Does this answer your question?

Stella: *Yes, it does. Thank you.*

Q: *And what is "the crown of life"?*
A: Eternal life if you choose to go on.

2:11 - He that hath an ear, let him hear what the Spirit saith unto the churches; He that overcometh shall not be hurt of the second death.

Q: *What is the "second death"?*

A: After mortal death you are given one more chance, from your new vantage point in heaven, to make a final choice — either to go on eternally or to choose oblivion. There is no reprieve from this final second choice. If you choose oblivion, your worthwhile energies and thoughts go into the collective mind.

Q: *Who or what is able to use these energies and thoughts?*
A: They are used by God the Supreme as he gathers

experiences for his evolutionary growth. [See the teachings on "evolutionary deity" in *UB*:1260ff.]

Q: Can other people tap into this collective mind?

A: Yes, people under stress who have personal problems to solve can tap into this vast reservoir of knowledge. The best way to do this is through meditation and prayer. Answers may come through dreams, hunches or unusual occurrences which may seem coincidental, but really are not.

Message to Pergamos

2:12 - And to the angel of the church in Pergamos write; These things saith he which hath the sharp sword with two edges.

See 1:16 for a discussion of the two-edged sword, which symbolizes choosing evil or good.

2:13 - I know thy works, and where thou dwellest, even where Satan's seat is: and thou holdest fast my name, and hast not denied my faith, even in those days wherein Antipas was my faithful martyr, who was slain among you, where Satan dwelleth.

Q: What and where is "Satan's seat" today?

A: He was once held in a celestial prison world, where he was interred after Jesus' resurrection. But today Satan exists no more. Anyone who still thinks he is still around is incorrect.

Q: But isn't his influence still with us?

A: Yes, but only to a certain extent. Your planet has progressed admirably technologically but you have not kept pace spiritually. Much of this is due to two tragic events in the history of your planet that are clearly explained in your *Urantia Book* in. Papers 53-4. These events were the so-called Caligastia betrayal at the behest of Satan, which occurred about 200,000 years ago, and the default of Adam and Eve, 38,000 years ago.

THE TRAGIC HISTORY OF OUR PLANET

Caligastia was the "planetary prince" of your world (see "Caligastia" in the glossary). Caligastia's downfall retarded the spiritual growth of humanity by failing to eradicate much of your animal-like tendency towards violence, greed, and selfishness. Those who have a propensity towards these evil ways continue to act in a manner contrary to the loving plan of God. While Caligastia and Satan did retard planetary evolution, in reality the evil you see today is the result of human choice.

Although Adam and Eve's (see glossary) actions were contrary to the edicts of the celestial beings in charge of this planet, they never set themselves above God, as Caligastia tried to do. (This event is taken up in detail later in the book.)

The nefarious three, Caligastia, Lucifer and Satan, are now no more. (See "Lucifer Rebellion" in the glossary.) Although much of your planet is still in spiritual darkness, we see spiritual awakening taking place throughout your world, and we are very pleased. Does this answer your question?

Stella: Yes, indeed, it does. Thank you.

A: You are welcome.

Q: Another question: Does "I know thy works" apply to the individual or to the church as a whole?

A: To the church as a whole, although the church includes individuals, of course.

Q: Who was Antipas?

A: A good man and friend of the church who was zealous in the proclamation of the gospel of Jesus. He was killed—stoned to death by ignorant tribesmen who could not understand his loving teachings. He is safe now on the mansion worlds away from the tormentors who killed him.

Q: That section of 2:13 which reads "where Satan dwelleth" appears different than "Satan's seat."

A: In this instance it refers to the evil that dwells in people's hearts.

2:14 - But I have a few things against thee, because thou hast there them that hold the doctrine of Balaam, who taught Balac to cast a stumbling block before the children of Israel, to eat things sacrificed unto idols, and to commit fornication.

2:15 - So hast thou also them that hold the doctrine of the Nicolaitanes, which thing I hate.

See 2:6 for an explanation of the Nicolaitanes, a minor sect in Jerusalem that worshipped Baal.

2:16 - Repent; or else I will come unto thee quickly, and will fight against them with the sword of my mouth.

See 1:16 - "Sword of my mouth" is equivalent to the two-edged sword.

2:17 - He that hath an ear, let him hear what the Spirit saith unto the churches; to him that overcometh will I give to eat of the hidden manna, and will give him a white stone, and in the stone a new name written, which no man knoweth saving he that receiveth it.

Q: What are the meanings of "hidden manna," the "white stone," and "in the stone a new name"?

A: Hidden manna is God's spiritual grace given to all who truly love the Lord and try to do his will. The white stone is that upon which is written the record of your life; it refers to the record which the angels faithfully make of what you have done in your life. It is like a stone; it can never be effaced.

Once you fuse with your God fragment, i.e., the so-called "thought adjuster" (see glossary), you are given a new name. *The Urantia Book* (see 1186-87) describes the Thought Adjuster as a "fragment of God" which is bestowed upon a child when that child makes his or her first moral choice without the prompting of an adult. This God fragment remains with each normal-minded person as their divine pilot throughout their lives, until the point of fusion which usually occurs in the afterlife.

Message to Thyatira

2:18 - And unto the angel of the church in Thyatira write; These things saith the Son of God, who hath his eyes like unto a flame of fire, and his feet are like fine brass;

2:19 - I know thy works, and charity, and service, and faith, and thy patience, and thy works; and the last to be more than the first.

Q: *What does "the last to be more than the first" mean?*
A: Although you may be the last to believe in God, you will be on an equal basis with those who believed first. The latecomers will be greeted joyously.

2:20 - Not withstanding I have a few things against thee, because thou sufferest that woman Jezebel, which calleth herself a prophetess, to teach and to seduce my servants to commit fornication, and to eat things sacrificed unto idols.

Q: *Corelli, what is the significance of this reference to Jezebel?*
A: Jezebel was a whore who led many men into perdition. Unfortunately, she became a symbol of all that is bad, all those unsavory things that men are prone to do. Jezebel did not survive into the afterlife. She refused to repent, but her legacy still lives on in those activities which are detrimental to spiritual growth. The original message to men in this verse was to not leave your wives for the temptations of harlots.

2:21 - And I gave her space to repent of her fornication; and she repented not.

2:22 - Behold, I will cast her into a bed, and them that commit adultery with her into great tribulation, except they repent of their deeds.

Q: Can you tell me what is meant by "I will cast her into a bed"?

A: "Cast her into a bed" means those who commit immoral acts will be cast into beds of their own making—in other words, into the results of their own iniquity, which means reducing their chances of eternal life by their own immoral behavior.

Q: Who will do the casting? God? Jesus?

A: No, again, "I" is a figure of speech. The people of those times ascribed everything to God. This should have read "they will be cast."

2:23 - And I will kill her children with death; and all the churches shall know that I am he which searcheth the reins and hearts: and I will give unto every one of you according to your works.

Q: Why punish the children? This is hardly the act of a loving God.

A: This is not at all what John intended. Parents have a responsibility to teach their children morals; and if they fail to teach their children about God, these children may suffer the same fate as their parents. This does not mean that God willingly punishes the children for the misdeeds of their parents, but rather that parents' behavior has a profound influence on their children.

2:24 - But unto you I say, and unto the rest in Thyatira, as many as have not this doctrine, and which have not known the depths of Satan, as they speak; I will put upon you none other burden.

Q: What does this verse mean, especially "none other burden"?

A: It means that all those who have not heard Christ's message will not be burdened by guilt because they did not know any better. But those who have heard Jesus' loving message and turned away will be held accountable for their misdeeds. Does this answer your question?

Stella: Yes, I guess so.

2:25 - But that which you have already hold fast till I come.

Q: *Hold fast to what?*

A: Hold fast to your belief in God.

2:26 - And he that overcometh, and keepeth my works unto the end, to him will I give power over the nations:

Q: *What does "power over nations" mean?*

A: Power over nations simply means the power to influence humanity towards God by their own right living.

2:27 - And he shall rule them with a rod of iron; as the vessels of a potter shall they be broken to shivers: even as I received of my Father.

Q: *What does "He shall rule them with a rod of iron" mean?*

A: This paragraph seems so convoluted even we are having trouble understanding it. This was not a part of John's original script.

2:28 - And I will give him the morning star.

Q: *What is the meaning of "morning star"?*

A: The morning star is Gabriel, the first-born child of the Creator Son (Jesus Christ) and the Mother Spirit. (*see UB*:407.) Why it was placed in this verse, we do not know.

2:29 - He that hath an ear, let him hear what the Spirit saith unto the churches.

As we know, the Spirit is a universal presence, a cosmic power, ever leading one to God.

These answers to my question about why John was told to write to the churches were certainly revealing, as were the answers to my many questions regarding the symbolism in the verses. I hope they are as revealing to you as they are to me. The next chapter continues the questions and answers about these intriguing symbols, but also contains some new surprises.

Highlights from Chapter 2

— The Eternal Son, "he who holds the seven stars" (2:1) tells John to write to the churches in the far regions to combat their brutishness and to instill faith in a loving God.

— John cites the churches' good works; then admonishes them to listen to the prompting of the Infinite Spirit.

— Those who turn to God will be given eternal life in Paradise, and will "eat of the Tree of Life" (2:7).

— The devil, "who shall cast some of you into prison" (2:10), is a being who really did exist, but can also be seen as a symbol that we are our own worst enemy.

— Everyone is given a second chance *after death* to go on or not go on. For those who refuse eternal life, the result is a "second death' (2:11), i.e., final extinction.

— Satan, Lucifer, and the other participants in the rebellion exist no more; they met final extinction in the recent adjudication.(See glossary.)

— The chaos we see today is the residue of human choices made in the aftermath of the rebellion led by Satan and Caligastia (see glossary) on this planet.

— Two tragic events completely altered the history of our planet: the Caligastia betrayal at the behest of Satan (*UB*: 601), and the default of Adam and Eve.

— "He who overcometh" (2:17) will get a new name. That is he will one day fuse with the indwelling God-fragment in the afterlife, after which we will literally be given a new name.

— Those who have not heard of Christ's message will not be burdened by guilt because they did not know any better.

3

King James Translation

1 And unto the angel of the church in Sardis write; These things saith he that hath the seven Spirits of God, and the seven stars; I know thy works, that thou hast a name that thou livest, and art dead.

2 Be watchful, and strengthen the things which remain, that are ready to die: for I have not found thy works perfect before God.

3 Remember therefore how thou hast received and heard, and hold fast, and repent. If therefore thou shalt not watch, I will come on thee as a thief, and thou shalt not know what hour I will come upon thee.

4 Thou hast a few names even in Sardis which have not defiled their garments; and they shall walk with me in white: for they are worthy.

5 He that overcometh, the same shall be clothed in white raiment; and I will not blot out his name out of the book of life, but I will confess his name before my Father, and before his angels.

6 He that hath an ear, let him hear what the Spirit saith unto the churches.

7 And to the angel of the church in Philadelphia write; These things saith he that is holy, he that is true, he that hath the key of David, he that openeth, and no man shutteth; and shutteth, and no man openeth;

8 I know thy works: behold, I have set before thee an open door, and no man can shut it: for thou hast a little strength, and hast kept my word, and hast not denied my name.

9 Behold, I will make them of the synagogue of Satan, which say they are Jews, and are not, but do lie; behold, I will make them to come and worship before thy feet, and to know that I have loved thee.

10 Because thou hast kept the word of my patience, I also will keep thee from the hour of temptation, which shall come upon all the world, to try them that dwell upon the earth.

11 Behold, I come quickly: hold that fast which thou hast, that no man take thy crown.

12 Him that overcometh will I make a pillar in the temple of my God, and he shall go no more out: and I will write upon him the name of my God, and the name of the city of my God, which is new Jerusalem, which cometh down out of heaven from my God: and I will write upon him my new name.

13 He that hath an ear, let him hear what the Spirit saith unto the churches.

14 And unto the angel of the church of the Laodiceans write; These things saith the Amen, the faithful and true witness, the beginning of the creation of God;

15 I know thy works, that thou art neither cold nor hot: I would thou wert cold or hot.

16 So then because thou art lukewarm, and neither cold nor hot, I will spue thee out of my mouth.

17 Because thou sayest, I am rich, and increased with goods, and have need of nothing; and knowest not that thou art wretched, and miserable, and poor, and blind, and naked:

18 I counsel thee to buy of me gold tried in the fire, that thou mayest be rich; and white raiment, that thou mayest be clothed, and that the shame of thy nakedness do not appear; and anoint thine eyes with eyesalve, that thou mayest see.

19 As many as I love, I rebuke and chasten: be zealous therefore, and repent.

20 Behold, I stand at the door, and knock: if any man hear my voice, and open the door, I will come in to him, and will sup with him, and he with me.

21 To him that overcometh will I grant to sit with me in my throne, even as I also overcame, and am set down with my Father in his throne.

22 He that hath an ear, let him hear what the Spirit saith unto the churches.

3

revised

In chapter 2, the Asian churches were admonished to listen to the Infinite Spirit, and assured that if they do, they will partake of the good news of eternal life in Paradise. But this chapter has a different tone. For example,it implies certain ominous threats such as in 3:3 where Christ "will come on thee as a thief; in 3:16: "I will spue thee out of my mouth"; and in 3:19: "I rebuke and chasten."

In my early conversations with Corelli, she assured me that we are safe in disregarding anything of a negative nature in this rather negative chapter. She reminded me that John's message was always one of hope and love.

Then on March 6, 1997, Corelli made an astonishing statement when I had asked her what she really thought of chapter 3. This is how she answered:

> A: We don't think anything about it. It really was not dictated by John. This chapter was a compilation of many writers and priests recording what they thought should be included. These are not John's thoughts, so

you can indicate that in your writings, unless, of course, you care to write what you think may be the message that was intended by these other writers. Otherwise just note briefly that John did not write it. Feel better?

Stella: Yes, thank you.

Though surprised, I was not fully satisfied with this answer. I did not trust myself to interpret chapter 3 correctly, although I did attempt to write out some interpretations based on previous communications and on some research in *The Urantia Book*. Although I was told to research the chapter myself, I thought my celestial guides might give me some information anyway. And they did!

A few days later, on March 13, 1997, I again asked whether John or someone else wrote this chapter. I needed confirmation that I had heard correctly. The following is a transcript of what occurred:

Q: *Did John write this chapter?*
A: No he did not.

Q: *Who did?*
A: We do not know. It was inserted long after John's death.

Q: *But it sounds so much like the rest of it.*
A: We know. It was a clever forgery never detected by anyone, until now when you questioned our original statement. It is clearly drafted to confuse a gullible public.

Q: *Nevertheless, the message contains some great truths. How about 3:3: "I will come on thee as a thief, and thou shalt not know what hour I will come upon thee"?*
A: But this was implied as a threat—that if one does not behave, God will strike and punish you. This is not John's original statement. For example, he wrote: "Be ye great in God's favor, for all who loveth him and keep his commandments of loving one another, he will seek and embrace you with loving concern. So it

is and it will ever be." This is quite different than the meaning as stated in the present version.

Stella: Well, that's quite a repudiation of 3:3.

Nevertheless, I was still curious about what they would say about the rest of the verses in chapter 3. So, with my teachers's assistance, I went back to the beginning and plowed through these verses which—although not written by John—have been studied by Christians for centuries.

Message to the church at Sardis

> 3:1 - And unto the angel of the church in Sardis write; These things saith he that hath the seven Spirits of God, and the seven stars; I know thy works, that thou has a name that thou livest, and art dead.

As we learned in 1:4, the "seven Spirits of God" referred to in this verse are the supreme directors of the created universe—which consists of seven superuniverses—and that the seven stars (see 1:16) represent the seven capital cities in each of these universes. On December 4, 1998, I asked Corelli to clarify the meaning of the "cities." She said that they are actually planets or celestial worlds—headquarters worlds of each superuniverse.

As a reminder, the "angel of the church" referred to in 3:1 (e.g., the Church at Sardis) is actually one of the so-called "religious guardians" who seek to preserve moral values (see 1:20). Following is a description of this order of angels from *The Urantia Book:*

> The religious guardians are the "angels of the churches," the earnest contenders for that which is and has been. They endeavor to maintain the ideals of that which has survived for the sake of the safe transit of moral values from one epoch to another. They are the checkmates of the angels of progress, all the while seeking to translate from one generation to another the imperishable values of the old and passing forms into the new and therefore less stabilized patterns of thought and conduct. These angels do contend for spiritual forms, but they are not

the source of ultra-sectarianism and meaningless controversial divisions of professed religionists. (1255)

But I remained confused about this verse. In my first transmission regarding 1:16, I was told that the seven stars referred to seven capital cities. Yet, 1:20 states the seven stars are the angels of the churches. So after my research above on 3:1, I of course had to ask which was correct. Does the angel in 3:1 refer to a capital city or to an angel who is a religious guardian? This time it was Aflana who answered my question.

A: In this case, seven angels are correct.

Aflana also told me that she did not know why John chose the same metaphors (which are obviously being carried forward into this chapter by the forgers of chapter 3). This certainly made things confusing—but luckily, Aflana offered to ask John about this. After a pause, Aflana returned and gave John's reply:

A: John chose dual metaphors because it was easier for the people to understand angels as being guardians of the churches. The idea of the seven stars referring to the seven capitals of the superuniverses was utterly beyond their comprehension. She also relayed this message from John to me:"We are glad you are attempting to correct and explain this"— which she said he graciously added.

3:2 - Be watchful, and strengthen the things, which remain, that are ready to die: for I have not found thy works perfect before God.

Aflana: This was not written by John but can remain as stated.

3:3 - Remember therefore how thou hast received and heard, and hold fast and repent. If therefore thou shalt not watch, I will come on thee as a thief, and thou shalt not know what hour I will come upon thee.

See beginning of this chapter for John's actual words which should substitute for the passage. The idea that "I will come on thee as a thief..." was written as an implied threat, but not by John.

> 3:4 - Thou has a few names, even in Sardis, which have not defiled their garments; and they shall walk with me in white; for they are worthy.

Aflana commented: Seems all right. The intent is a loving one and can be kept in.

> 3:5 - He that overcometh, the same shall be clothed in white rainment; and I will not blot out his name out of the book of life, but I will confess his name before my Father, and before his angels.

Aflana: With belief in God and a spiritual way of life, your name will not be erased from the record or book of life.

> 3:6 - He that hath an ear, let him hear what the Spirit saith unto the churches.

See 2:7 for an explanation of Infinite Spirit (in regard to "the Spirit saith"). As a reminder, the Infinite Spirit is the third person of the Trinity, and is a divine and cosmic power exerting a "holy" influence on all created beings. This explanation applies to all the verses dealing with "He that hath an ear..." Aflana confirmed that I have explained 2:7 and 3:6 correctly.

Message to the church at Philadelphia

> 3:7 - And to the angel of the church in Philadelphia write; These things saith he that is holy, he that is true, he that hath the key of David, he that openeth, and no man shutteth; and shutteth, and no man openeth;

In this verse, the "key of David" refers of course to Jesus who was presumed to have been of the line of King David. But it turns out that, according to *The Urantia Book*, Jesus was *not* a descendant of David.

> Joseph was not of the line of King David. Mary had more of the Davidic ancestry than Joseph. True, Joseph did go

to the City of David, Bethlehem, to be registered for the Roman census, but that was because, six generations previously, Joseph's paternal ancestor of that generation, being an orphan, was adopted by one Zadoc, who was a direct descendent of David; hence was Joseph accounted as of the house of David...Jesus himself one-time publicly denied any connection with the royal house of David. (1347-8)

3:8 - I know thy works: behold, I have set before thee an open door, and no man can shut it: for thou hast a little strength, and hast kept my word, and hast not denied my name.

Aflana continued: "Open door" in this verse refers to the door of eternal life, which is wide open to all. Even when there is doubt regarding the sincerity and whole-heartedness of a person's devotion to the kingdom, the judges of men receive the doubtful candidate.

3:9 - Behold, I will make them of the synagogue of Satan, which say they are Jews, and are not, but do lie; behold, I will make them to come and worship before thy feet, and to know that I have loved thee.

"Synagogue of Satan" most likely refers to those temples devoted to the worship of pagan deities, Baal. (See 2:9.) But this verse seemed somewhat convoluted to me, so I asked for the meaning of, "I will make them to come and worship before thy feet, and to know I have loved thee."

A: Those who are in doubt may come at any time to worship God through the Master. He will never turn anyone away who prays with a sincere heart.

3:10 - Because thou hast kept the word of my patience, I also will keep thee from the hour of temptation, which shall come upon all the world, to try them that dwell upon the earth.

Q: What does "I will keep thee from the hour of temptation which shall come upon all the world to try them that dwell upon the earth" mean?

A: The phrase "I also will keep thee from the hour of temptation" is not correct in its implication. God shows us the way, but the decision to turn from temptation is only yours. But if you are sincere in your faith, you will be protected in your hours of adversity.

Q: *On another point, a year ago or so you said John did not write this chapter, and somewhere along the way I got the impression that there were many who contributed to writing this chapter, adding passages which they thought fit. Were my impressions correct?*

A: Yes, indeed. Many others took John's original message and simply wrote in what they thought should be inserted. The results were often a mixture of half-truths and innuendoes. You are safe in clarifying this chapter as you have already done and according to what we have told you. Bear in mind that John's ultimate message was: "Love ye one another as I have told you," which Jesus stated over and over. John's final message was: "My children, love you one another." Much else can be disregarded except as to the truths contained in what Jesus actually taught.

Q: *And what are these truths?*

A: Much of what Jesus actually said and did can be found in *The Urantia Book*. This is almost a verbatim account of what he said and how he lived his life, a life of majestic splendor.

3:11 - Behold I come quickly: hold that fast which thou hast, that no man take thy crown.

A: This can mean that you should let no man influence you away from your goal of eternal life.

3:12 - Him that overcometh will I make a pillar in the temple of my God, and he shall go no more out: and I will write upon him the name of my God, and the name of the city of my God, which is New Jerusalem, which cometh down out of heaven from my God: and I will write upon him my new name.

Q: *What does this section mean?*

A: We think this addition could mean that once you have made your final decision for eternal life, you are then assured of eternal life.

ETERNAL LIFE AND THE EXPERIENCE OF "FUSION"

Later in this book we will encounter other references to receiving "a new name" (as in, "I will write upon him a new name" at 3:12 just above). Corelli indicated to me that receiving a "new name" refers to the ultimate experience in the spiritual life: our eventual fusion with the spirit of God within, or "fragment of God." In the Urantia Revelation this entity is called by the odd name of "thought adjuster" (see glossary). At the moment of fusion with this inner gift of God, the *UB* teaches that we will indeed receive a new name. This name will go with us for the rest of eternity as an indication of our assurance of eternal life. In other words, at the point of fusion, you need never again fear that eternal life cannot be yours. (The same interpretation could also apply, she said, to phrases like "he shall go no more out" at 3:12.)

As we pointed out before, you retain the choice of going on in the afterlife, or stopping at any point-up until this point of fusion. As you first enter the afterlife, you are counseled as to your choices and encouraged to repent of your misdeeds in the mortal life. If in the final analysis you refuse to repent, you are judged and given the second or final death. There is no third chance. But if you choose to go on and continue to experience the glories of the morontia life, fusion with the God-fragment will be your goal.

Here are some additional points of information from *The Urantia Book* (see Papers 107-112, pages 1176-1241) about this extremely important concept:

1. At the moment that a child makes his or her first moral choice—which usually occurs at about the ages of five or six—a fragment of God (i.e., Thought Adjuster, and also sometimes called the "Mystery Monitor") is immediately assigned to that child.

2. Your mortal human mind and this fragment of God work together during your lifetime to create your immortal soul. Your soul is a direct creation of your God-fragment, using as its basis the actual moral choices of your human mind.

3. At death, the Thought Adjuster leaves immediately, but is subsequently reunited with you and your soul at the moment of your resurrection in the afterlife. (The material body and brain/mind return to dust of course, but as noted previously, we receive a new morontia body at the point of resurrection.)

4. Your Thought Adjuster and soul stay with you as you continue upon your eternal journey—if you choose it. At some point in the afterlife when you are sufficiently spiritualized, fusion occurs between these two entities. When that happens, you are assured of eternal life. Sometimes (but rarely for our planet) fusion can occur during the mortal life, in a flash of combustion of sorts. (As we will see later, Enoch was the first human to fuse.)

5. If you decide not to continue eternal life and choose oblivion, all your good deeds and spiritual memories remain in the permanent custody of your former God-fragment. It is subsequently assigned to another child. As a consequence, these memories become the legacy of another human being.

6. Throughout this tremendous process, our "pre-personal" but infinite and eternal God-fragment is trying to achieve union with you, a human personality. According to the Urantia Revelation, "personality" is that unchanging part of you which is absolutely and uniquely you. Your personhood is a divine gift to you from God (in addition to the gift of the thought adjuster).

7. You and I, for our part, can aspire to divinity through the urgings of this divine spark within. But we must determine for ourselves that we will yield to these leadings by the decisions of our mortal mind. When final fusion occurs, both God and man have achieved their goals, and, as it says at 3:12, you "shall go no more out." You will then be given a "new name."

> 3:13 - He that hath an ear, let him hear what the Spirit saith unto the churches.

Once again, the Infinite Spirit is guiding the churches onward.

Message to the church at Laodicia

3:14 - And unto the angel of the church of the Laodiceans write; These things saith the Amen, the faithful and true witness, the beginning of the creation of God;

3:15 - I know thy works, that thou art neither cold nor hot: I would thou wert cold or hot.

3:16 - So then because thou art lukewarm, and neither cold nor hot, I will spue thee out of my mouth.

3:17 - Because thou sayest, I am rich, and increased with goods, and have need of nothing; and knowest not that thou art wretched, and miserable, and poor, and blind, and naked:

A: Generally, this message to the Laodicians indicates that earthly riches are of no use in the after life. There is nothing wrong with having earthly possessions, as long as they are used for the good of humanity. Were these possessions gained at the cost of oppressing those who created the wealth? In that case you will be judged by your motives, not by what you possessed.

3:18 - I counsel thee to buy of me gold tried in the fire, that thou mayest be rich; and white raiment, that thou mayest be clothed, and that the shame of thy nakedness does not appear; and anoint thine eyes with eye salve, that thou mayest see.

Q: What is the "gold tried in the fire"?

A: The gold signifies those spiritual treasures that you have stored up in heaven while on earth. This is the gold that has eternal value. You will one day be clothed in fine "white raiment," when you have become worthy to stand before the throne of God.

3:19 - As many as I love, I rebuke and chasten: be zealous therefore, and repent.

A: Can remain as is.

Promise of reward to the faithful

3:20 - Behold, I stand at the door, and knock: if any man hear my voice, and opens the door, I will come in to him, and will sup with him, and he with me.

3:21 - To him that overcometh will I grant to sit with me in my throne, even as I also overcame, and am set down with my Father in his throne.

3:22 - He that hath an ear, let him hear what the Spirit saith unto the churches.

Although John did not write 3:20-22, Corelli told me they could remain.

Some surprising additional information came through after I questioned Corelli and Aflana many times on this chapter. Why I asked the following question, I do not know:

Q: Did John really write to seven churches?

A: No, he did not. He only wrote to five. Laodicia was the last of these, and most of that section was never incorporated into the biblical text and was lost. The only portions of chapter 3 that can stand as a worthwhile message—although not written by John—are verses 3:20-22.

Q: Corelli, Can you tell me why John only wrote to five churches and why Sardis and Philadelphia were added?

A: Yes, we can. Sardis was a very small hamlet without a church of any significance. Philadelphia was also small but somewhat off the beaten path so that the runner didn't think it important to deliver the small note from John. When these two towns grew larger, the priests at that time thought it would be a good idea to create letters along the lines of the original five letters written by John. Consequently, they wrote what they considered would be good letters of instructions containing warnings to repent.

Thus ended the sessions on a chapter not written by John, but, nevertheless, one that adds new and surprising information. John wrote only to five churches and not to Sardis and Philadelphia, and almost the entire chapter is a clever forgery by those who came after him.

Recall John's original statement at 3:3 that was lost: "Be ye great in God's favor, for all who loveth him and keep his commandments of loving one another, he will seek and embrace you with loving concern. So it is and it will ever be." What a hopeful and reassuring message!

Highlights from Chapter 3

— Chapter 3 was neither dictated nor recorded by John, and is actually a "clever forgery"—a compilation of many writers and priests who came after him.

— The "angel of the church"(3:1) is one of the so-called religious guardians who seek to transmit moral values from one epoch to another. (*UB*: 1225)

— John never wrote the well-known passage at 3:3:" I will come on thee as a thief, and thou shall not know what hour I will come upon thee." John's original statement was: "Be ye great in God's favor, for all who loveth him and keep his commandment of loving one another, he will seek and embrace you with loving concern. So it is and it will ever be."

— Mary had more of the Davidic ancestry than did Joseph. Jesus was not in the direct bloodline of King David. (*UB*: 1347)

— Much of what Jesus actually said and did can be found in Part IV of *The Urantia Book*, which is an almost verbatim account of his life.

— At 3:12, the references to you "shall no more go out", and will be given a "new name" can be said to refer to our destiny of one day fusing with the God-fragment within us—also known as the "thought adjuster". This is a very important concept introduced in the Urantia Revelation (*UB*: 1176-1241). The inner God fragment and the human mind work together to co-create our soul, which survives in the afterlife.

— John wrote only to only five churches; he never did communicate with the churches at Sardis and Philadelphia. All that he wrote in this chapter was lost .

4

King James Translation

1 After this I looked, and, behold, a door was opened in heaven: and the first voice which I heard was as it were of a trumpet talking with me; which said, Come up hither, and I will shew thee things which must be hereafter.

2 And immediately I was in the spirit: and, behold, a throne was set in heaven, and one sat on the throne.

3 And he that sat was to look upon like a jasper and a sardine stone: and there was a rainbow round about the throne, in sight like unto an emerald.

4 And round about the throne were four and twenty seats: and upon the seats I saw four and twenty elders sitting, clothed in white raiment; and they had on their heads crowns of gold.

5 And out of the throne proceeded lightnings and thunderings and voices: and there were seven lamps of fire burning before the throne, which are the seven Spirits of God.

6 And before the throne there was a sea of glass like unto crystal: and in the midst of the throne, and round about the throne, were four beasts full of eyes before and behind.

7 And the first beast was like a lion, and the second beast like a calf, and the third beast had a face as a man, and the fourth beast was like a flying eagle.

8 And the four beasts had each of them six wings about him; and they were full of eyes within: and they rest not day and night, saying, Holy, holy, holy, Lord God Almighty, which was, and is, and is to come.

9 And when those beasts give glory and honour and thanks to him that sat on the throne, who liveth for ever and ever,

10 The four and twenty elders fall down before him that sat on the throne, and worship him that liveth for ever and ever, and cast their crowns before the throne, saying,

11 Thou art worthy, O Lord, to receive glory and honour and power: for thou hast created all things, and for thy pleasure they are and were created.

4
revised

This chapter contains symbols already encountered previously, such as the seven spirits of God. But it also introduces intriguing new images, including the twenty-four elders, the sea of glass, and the four beasts. To the amazement of some, we will discover that most of the odd material presented in this chapter has literal reality according to the Urantia Revelation. All we have to do is "decompress" the images.

I began to question Corelli regarding this chapter on March 13, 1996. As I explained previously, I focused on items that initially caught my attention; I had no plan to write a book in the early days of my research. For example, I was curious right away about the meaning of the symbol of the "four beasts" at 4:6. I went into meditation and this is what came through from Corelli:

A: When John received his revelation there were no words for such things as energy, so he resorted to allegories to convey his meanings. Regarding the four beasts, the word "beast" in Hebrew is *nebbish*. The four beasts—the lion, the calf, the beast with a face like a man, and the flying eagle—each had a particular characteristic the audience could understand. For example, the lion is understood to be strong and majestic, the king of all that he surveys.

This sent me once again to *The Urantia Book*. Here I read that the four beasts that John saw are actually "power centers" that emanate cosmic energies. (Verse 4:8 is correct when it says: "They rest not night and day.") Then I wondered if perhaps each of the power centers has a specialized function, or does each "beast" contain all four characteristics within himself?

Corelli continued: The Bible does not convey this correctly. Each "beast" actually contains all four characteristics—the qualities of the lion, face of man, calf and flying eagle. The "face of man" image points to the humanity of God; the calf represents Jesus or the lamb of God; and the flying eagle symbolizes forces or wings that send out cosmic energies.

Later I looked up nebbish in Webster's *New World Dictionary*, Second College Edition. It means "a person who is pitifully inept, ineffectual, shy, dull." This did not seem to fit —but *neb* does fit. It means the bill of a bird, the snout of an animal, or the nose or mouth of a person. It seems I picked up on something important, however unwittingly. Almost two years later, on February 6, 1998, I decided to try to verify what I had been told initially, so I asked Corelli if, centuries ago, nebbish meant animal-like.

A: Yes, that is correct. Meanings do change over time. Today nebbish refers to a person who is ineffective and shy; then it meant animal-like. John tried to portray the characteristics or traits of certain creatures. Again, each of these "beasts" had all four traits;

as I said previously, there was an error in the way it was originally written.

I went back to *The Urantia Book* and was utterly fascinated with what I read. (See verse 4:5 below and *UB*:378.) Its explanations of the symbols were so clear and detailed that I felt there was no need to get further clarification from Corelli, other than to ask her if what I read in *The Urantia Book* was true.

A: Yes it is, Stella. Still, there is much more that we didn't go into in *The Urantia Book*. In fact there is so much, you would be astonished and pleased. John also saw many things that he did not include in his revelation. Besides, the people of those times would not have comprehended the workings of the cosmos, its energies, your solar system, and the mansion worlds—all of which were revealed to John. There is a great and glorious heaven waiting for those who choose to continue. Be not afraid of death, you who read this. Life after death is a safe haven—or heaven, as you call it.

The rest of my interpretations in this chapter are guided by a close reading of passages in *The Urantia Book* based on guidance by Corelli.

The scene in heaven before the breaking of the seals

4:1 - After this I looked, and, behold, a door was opened in heaven: and the first voice which I heard was as it were of a trumpet talking with me; which said, Come up hither, and I will shew thee things which must be hereafter.

A: This verse indicates that John's visions are beginning.

4:2 - And immediately I was in the spirit: and, behold, a throne was set in heaven, and one sat on the throne.

A: John is in a state of shock as this experience overtakes him, yet he is in control of his mind. "I was in the spirit" in this sense indicates his state of mind.

As we saw in chapter 2, the "throne set in heaven" represents the judgment seat of the presiding archangel. Technically speaking, it is the throne of the "resurrection roll call" for those who have survived death, Corelli indicated.

"One sat on the throne" refers ultimately to the Eternal Son. As we learned at 1:8, the Eternal Son is the second person of the Trinity, who acts in this local universe through his Sons (in our case Jesus), through the Ancients of Days, through the archangel of life, and through other agencies.

> 4:3 - And he that sat was to look upon like a jasper and a sardine stone: and there was a rainbow round about the throne, in sight like unto an emerald.

John is privileged to see beautiful colors radiating about the throne. I learned in my research that the Greek translation for sardine is "sardius," which is a gemstone somewhat like a ruby or sard worn on a Hebrew high priest's breastplate.

The four beasts and the enthroned elders

> 4:4 - And round about the throne were four and twenty seats: and upon the seats I saw four and twenty elders sitting, clothed in white raiment; and they had on their heads crowns of gold.

Over the centuries of interpretation of the Book of Revelation, many have wondered—Who are the mysterious elders of 4:4?

THE TWENTY-FOUR ELDERS

The Urantia Book reveals that the twenty-four elders are a real body of celestial counselors who oversee the evolution of our planet. Most were placed in this high position by Christ Michael (Jesus), just after his life on earth. These elders wear crowns that indicate their authority; indeed, they are the personal agents of Jesus. (At 4:5 we learn about their location in the heavenly realms.)

The Urantia Book indicates that these twenty-four high counselors are recruited from the eight Urantia races. Fifteen of them are highly spiritualized individuals who lived before the time of Christ. They have the authority to represent him and to also carry out special requests of Gabriel not only on our planet but even on other planets as well. (See *UB*:513-4.)

Summarized below are a selection of these individuals, including their chief earthly achievements. [Note to reader: To really understand their significance in planetary history, a good acquaintance with *The Urantia Book* is necessary. Many of these teachers and leaders are pre-historic.]

1. Onamonalonton—a far-distant leader of the red man who directed this race to the veneration of "The Great Spirit."

2. Singlangton—an early teacher of the yellow race who taught "One Truth"—one God instead of many.

3. Adam

4. Eve (the full stories of Adam and Eve are covered later)

5. Enoch—first mortal to fuse with his thought adjuster (fragment of God). See the end of this chapter for more on Enoch.

6. Moses—revived worship of the Universal Father under the name of "The God of Israel."

7. Elijah—a soul of brilliant spiritual achievement.

8. Machiventa Melchizedek—the so-called "sage of Salem" in the days of Abraham. Machiventa is a very important figure to our planet, according to the Urantia Revelation. (See glossary.)

9. John the Baptist—the forerunner of Jesus' mission on Urantia.

The Urantia Book also tells us that eight of the seats on the council are always filled temporarily in order to be available for great spiritual teachers of subsequent ages.

> 4:5 - And out of the throne proceeded lightnings and thunderings and voices: and there were seven lamps of fire burning before the throne, which are the seven Spirits of God.

The Urantia Book states that John did indeed see seven spirits of God as these were burning like lamps before a throne. But in truth he is speaking here of a different throne than that referred to in 4:5; for it is not true that the seats of the four and twenty are assembled around these seven spirits.

> This record represents the confusion of two presentations, one pertaining to the universe headquarters and the other to the system capital. The seats of the four and twenty elders are on Jerusem, the headquarters of our local system of inhabited worlds. The seven...spirits are at Salvington [the headquarters of the local universe]. (See *UB*:378.)

The phrase "...out of the throne proceeded lightnings and thunderings" refers to "universe broadcasts" which regularly occur on Salvington.

THE SEA OF GLASS

4:6 - And before the throne there was a sea of glass like unto crystal: and in the midst of the throne, and round about the throne, were four beasts full of eyes before and behind.

Liberal-minded Christians will also be surprised to learn that, according to *The Urantia Book* (486-7), the crystalline sea of glass is literally real. It is the routine receiving area on heavenly spheres, the equivalent of an airport. It is an enormous circular crystal of very large circumference and depth. "This magnificent crystal serves as the receiving field for all...beings arriving from points outside the sphere...." (*UB*: 487)

> 4:7 - And the first beast was like a lion, and the second beast like a calf, and the third beast had a face as a man, and the fourth beast was like a flying eagle.

See earlier in this chapter for explanations of the four beasts which are, in reality, living beings who function as power centers that emanate directional energies through the local universe. In this passage *The Urantia Book* makes explicit reference to John's vision of the "beasts":

> He [John] also envisaged the directional control creatures of the local universe, the living compasses of the headquarters world. This directional control in Nebadon is maintained by the four control creatures of Salvington, who operate over the universe currents....But the description of these four creatures, called beasts, has been sadly marred; they are of unparalleled beauty and exquisite form." (*UB*: 378)

> 4:8 - And the four beasts had each of them six wings about him; and they were full of eyes within: and they rest not day and night, saying, Holy, holy, holy, Lord God Almighty, which was, and is, and is to come.

According to Corelli, the eyes on each beast symbolize beams of light; the six wings represent cosmic forces that send energies into space.

> 4:9 - And when those beasts give glory and honour and thanks to him that sat on the throne, who liveth for ever and ever,

> 4:10 - The four and twenty elders fall down before him that sat on the throne, and worship him that liveth for ever and ever, and cast their crowns before the throne, saying,

> 4:11 - Thou art worthy, O Lord, to receive glory and honour and power: for thou hast created all things, and for thy pleasure they are and were created.

The symbols in 4:9-11 are already explained above.

THE MAGNIFICENT ENOCH

According to legend, Enoch was caught up into the heavens and then returned to earth to tell his sons what he had seen. I wondered what Corelli could tell me about him so I questioned her:

Q: *When did Enoch live?*

A: He actually lived before the arrival of Adam and Eve. Enoch lived in Canaan and was a deeply spiritual man, extraordinary for those times. He loved God wholeheartedly and tried to instill this love in his children, but did not wholly succeed. He was a unique personality, a man so spiritual that he actually fused in this life—an extremely rare occurrence. We were so glad for him and for us. His fusion meant that the plan for ascension was really working; we had held our breath for so long wondering if it would ever occur. He was an inspiration to many—even to Jesus. He was a man way ahead of his time, a forerunner and example for others to follow.

Highlights from Chapter 4

- There is a great deal that John saw that he did not include in his revelation; there is likewise much that was left out of *The Urantia Book* as well. "There is a great and glorious heaven waiting for those who go on." (—Corelli)

- After Jesus' resurrection, he placed in position twenty-four "elders" (4:4) who have the authority to represent him and Gabriel and who oversee the spiritual evolution of our planet. These twenty-four are former humans who were highly spiritualized leaders of their respective races. Eight seats are temporarily filled, and are kept open for great spiritual teachers of subsequent ages. (*UB*:513)

- The sea of glass (4:6) is not a metaphor but actually refers to a real crystal. It is literally a "landing field" and receiving area that is found on almost all heavenly spheres.

- The four beasts (4:6) are real celestial creatures who function as "power centers". They are in reality beings of unparalleled beauty. (*UB*:378)

- Enoch, who is one of the elders, was the first mortal on our planet to fuse with the indwelling fragment of God (or Thought Adjuster).

5

King James Translation

1 And I saw in the right hand of him that sat on the throne a book written within and on the backside, sealed with seven seals.

2 And I saw a strong angel proclaiming with a loud voice, Who is worthy to open the book, and to loose the seals thereof?

3 And no man in heaven, nor in earth, neither under the earth, was able to open the book, neither to look thereon.

4 And I wept much, because no man was found worthy to open and to read the book, neither to look thereon.

5 And one of the elders saith unto me, Weep not: behold, the Lion of the tribe of Judah, the Root of David, hath prevailed to open the book, and to loose the seven seals thereof.

6 And I beheld, and, lo, in the midst of the throne and of the four beasts, and in the midst of the elders, stood a Lamb as it had been slain, having seven horns and seven eyes, which are the seven Spirits of God sent forth into all the earth.

7 And he came and took the book out of the right hand of him that sat upon the throne.

8 And when he had taken the book, the four beasts and four and twenty elders fell down before the Lamb, having every one of them harps, and golden vials full of odours, which are the prayers of saints.

9 And they sung a new song, saying, Thou art worthy to take the book, and to open the seals thereof: for thou wast slain, and hast redeemed us to God by thy blood out of every kindred, and tongue, and people, and nation;

10 And hast made us unto our God kings and priests: and we shall reign on the earth.

11 And I beheld, and I heard the voice of many angels round about the throne and the beasts and the elders: and the number of them was ten thousand times ten thousand, and thousands of thousands;

12 Saying with a loud voice, Worthy is the Lamb that was slain to receive power, and riches, and wisdom, and strength, and honour, and glory, and blessing.

13 And every creature which is in heaven, and on the earth, and under the earth, and such as are in the sea, and all that are in them, heard I saying, Blessing, and honour, and glory, and power, be unto him that sitteth upon the throne, and unto the Lamb for ever and ever.

14 And the four beasts said, Amen. And the four and twenty elders fell down and worshipped him that liveth for ever and ever

5

revised

This chapter is written in John's usual cryptic code, but with Corelli's help it was relatively easy to interpret. It deals with life after death and how we are judged according to our actions through "the seven stages of life." These stages correlate with the opening of the symbolic "seven seals" for which this chapter is famous.

Chapter 5 also presents the key image of the throne of judgment—but it is not clear who sits on the throne. Is it Jesus or is it the Eternal Son who presides at that awesome event? I questioned Corelli many times about this because I wanted to be certain I had heard correctly. She usually answered the Eternal Son, but at one point she said it was a presiding Angel of Life. So which is correct, I wondered?

As always, her answers opened up new vistas of thought and led to new questions. For example, why do some people choose extinction? How do the so-called seven spirits of God actually relate to our lives? Who exactly are the "Ancients of Days"?

Early in 1996 I continued my almost haphazard questioning of Corelli. I was eager to get as many questions answered before this strange series of celestial contacts ended. When I later realized that this contact would continue, I made sure the questions and answers followed verse by verse.

I began on March 13, 1996, with the following series of questions:

The book of the seven seals

5:1- And I saw in the right hand of him that sat on the throne a book written within and on the backside, sealed with seven seals.

Q: *Who actually sits on the "throne," Corelli?"*

A: God, of course. (But Corelli amends this answer below.)

Q: *And what is the meaning of the seven seals?*

A: The seals do not refer to secret prophecies, as Christians have thought. They refer to the Book of Life—the celestial record of all those who have lived and died. It is only to be opened by the Archangel of Life when a final decision has been made as to going on for eternal life or refusing to go on. That decision is final and takes place in the Halls of Learning; it is obviously a most profound event in the life of any individual. Many are chosen but few accept this extraordinary invitation.

Q: *Why not?*

A: Many fear the extra effort that will be required to do God's will and they back out at the last minute— eternal life somehow doesn't hold their interest and they choose oblivion. It is sad but true: They are tired at the thought of an eternal struggle and cannot comprehend the eventual rewards.

Q: *"Many are chosen, but few accept"? Is this really true?*

A: Yes, it's hard to believe. As we told you, many find that they are tired of going on.

Q: But in all the universes, aren't there trillions who choose to go on?

A: Yes, that is also true. Those who choose eternal life are the eager, curious ones who consider life to be an adventure to be lived as long as possible; they are thrilled when after mortal death they find they are still alive and are overwhelmed with thankfulness. Usually, those who choose to go on prove most useful as they continue the magnificent journey of eternity. You, too, will be enchanted as new opportunities to serve are given to you during your ascension career.

Q: At what point do people actually choose extinction?

A: It can be at any point—usually when they think they have failed at a task, and their disappointment is great. We do try to counsel them, but sometimes we just cannot reach them.

Q: What percentage of them actually chooses extinction, Corelli?

A: The amount happens to be about seven percent.

Months and sometimes years may elapse before another question occurs to me on a topic previously covered. On February 7, 1998, I returned to chapter 5 and questioned Corelli's answer of March 13, 1996, when she said that God sat on the "throne"—whereas as we saw in chapter 2, we learned that that "throne" refers to the seat of judgment. Which is correct?

A: Judgment seat is correct. God, of course, has authorized the process by which all are judged—but judgment is the province of the presiding archangel.

Q: Who is this presiding archangel?
A: The Eternal Son.

Q: So why call him a presiding archangel?
A: The presiding archangel, or Angel of Life, has the authority to speak for the Eternal Son on occasion.

Q: But The Urantia Book *does not mention an Archangel of Life. Is there really such a being?*

A: Yes, there is. This archangel is well trained to adjudicate the progress of a mortal. His judgment carries great weight with the Ancients of Days.

Q: *What is the Hall of Learning?*

A: The Hall of Learning is where you receive an account of what your life has been. It has many divisions.

I was still trying to understand who we stand before at the time of judgment, so I asked about about this yet again.

Corelli answered: Ultimately the Ancients of Days make the final judgment, but before then there are various stages of evaluation at the learning and training schools. You will stand in the presence of Christ in a far distant time, but you ultimately stand before the Ancients of Days.

Q: *Corelli, when John saw the being holding a book in his right hand, was this the Ancients of Days?*

A: No. John saw what occurs at the Hall of Learning when you are given an account of your life. John actually saw a presiding archangel, but he used the term "lamb" which people understood to be Jesus. The people of those times could not have comprehended the various levels of judgment one undergoes before reaching the courts of the Ancients of Days who make the final decision as to whether you are considered worthy to continue eternal life or not. Does this help?

Stella: *I guess so.*

The Urantia Book explains all this clearly. For example, it states that "Cessation of existence is usually decreed at the dispensational or epochal adjudication.... by co-ordinate action of all tribunals of jurisdiction, extending from the planetary council up through the courts of the Creator Son [Jesus] to the judgment tribunals of the Ancients of Days." (UB:37)

Naturally I wanted to know more about the Ancients of Days.

For this I went again to The Urantia Book: It explains that each superuniverse (of which there are seven) is ruled by three Ancients of Days. They are among the highest created beings. These personalities have the ultimate power of decision..."when each individual's right to unending life comes up for adjudication." (*UB*:314)

> 5:2 - And I saw a strong angel proclaiming with a loud voice, Who is worthy to open the book, and to loose the seals thereof?
>
> 5:3 - And no man in heaven, nor in earth, neither under the earth, was able to open the book, neither to look thereon.
>
> 5:4 - And I wept much, because no man was found worthy to open and to read the book, neither to look thereon.
>
> A: No one at this point has the authority to open the Book of Life, save the Archangel of Life. (See above.)

Christ alone is worthy of opening the book

> 5:5 - And one of the elders saith unto me, weep not: behold the lion of the tribe of Judah, the root of David, hath prevailed to open the book and to loose the seven seals thereof.

Christ is sometimes referred to in the Bible as being the "Lion of Judah" as well as being of the root of David.

Corelli's answer on March 13, 1996, was enlightening regarding my question as to the meaning of seven seals. However, on December 20, 1999, I decided to try to get more information as to what are the actual meanings of the seven seals.

This is how she replied:

> A: The seals actually refer to seven stages of human development: Birth to 5 years; age 6-12; 13-21; 22-28; 29-35; 36-50; and beyond 50. All these stages are evaluated regarding your successes as a human

being. Have you been thoughtful, loving, believing in God—or have you gone through life taking for personal gain and disregarding the welfare of others? What was your intent? Even if you failed in your accomplishments, you are weighed as to what you intended to do.

If your intentions and actions are judged as not noble, you will still have the opportunity to repent, and you will be judged again accordingly. There is much flexibility in judging anyone, and there is ample time to decide if you wish to repent. As we said before, there is no precise timeline.

But once you decide, that is considered final. Many choose not to go on. In that case, oblivion will be your chosen fate, for there is no hell. If you choose to go on, the adventure of eternal life is yours.

5:6 - And I beheld, and, lo, in the midst of the throne and of the four beasts, and in the midst of the elders, stood a lamb as it had been slain, having seven horns and seven eyes, which are the seven spirits of God sent forth into all the earth.

See 5:1 above in which "throne" is referred to as the judgment seat.

We have previously explored the figures of the four beasts and the twenty-four elders. But the slain lamb with seven horns and seven eyes presents yet another new symbolism!

It turns out that this refers to the so-called "adjutant spirits" spoken of in *The Urantia Book*, and also referred to previously as "the seven spirits of God." This is clarified in the following questions:

Q: What are the meanings of "seven horns and seven eyes"?

A: The seven horns are the seven adjutant mind-spirits. The horns represent specialized spiritual influences which, as *The Urantia Book* explains, are beamed to the local universe. [Note: these influences are not to be confused with the "directional" energies emanated to the universe by the "four beasts."] The eyes, symbolically, are able to see the far-distant places to which these influences are encircuited.

THE SEVEN SPIRITS
AND THE MOTHER SPIRIT

The Urantia Book (378) explains that the seven adjutant mind-spirits are the creation of the Mother Spirit of a local universe. And she is revealed to be the divine and "feminine" complement of Christ Michael; together, the two of them are the actual creators of our local universe! An entire paper in the Urantia Revelation is devoted to the Mother Spirit. (See Paper 34, page 374ff.)

These seven mind-spirits of the Mother Spirit are the "seven spirits of God," "like lamps burning before the throne," which we have encountered previously. These "lamps" are the spirits of wisdom, worship, counsel, knowledge, courage, understanding, and intuition. These mind-spirit forces are beamed to the Mother's universe in successive stages. In gradations, they first endow vegetative life, then animal organisms, and then continuing on up to the first and then more advanced levels of human consciousness. Animals, for example, receive the first five of the seven mind-spirit endowments. Humans receive all seven.

These forces support life-evolution on all inhabited planets; they are the living architecture of the evolution of life and of consciousness from single cells through the most advanced human being.

On February 6, 1998 (two years after the first questions on Chapter 5), it occurred to me to ask why 5:6 has the image of a little lamb standing as if slain.

> Q: *What does this image mean, Corelli? This lamb has seven horns and seven eyes, and you've already explained what these symbols mean. But why represent the lamb as if killed?*

A: The lamb is Jesus, of course. But what John saw did not have horns and eyes, and the lamb was not dead. This is simply an erroneous representation.

5:7 - And he came and took the book out of the right hand of him that sat upon the throne.

Here John witnesses as Christ receives the Book of Life.

5:8 - And when he had taken the book, the four beasts and four and twenty elders fell down before the lamb, having every one of them harps, and golden vials full of odours, which are the prayers of saints.

According to Corelli, the "harp" refers to the so-called harp of God, which *The Urantia Book* explains (539) is a "perfected contrivance for space communications" that is carried by celestial beings.

On March 14, 1996, I asked Corelli the meaning of "golden vials" in verse 5:8.

A: The golden vials are a figure of speech representing the desires and longings of humanity. The odours represent the "fragrances" of saints who have been found worthy, and hence are sending thanks to God in the form of essences.

Solemn worship of the lamb

5:9 - And they sung a new song, saying, thou art worthy to take the book, and to open the seals thereof: for thou wast slain, and hast redeemed us to God by thy blood out of every kindred, and tongue, and people, and nation;

In this vision John watches as the the heavenly hosts worship Christ through song.

Q: *Corelli, I need you!*

A: Yes, I am here. How can I help you?

Q: *What does "...hast redeemed us to God by thy blood" mean?*

A: It does not mean that Christ had to shed his blood to redeem the human race. Rather, Christ lived on earth to show God's way of grace to all who repent; they are thereby saved—not by his blood, but by his grace. As we discussed in chapter 1, this notion of redemption by blood was a belief based on old tribal customs that used sacrifice as a way of propitiating the gods. But God never could be so cruel as to give his blameless son to die for people to redeem them; God is all-forgiving. The blood reference was inserted long after John was dead; it has no place in Christ's redeeming message.

Stella: Thank you, Corelli.

A: You are welcome. [See also 1:5 for more on the shedding of blood and the atonement doctrine of Christianity.]

5:10 - And hast made us unto our God kings and priests: And we shall reign on the earth.

Q: Corelli, what does this one mean?

A: This was inserted long after John died and was meant to tell people that kings and priests were anointed by God, and therefore must be obeyed. There is absolutely no truth in this statement and it should therefore be disregarded; all are equal before the Lord.

The only valid communication is between yourself and God. This is the pearl beyond price: that fragment of God within you—who is always there, gently, never coercing you, but leading you upward to a more spiritual life.

Q: About a year later, I again asked Corelli, "Did Jesus intend for kings and priests to reign on earth?" [I had forgotten I'd asked her about this same question two years previously. Her answer was almost the same.]

A: Of course not. This was inserted by priests at the behest of kings to legitimize their claims to be rulers, and this is probably where the idea of the divine right of kings came into being. But no one has a divine right to rule over anyone. Unfortunately, many people once believed in the divine right of rulership, whether in church or state. This is a totally false concept.

5:11 - And I beheld, and I heard the voice of many angels round about the throne and the beasts and the elders: and the number of them was ten thousand ten thousand, and thousands of thousands;

5:12 - Saying with a loud voice, Worthy is the Lamb that was slain to receive power, and riches, and wisdom, and strength, and honour, and glory, and blessing.

5:13 - And every creature which is in heaven, and on the earth, and under the earth, and such as are in the sea, and all that are in them, heard I saying, Blessing, and honour, and glory, and power, be unto him that sitteth upon the throne, and unto the Lamb for ever and ever.

5:14 - And the four beasts said, Amen. And the four and twenty elders fell down and worshipped him that liveth for ever and ever.

Verses 5:11 through 5:14 are explained above except for the meanings of the "thousands" in 5:11. When I asked Corelli for the meanings of these numbers, this is how she replied:

A: They are all those many souls who have made the long climb through eternal life, and who now stand before the throne of the Eternal Son.

On March 17, 1997, Corelli and Aflana said: "The rest of chapter 5 is essentially correct. You have explained the symbols quite accurately. We thank you and love you."

Highlights from Chapter 5

— The "seven seals" (5:1 and 5:5) do not actually signify prophecies of future events. Instead they refer to the seven possible stages of human development, as these are recorded in the Book of Life for each person.

— The seals can be opened by a representative of the Eternal Son. The Archangel of Life acts for him at the time of judgment.

— There are intervening stages of evaluation at the "learning and training schools" on high, when recommendations are made regarding eternal life.

— In a far distant time, we will stand before Christ. When ultimate questions arise as to whether a person is worthy of eternal life, the final judgment is made by the so-called Ancients of Days. (Each of the seven superuniverses are supervised by three Ancients of Days.)

— A small percentage of individuals choose oblivion, as they have been given their options and have decided on their own to reject eternal life. All individuals are given many chances to decide; the final decision is theirs. But final cessation of existence is by "the coordinate action of all tribunals of jurisdiction." (*UB*:37)

— The "seven spirits of God", and the "seven horns" (5:6) are actually spiritual circuits emanating from the Mother Spirit (see glossary) in support of the seven gradations of all life.

— It is a great fallacy to believe that kings and priests were annointed by God "to reign on the earth" (5:10). No one has a divine right to rule over any one.

6

King James Translation

1 And I saw when the Lamb opened one of the seals, and I heard, as it were the noise of thunder, one of the four beasts saying, Come and see.

2 And I saw, and behold a white horse: and he that sat on him had a bow; and a crown was given unto him: and he went forth conquering, and to conquer.

3 And when he had opened the second seal, I heard the second beast say, Come and see.

4 And there went out another horse that was red: and power was given to him that sat thereon to take peace from the earth, and that they should kill one another: and there was given unto him a great sword.

5 And when he had opened the third seal, I heard the third beast say, Come and see. And I beheld, and lo a black horse; and he that sat on him had a pair of balances in his hand.

6 And I heard a voice in the midst of the four beasts say, A measure of wheat for a penny, and three measures of barley for a penny; and see thou hurt not the oil and the wine.

7 And when he had opened the fourth seal, I heard the voice of the fourth beast say, Come and see.

8 And I looked, and behold a pale horse: and his name that sat on him was Death, and Hell followed with him. And power was given unto them over the fourth part of the earth, to kill with sword, and with hunger, and with death, and with the beasts of the earth.

9 And when he had opened the fifth seal, I saw under the altar the souls of them that were slain for the word of God, and for the testimony which they held:

10 And they cried with a loud voice, saying, How long, O Lord, holy and true, dost thou not judge and avenge our blood on them that dwell on the earth?

11 And white robes were given unto every one of them; and it was said unto them, that they should rest yet for a little season, until their fellow servants also and their brethren, that should be killed as they were, should be fulfilled.

12 And I beheld when he had opened the sixth seal, and, lo, there was a great earthquake; and the sun became black as sackcloth of hair, and the moon became as blood;

13 And the stars of heaven fell unto the earth, even as a fig tree casteth her untimely figs, when she is shaken of a mighty wind.

14 And the heaven departed as a scroll when it is rolled together; and every mountain and island were moved out of their places.

15 And the kings of the earth, and the great men, and the rich men, and the chief captains, and the mighty men, and every bondman, and every free man, hid themselves in the dens and in the rocks of the mountains;

16 And said to the mountains and rocks, Fall on us, and hide us from the face of him that sitteth on the throne, and from the wrath of the Lamb:

17 For the great day of his wrath is come; and who shall be able to stand?

revised

Perhaps no other image in the Book of Revelation has induced more terror in the hearts of believers than that of the Four Horsemen of the Apocalypse. These chilling figures have inspired countless artists, sculptors, and writers down through the centuries to create depictions of God's vengeance spewing forth as war, pestilence, famine, death, and earthquakes. But are such catastrophes a reality of the divine plan for the human race? Or are they simply misconstrued prophecies as already indicated in chapter 5? John wrote in code, but what did he really intend to convey in this regard?

My often naïve questions about this chapter began on March 18, 1996, followed by more questions throughout the ensuing years as I became more aware of the significance of John's awesome revelation.

The voice of conquest

Q: Corelli, I am puzzled. I can understand how the seals are related to the Books of Life, the records of all who have lived that you explained in 5:1. Now, chapter 6 speaks of the breaking of each seal. Is each seal indicative of what every person goes through more or less in his or her life?

A: Yes, these are phases of development that each person must go through on their spiritual journey to God. Each person, at various thresholds in their lives, is faced with particular circumstances; the test is in how they react to these conditions. Some may be faced with very difficult circumstances—as in the case of war—but ultimately these circumstances will not adversely affect their spiritual destiny. Rather, such experiences will only enhance their worthiness in the eyes and ears of God.

So do not worry, for there is justice in the long run. You humans worry needlessly. Justice is swift and sure when measured by our time.

6:1 - And I saw when the Lamb opened one of the seals, and I heard, as it were the noise of thunder, one of the four beasts saying, Come and see.

Q: Did Christ, the Lamb, open the first seal?

A: Yes, Christ is the final adjudicator of who is worthy to go on into the eternal journey—followed as we have seen by the Ancient of Days when there is a critical question as to whether an individual should continue. But all that occurs in a far distant time after you have obtained much experience in your morontia life. [Morontia is the term used in the *The Urantia Book* to indicate the first lengthy phase of life after death.]

Q: Are the four beasts in this case the power controllers? Why would they be the ones to say "come and see"? I thought their only function was the control of the energies, rather than spiritual progress.

A: In this case the four beasts actually refer to those angels of God whose duties are to welcome newcomers to that celestial world to which they have been assigned.

STAGES OF THE ASCENSION CAREER

Please understand that there are three grand stages of your eternal career: First, of course, is the physical phase, which you leave behind at death; second is the morontial, in which you still have vestiges of a physical life, i.e., human thoughts and emotions; and third, an unending spiritual phase.

Your first introduction to the morontial phase is by the welcoming angels mentioned in this passage. Your morontial life will continue for many lifetimes or translations, always becoming increasingly spiritualized until you literally stand before Christ himself. It is then that the third and spiritual phase of your eternal career actually begins. [Note to the reader: "Lifetimes" or "translations" do not refer to reincarnation, but rather to eternal life on higher spheres in increasingly finer bodies. According to the Urantia Revelation, we never return to this planet.]

6:2 - And I saw, and behold a white horse: and he that sat on him had a bow; and a crown was given unto him: and he went forth conquering, and to conquer.

Q: *What do the images of the white horse and bow mean?*

A: The man on the white horse and his bow represent the man who is chaste and honorable who wishes to impart his goodness to humanity. The bow represents sending out or reaching out by every honorable means.

Q: *Why was the crown given to him?*

A: He will be rewarded for his efforts; hence the golden crown of goodness.

We see you seem puzzled, but we assure you, all these meanings will fall in place.

You ask whether John of Patmos is pleased that you are doing this. John has expressed regret that through the centuries his message was distorted. He feels the time has come when new meanings will lead to a better understanding of God and the universes. The time is ripe for a major renaissance in the lives of all men and women.

There are many souls sorely troubled by the message of doom and gloom in the Book of Revelation, but we repeat: There is no hell except the one of man's own making. John's message was to have been one of joy and hope and not the prospect of a destroyed world. The image of the Rapture is a figment of one man's imagination and certainly is not a message that God would ever countenance. Your world is marching towards an era of Life and Light [see glossary] despite the efforts of doomsayers to block this progress.

Q: Where is John now?

A: He is on Salvington watching what you are doing with interest. You seem overwhelmed by what you consider to be an awesome job. Not really true; you will see that it will go quite easily. [This answer came from Solonia, who is introduced later in this chapter.]

Stella: Thank you. I'm impressed.

Vision of war

6:3 - And when he had opened the second seal, I heard the second beast say, Come and see.

Regarding the reference to beasts, see 6:1 above.

6:4 - And there went out another horse that was red: and power was given to him that sat thereon to take peace from the earth, and that they should kill one another: and there was given unto him a great sword.

Q: Can you explain the symbolism of the red horse?

A: The red horseman means the possibility of war, anger, revolt—all manner of evildoing.

Vision of famine

6:5 - And when he had opened the third seal, I heard the third beast say, Come and see. And I beheld, and lo a black horse; and he that sat on him had a pair of balances in his hand.

Q: Why is this a vision of "famine"?

A: Man must prepare for our sustenance by prudence and diligence. If he fails to provide for himself or humankind collectively, the result is famine. Mankind has the power to eradicate poverty and disease. A well-regulated society must care for its weak and elderly until such time when this type of care is no longer needed.

Q: Is death the real meaning of the black horse?

A: It refers to death to the past as well as to literal death. Death is to be no more—unless one chooses death. It also means death to the rehashing of old problems, which no longer have a bearing on the present. Life should be lived in the immediate present; "suffice unto the day."

6:6 - And I heard a voice in the midst of the four beasts say, a measure of wheat for a penny, and three measures of barley for a penny; and see thou hurt not the oil and the wine.

On March 19, 1997, I called upon Corelli for advice.

A: Yes, I'm here.

Q: What does "a measure of wheat for a penny and three measures of barley for a penny" mean?

A: This is a measure of food for which they paid these amounts. These are figures of speech encouraging the reader to be prudent, to save money, to be able to purchase these foods in times of famine.

Q: Why not hurt the oil and the wine?

A: Again a figure of speech. Take care to see that these are not spoiled through carelessness.

Vision of death

6:7 - And when he had opened the fourth seal, I heard the voice of the fourth beast say, come and see.

See 6:1 regarding the angels of God welcoming newcomers to the celestial worlds.

6:8 - And I looked, and behold a pale horse: and his name that sat on him was Death, and Hell followed with him. And power was given unto them over the fourth part of the earth, to kill with sword, and with hunger, and with death, and with the beasts of the earth.

Q: *What does this whole paragraph mean? What is the difference between black horse and pale horse?*

A: Yes, there is a difference. The black horse does mean death, whereas the pale horse refers to all manners of sickness, to be controlled by cleanliness. The need for basic hygiene was a hard concept for people of those times to understand. For example, few even bathed except possibly in public baths; the hygiene was slovenly. People were also careless in the preservation and cooking of food. This had a bad effect on children as well as adults. The message of this paragraph was to take heed, to live your lives in a more careful, orderly fashion.

Q: *And "power given unto them over the fourth part of the earth"? What power and to whom?*

A: This is difficult to understand in terms of the writer's intentions, for John did not actually write this passage. But he did write about the pale horse, and the meaning was, as I explained, about sickness and disease. Beyond that we cannot answer your question.

Vision of martyrs

6:9 - And when he had opened the fifth seal, I saw under the altar the souls of them that were slain for the word of God, and for the testimony which they held:

Q: Corelli, who are these souls John sees under the altar?

A: We will try to answer. Those are all the martyrs who died for Christ's sake. They could not deny the fact that they believed Christ was the Son of God.

The early Christians were a godly lot. They fervently believed in Jesus' teachings of loving one another. They could not envision denying this new life of love and caring and going back to old religious beliefs that were pagan and decidedly not loving. Many died in great torment and were harassed and persecuted before they died. They are now safe and cared for on the morontia worlds.

6:10 - And they cried with a loud voice, saying, how long, O Lord , holy and true, dost thou not judge and avenge our blood on them that dwell on the earth?

Q: What does this verse mean?

A: This is a cry of anguish by the Jewish people asking God how long they must suffer before the Messiah comes. This passage was inserted much later by a Jewish scribe. Many Jews, at that time, were praying for vengeance against those who persecuted them. Of course, God cannot grant such a request. Calling upon God to avenge your enemies is a perversion of God's intent. Even under these circumstances, one must love one's enemies. It is better for mankind to settle their grievances through communication, tolerance and love. Nothing else will ever settle a conflict.

6:11 - And white robes were given unto every one of them; and it was said unto them, that they should rest yet for a little season, until their fellow servants also and their brethren, that should be killed as they were, should be fulfilled.

Q: And this paragraph?

A: Again, this is a cry for vengeance. The first part of

the verse is all right and should end after "a little season." Beginning with "until their fellow servants" to the end of the sentence should be eliminated.

The white robes are a symbol of purity which you will be entitled to wear once you have been adjudicated as worthy to go on to eternal life. Does this answer your question?

Stella: Yes, thank you.

Vision of the day of the Lord

6:12 - And I beheld when he had opened the sixth seal, and lo, there was a great earthquake; and the sun became black as sackcloth of hair, and the moon became as blood;

Q: What does the earthquake really mean?

A: This is when the realization dawns on man as to what he has done with his life, with his actions. This can be likened to an earthquake.

6:13 - And the stars of heaven fell unto the earth even, as a fig tree casteth her untimely figs, when she is shaken of a mighty wind.

Q: What does "stars of heaven fell on the earth" mean?

A: These are energies or blessings falling upon all humankind, even on those not necessarily deserving.

6:14 - And the heaven departed as a scroll when it is rolled together; and every mountain and island were moved out of their places.

Q: "Heaven departed as a scroll..."?

A: This was a metaphor for John's being taken up into the mansion worlds. It was as if the heavens parted, and he was able to see the earth, the clouds, from a distance. It was indeed a glorious sight. [The Greek translation reads "separated" rather than "departed."]

6:15 - And the kings of the earth, and the great men, and the rich men, and the chief captains, and the mighty men, and every bondman, and every free man hid themselves in the dens and in the rocks of the mountains;

Q: What is the meaning of this verse?

A: This is when men and women are frightened of the consequences of their actions and ask for punishment or try to run from God's awareness. But no one escapes from the results of their actions. "God is not mocked—but as ye sow, so shall you reap." People sow the seeds of their own destruction.

God is loving and kind. He is not the wrathful God as portrayed in the Book of Revelation. Fear not God, but fear the results of your own actions if they are not in keeping with the will of God, which is the supreme epitome of justice.

That will be all for now. We love you and thank you for your diligence.Speaking are Solonia and Eckert.

Q: Who are Solonia and Eckert?

A: Solonia belongs to the fifth order of angels, the planetary helpers, who accompanied Adam and Eve to this planet.

She was the "angel of the garden" who admonished Adam and Eve in the Bible ("the voice of the Lord God" at Genesis 3:8). In truth, her admonition was that they had gone against the divine plan for an orderly upstepping of the human races. (See *UB*:583 and 843.)

And Eckhart is a new assistant entrusted with your care. He will watch over you and try to guide you in your affairs.

Stella: Thank you so much.

In my early transmissions I thought I was hearing the name "Eckert." As I later discovered, this being is actually Meister Eckhart, the famed medieval mystic!

6:16 - And said to the mountains and rocks, Fall on us, and hide us from the face of him that sitteth on the throne, and from the wrath of the Lamb:

6:17 - For the great day of his wrath is come; and who shall be able to stand?

Q: What is meant by the wrath of God in this case?

A: Wrath was the word used for all problems that beset humans. At that time it did not mean that God was personally doing these things, but since then it has taken on that meaning that God supposedly causes terrible things to happen.

The so-called "wrath of God" is personified by the Four Horsemen of the Apocalypse and was a way of warning people about what can occur if humankind does not live in harmony with the plan of God. The terrifying images of the Four Horsemen as portrayed by many artists and writers were merely the figments of their imaginations and are incorrect.

We are all ultimately responsible for putting God's loving plan into action.

Highlights from Chapter 6

— Four beasts in this chapter are actually angels of God who welcome newcomers to the celestial worlds.

— John's so-called visions of the Four horsemen of the Apocalypse are a product of artistic invention. Below are the real meanings of these figures:

  - The White horse represents men who are chaste and honorable.
  - The Black horse is literal death or death to a rehash of old problems.
  - The Red horse is the possibility of war, anger, and evil.
  - The Pale horse represents sickness that can be controlled by cleanliness.

— There are three stages of life in our ascension: physical, morontial (the stage after death between physical and spiritual) and spiritual.

— John's message is of hope and joy, not destruction of world.

— The earthquake in chapter 6 signifies the shock of realization when one reviews one's own life in detail.

— There is no such things as the "wrath of God." Further, it is useless to ask God to avenge your enemies ("Settle your grievances through communication." —Corelli)

— Fear not God. Only fear the *results of your own unwise actions.*

7

King James Translation

1 And after these things I saw four angels standing on the four corners of the earth, holding the four winds of the earth, that the wind should not blow on the earth, nor on the sea, nor on any tree.

2 And I saw another angel ascending from the east, having the seal of the living God: and he cried with a loud voice to the four angels, to whom it was given to hurt the earth and the sea,

3 Saying, Hurt not the earth, neither the sea, nor the trees, till we have sealed the servants of our God in their foreheads.

4 And I heard the number of them which were sealed: and there were sealed an hundred and forty and four thousand of all the tribes of the children of Israel.

5 Of the tribe of Juda were sealed twelve thousand. Of the tribe of Reuben were sealed twelve thousand. Of the tribe of Gad were sealed twelve thousand.

6 Of the tribe of Aser were sealed twelve thousand. Of the tribe of Nepthalim were sealed twelve thousand. Of the tribe of Manasses were sealed twelve thousand.

7 Of the tribe of Simeon were sealed twelve thousand. Of the tribe of Levi were sealed twelve thousand. Of the tribe of Issachar were sealed twelve thousand.

8 Of the tribe of Zabulon were sealed twelve thousand. Of the tribe of Joseph were sealed twelve thousand. Of the tribe of Benjamin were sealed twelve thousand.

9 After this I beheld, and, lo, a great multitude, which no man could number, of all nations, and kindreds, and people, and tongues, stood before the throne, and before the Lamb, clothed with white robes, and palms in their hands;

10 And cried with a loud voice, saying, Salvation to our God which sitteth upon the throne, and unto the Lamb.

11 And all the angels stood round about the throne, and about the elders and the four beasts, and fell before the throne on their faces, and worshipped God,

12 Saying, Amen: Blessing, and glory, and wisdom, and thanksgiving, and honour, and power, and might, be unto our God for ever and ever. Amen.

13 And one of the elders answered, saying unto me, What are these which are arrayed in white robes? and whence came they?

14 And I said unto him, Sir, thou knowest. And he said to me, These are they which came out of great tribulation, and have washed their robes, and made them white in the blood of the Lamb.

15 Therefore are they before the throne of God, and serve him day and night in his temple: and he that sitteth on the throne shall dwell among them.

16 They shall hunger no more, neither thirst any more; neither shall the sun light on them, nor any heat.

17 For the Lamb which is in the midst of the throne shall feed them, and shall lead them unto living fountains of waters: and God shall wipe away all tears from their eyes.

revised

"Hurt not the earth or the seas for the sake of generations to come"—this prophetic declaration summarizes the original intent of John's message in 7:3. Those who know their Bible well will recognize just how different this message is from the strange and confusing statements that open this chapter, such as the image of four angels "holding the four winds," followed by instructions to "hurt the earth and the sea." Even more confusing is the fact that 7:3 directly contradicts 7:2, for the angels are now told not to hurt the earth until the servants of God are "sealed in their foreheads."

John's original admonition to us in this chapter—now recovered with the help of my celestial guides—is certainly a valid one today, almost two millennia later, for only we can stop the destruction of the soil and the air, and the pollution of our waters, which is occurring all around us.

But I wondered, what the four angels, the four winds, the sealing of the servants of God in their foreheads, the "144,000 who are sealed," and all the rest of this chapter have to do with John's basic message of not hurting the earth and sea.

I knew I had to get answers to these questions. The

answers I received ranged over a period of three years, and began as follows on March 28, 1996:

Visions of five angels

> 7:1 - And after these things I saw four angels standing on the four corners of the earth, holding the four winds of the earth, that the wind should not blow on the earth, nor on the sea, nor on any tree.

> Q: *Corelli, who are the four angels in this case?*

> A: As we have seen before, these four are the power organizers (i.e., the "beasts") in charge of directional energies beamed to the earth and the universes. Calling them angels is closer to their true appearance; they are the exquisite beings who we have met before. Note that in 7:2, an angel of God requests that these energies be used so that no harm befalls any planet.

Corelli answered my questions on the rest of the verses in chapter 7 over the coming years, but upon re-reading 7:1 more recently, I realized I hadn't asked for the meaning of the winds. I hoped I could still contact my celestial friends at this late date, June 24, 1999. Many months had elapsed since my last contact. Happily, Corelli, Solonia and Meister Eckhart were standing by. My naïve questions follow:

> Q: *What do the four angels holding the four winds really refer to? We have terrible hurricanes, tornadoes and winds that create great havoc. Why do we have these phenomena?*

> A: The energies that these beings send forth are strictly spiritual and fall equally on all, good and bad. They have nothing to do with physical energies such as rain, sleet, wind, etc., which are physical characteristics of a developing planet, for example, the trade winds that encircle the planet. Depending on many events—temperature of the seas, time of the year—these forces can work together to create monstrous winds. The planet Jupiter is subject to far greater wind storms than is Urantia. In time Jupiter's

wind patterns will moderate as have yours. By contrast the angelic energies are wholesome and life-giving, never destructive. Does this answer your question?

Q: Not really. I'm still puzzled. Tell me more about the angelic energies. What are they specifically?

A: We will try again. These angelic energies are energies of hope, love, of methods of behavior, all having to do with man's evolving spiritual being.

Q: So did John use wind as a metaphor for spirit energies?

A: Yes, he did. You cannot see the wind or spirit forces, but you can see their effects. This is another instance wherein the people of those times could not visualize spirit energies but could comprehend the force of the wind.

John also saw the four angels gathering spiritually receptive mortals for re-personalization after death. It was quite a remarkable experience for him to see angels ministering to mortals in this way. [This was Corelli speaking, I presumed. I don't always know who is contacting me.] John tried to convey the information that those who live spiritual lives are resurrected in three days, or periodically in a mass resurrection. This activity is accompanied by certain spirit forces.

7:2 - And I saw another angel ascending from the east, having the seal of the living God: and he cried with a loud voice to the four angels, to whom it was given to hurt the earth and the sea,

The meaning of this verse can be found above in 7:1 and below in 7:3.

7:3 - Saying, Hurt not the earth, neither the sea, nor the trees, till we have sealed the servants of our God in their foreheads.

Q: You have answered my questions about the winds, but what does "till we have sealed the servants of our God in their foreheads" mean?

A: This angel from the east is telling them that they are forbidden to remove the seals until all have truly repented.

Q: *"Until they have truly repented"*?
A: We will try to explain.

THE JUDGMENT AFTER DEATH

This verse means that survivors must realize what errors they have made in their mortal lives and that they should truly regret their actions if they hurt, maligned, or unfairly took advantage of anyone. If they truly repent and give permission for their seals to be opened, then the seals are opened and their life is reviewed. If they are found worthy, they will continue the eternal journey. If there is doubt as to whether they should continue, then they will be assigned to one of the courts of the Ancients of Days for final disposition. Everyone has a secret place in the most high.

Q: *Again, I interjected a question: What is this secret place in the most high?*
A: An Angel of Record records everything you have ever done. No one has access to this other than the Angel of Record. When you stand before the seat of judgment, this record of your life is reviewed. But the seal of life [i.e., the seal on the record] will not be opened until your permission to do so has been gained.

At that point the Angel of Resurrection will discuss with you your life and your choices—in other words, those actions that made you unique and determined what you became. That which is of no use in your spiritual growth will cease to exist. That which has redeeming value will remain in your memory as shadows of reality. The memories of your good deeds are forever sealed in your "forehead" and will stay with you throughout eternity.

On February 11, 1998, having completely forgotten what I transcribed two years ago on March 28, 1996, and thinking I was showing great depth of perception in detecting contradictions, I asked Corelli the following question:

> Q: *These first three verses of chapter 7 seem to be contradictory. For instance in 7:1, the four angels are holding the winds so that they should not blow on the earth. In 7:2, the four angels were given the task to "hurt" the earth and sea. Then in 7:3, they are told to not hurt the earth and sea. What does all this mean?*

A: It is a complete revision of what John actually said. His original message was this: "Hurt not the earth or the seas for the sake of generations to come."

The angels in 7:3 were merely metaphors for those people who lacked God's spiritual light, those people who were only interested in using the earth and sea for their own gains. Your present-day activists are as concerned today as John was in his time when he wrote those words. He well knew that man in his greed and lust for gain would use the soil and sea for personal gain. But this is not at all God's plan for humanity's sustenance. Is this clear?

> *Stella: Not really. To me it sounds as if it's all right to hurt the environment after people have been sealed with their thought adjusters.*

A: No, this is completely incorrect. Whoever wrote these lines merely guessed at the original meanings. From this you can see how difficult it is to correct words that others used incorrectly. Suffice it to say, *The Urantia Book* is correct in its explanations, and be assured that John's intent was as originally stated: "Hurt not the earth or the seas for the sake of generations to come."

Number of Israelites who were sealed

7:4 - And I heard the number of them which were sealed: and there were sealed an hundred and forty and four thousand of all the tribes of the children of Israel.

7:5 - Of the tribe of Juda were sealed twelve thousand. Of the tribe of Reuben were sealed twelve thousand. Of the tribe of Gad were sealed twelve thousand.

7:6 - Of the tribe of Aser were sealed twelve thousand. Of the tribe of Nepthalim were sealed twelve thousand. Of the tribe of Manasses were sealed twelve thousand.

7:7 - Of the tribe of Simeon were sealed twelve thousand. Of the tribe of Levi were sealed twelve thousand. Of the tribe of Issachar were sealed twelve thousand.

7:8 - Of the tribe of Zabulon were sealed twelve thousand. Of the tribe of Joseph were sealed twelve thousand. Of the tribe of Benjamin were sealed twelve thousand.

Corelli's response to my questions on verses 7:4-8 was a surprise to me when, on March 28, 1996, I asked:

Q: What does the 144,000 or 12,000 sealed in each tribe mean? Does that refer to all who received the sealing of their good deeds?

A: No, it is merely a figure of speech. There were many good people of many races who were "sealed" with their good deeds. The Jews who later inserted these paragraphs were determined to portray the exclusivity of their people by promulgating the myth of their superiority. These tribes really did not exist as such, but were a loose band of people living in the areas of these towns throughout this region.

Q: Which towns?

A: Generally speaking, these tribes tended to congregate in certain areas. Subsequently, these villages became known by the name of their tribal leaders. The Jews were not really a "chosen people," but they were chosen to spread the gospel of Jesus Christ— which they failed to do. So then this task was given to others. Notwithstanding their failure to spread the gospel, they are all equal before God.

Verses 4, 5, 6, 7 and 8 were not actually written by John, but were added later by Jewish scribes.

Salvation of the gentiles

7:9 - After this I beheld, and, lo, a great multitude, which no man could number, of all nations, and kindreds, and people, and tongues, stood before the throne, and before the Lamb, clothed with white robes, and palms in their hands;

A: (Solonia and Eckhart) Verse 9 is more accurate. It indicates that many people have been resurrected who are worthy to continue the eternal journey. This will be all.

7:10 - And cried with a loud voice, saying, Salvation to our God which sitteth upon the throne, and unto the Lamb.

A: This can remain as written. It indicates worship of God.

7:11 - And all the angels stood round about the throne, and about the elders, and the four beasts, and fell before the throne on their faces, and worshipped God.

Chapter 4:4 explains the meanings of throne, elders, and beasts.

7:12 - Saying, Amen: Blessing, and glory, and wisdom, and thanksgiving, and honour, and power, and might, be unto our God for ever and ever. Amen.

A: Self-evident. Refers to thankful worship.

7:13 - And one of the elders answered, saying unto me, What are these which are arrayed in white robes? and whence came they?

See 5:11-14. This refers to all those souls who have made the long journey through eternal life.

7:14 - And I said unto him, Sir, thou knowest. And he said to me, These are they which came out of great tribulation, and have washed their robes, and made them white in the blood of the Lamb.

7:15 - Therefore are they before the throne of God, and serve him day and night in his temple: And he that sitteth on the throne shall dwell among them.

7:16 - And they shall hunger no more, neither thirst any more; neither shall the sun light on them, nor any heat.

This verse correlates, perhaps, with the following description of the afterlife from *The Urantia Book*.

The shadow of the mortal nature grows less and less as these worlds are ascended one by one. You are becoming more and more adorable as you leave behind the coarse vestiges of planetary animal origin. "Coming up through great tribulation" serves to make glorified mortals very kind and understanding, very sympathetic and tolerant. (538)

7:17 - For the lamb which is in the midst of the throne shall feed them, and shall lead them unto living fountains of waters: and God shall wipe away all tears from their eyes.

The following quotation from *The Urantia Book* may pertain to this famous and beautiful verse:

Jesus at Capernaum, "I am this bread of life. Your fathers ate manna in the wilderness and are dead. But this bread which comes down from God, if a man eats thereof, he shall never die in spirit. I repeat, I am this living bread, and every soul who attains the realization of this united nature of God and man shall live forever. And this bread of life which I give to all who will receive is my own living and combined nature. The Father in the Son and the Son with the Father—that is my life-giving revelation to the world and my saving gift to all nations." (1711)

Highlights from Chapter 7

- John's original intent in this chapter was to admonish us to not despoil the earth, water and air, for the sake of future generations.

- Angelic energies are like the winds (7:1) in that only their effects can be directly seen. Angels are constantly showering humans with radiant energies for the specific purpose of spiritualizing the human race; angelic assistance is also used to gather mortals for repersonalization after death.

- "Before you are sealed"(7:3) in the afterlife, you must repent and realize what errors you have made; you must also experience regret for any hurtful or unfair actions. But the Angel of Record does not open the seal to review your life record until your have given permission to do so. At this point your life is reviewed and you are judged.

- Once you pass through judgment, the memories of your good deeds are "sealed in your forehead" and will stay with you throughout eternity.

- At the time of death, your resurrection can take place either after three days or when a mass resurrection occurs. At the time of resurrection you are reunited with your Thought Adjuster, and all worthwhile memories are retained (sealed in your forehead) throughout eternity if you choose to survive.

- Those verses pertaining to the so-called tribes of Israel were added long after John's death. The Jews were not a "chosen people." However, it is true that they were chosen to spread the Gospel of Jesus but failed as a group to accomplish this task.

8

King James Translation

1 And when he had opened the seventh seal, there was silence in heaven about the space of half an hour.

2 And I saw the seven angels which stood before God; and to them were given seven trumpets.

3 And another angel came and stood at the altar, having a golden censer; and there was given unto him much incense, that he should offer it with the prayers of all saints upon the golden altar which was before the throne.

4 And the smoke of the incense, which came with the prayers of the saints, ascended up before God out of the angel's hand.

5 And the angel took the censer, and filled it with fire of the altar, and cast it into the earth: and there were voices, and thunderings, and lightnings, and an earthquake.

6 And the seven angels which had the seven trumpets prepared themselves to sound.

7 The first angel sounded, and there followed hail and fire mingled with blood, and they were cast upon the earth: and the third part of trees was burnt up, and all green grass was burnt up.

8 And the second angel sounded, and as it were a great mountain burning with fire was cast into the sea: and the third part of the sea became blood;

9 And the third part of the creatures which were in the sea, and had life, died; and the third part of the ships were destroyed.

10 And the third angel sounded, and there fell a great star from heaven, burning as it were a lamp, and it fell upon the third part of the rivers, and upon the fountains of waters;

11 And the name of the star is called Wormwood: and the third part of the waters became wormwood; and many men died of the waters, because they were made bitter.

12 And the fourth angel sounded, and the third part of the sun was smitten, and the third part of the moon, and the third part of the stars; so as the third part of them was darkened, and the day shone not for a third part of it, and the night likewise.

13 And I beheld, and heard an angel flying through the midst of heaven, saying with a loud voice, Woe, woe, woe, to the inhabiters of the earth by reason of the other voices of the trumpet of the three angels, which are yet to sound!

8

revised

Chapter 8 presents a prophecy of the horrors that may occur if humankind continues on its path of destroying the ecology of the planet. However, as I researched this chapter, I found it comforting to learn that angels are always trying to influence receptive minds towards remedying the ills that plague us. There is profound hope if only we will listen to the whispers of the God within and to the celestial beings around us who are working so earnestly to uplift our disordered planet.

My questioning of Corelli about chapter 8 began on March 19, 1996.

Q: Corelli, this chapter depicts such a bloody and terrible future for the earth. What does it really mean?

A: Good morning, Stella. This chapter is completely symbolic and its primary purpose is to warn us about what may ensue if people turn away from God. Certainly this does not apply to all people, but only to those who persist in error.

Stella: But it seems to deal with the destruction of the earth itself.

A: (Solonia and Eckhart) Yes, we know—and are you not indeed on a path of destruction of the earth by your careless cutting of the forests and the wanton polluting of your air and water? Humankind can use its free will to either destroy or preserve Urantia.

The Book of Revelation was written in the symbolism of those times, and this makes it difficult for modern man to understand its true meaning. Suffice to say that this chapter is a genuine warning of what might happen but can be averted. Taking it literally word for word is not correct, but, overall, it is a warning of what could occur in ages to come. The cutting down of the rain forests must stop before it is too late.

That will be all for now. Be of good cheer.

Q: *[On March 20, 1997, I asked these follow-up questions.] I reread the information you gave me on March 19, 1996, almost one year ago. I understand that this chapter was mostly symbolic, but I do need further clarification. When I read chapter 8, it sounds to me as if the angels are causing all these calamities, rather than mankind. Can you speak to this?*

A: Yes, Stella, we understand your confusion. As we said before, this chapter is strictly symbolic. In ancient times, all calamities were attributed to a vengeful God. Humankind's understanding at that time could not comprehend that many so-called natural disasters were actually caused by human ignorance and greed. This was the warning being issued by John, but, alas, few understood, and fewer listened. Inform your readers that where you read that God or the angels caused these disasters, in reality, it is man himself. Only he can take the necessary steps to save the earth. We are glad you questioned this point.

Q: *I'm also wondering whether these angels of the trumpets are actually the angels of the nations as* The Urantia Book *describes on page 1255:*

The angels of nation life...are the "angels of the trumpets," directors of the political performances of Urantia national life. The group now functioning in the overcontrol of international relations is the fourth corps to serve on the planet. It is particularly through the ministry of this seraphic division that "the Most Highs rule in the kingdom of men."

Corelli continued: Yes, the seven trumpet angels are the angels of the nations who have charge of influencing legislators, presidents, and kings toward a peaceful way of adjudicating disagreements. Only communication, good will, and tolerance can change the makeup of nations. We try so hard, but often these pleas fall upon deaf ears. But let there be no doubt, Jesus' teachings of loving thy neighbor will some day prevail, although much suffering will ensue before mankind learns a bitter lesson.

Q: Corelli, every time I start a chapter I get so worried that I won't hear correctly, but then the answers appear so beautifully and sensibly. Thank you very much.
A: (Solonia and Eckhart) You are welcome.

Q: Oh, it's Solonia and Eckhart today. Where is Corelli?
A: She stepped aside so we could contact you.

Q: And Meister Eckhart, how is he?
A: He is fascinated with what you are doing, and wishes there had been someone like you in his day.

Q: But why? Certainly what he had to say as an influential priest was far more important than what a layperson can do.
A: True, but he needed someone who could talk to the people on their level as you, hopefully, will be doing.

At this point I felt a little overwhelmed by all this attention and responsibility.

Q: Does each of the seven angels have a specific duty?
A: Yes, each has the supervision of a specific portion

of the nation's activities, including agriculture, health, finance, medicine, wages, or government.

Q: How do they exert influence?

A: They try to arrange conditions by bringing people together who are qualified to handle these tasks. They do not and cannot influence minds unless that human already has a specific idea or ideal in their mind. The arrangement of events is much easier when we sense what that person has in mind.

Q: Were these verses prophecies of coming events, of wars?

A: In a sense, yes. By watching current events we can guess at their eventual outcomes, although everything is subject to human desires or manipulations. We do not predict as a rule, but from our long years of experience we can almost predict outcomes. Our goal is to seek out people who can be put in positions to effect resolutions through acting in accord with the will of God.

8:1 - And when he had opened the seventh seal, there was silence in heaven about the space of half an hour.

Q: What does "silence in heaven about the space of half an hour" mean?

A: This is a figure of speech. It means humankind is being given time to reflect on the effects of its actions.

8:2 - And I saw the seven angels which stood before God; and to them were given seven trumpets.

The angels are here given instructions to send out their messages.

8:3 - And another angel came and stood at the altar, having a golden censer; and there was given unto him much incense, that he should offer it with the prayers of all saints upon the golden altar which was before the throne.

Q: What is the meaning of the censer?

A: The censer refers to a device which propels special energies into the "harps" [see chapter 4 and 8:5] which receive the news broadcasts throughout the universes—something akin to your radio and television. The harp is handheld and is carried by most celestial beings.

8:4 - And the smoke of the incense, which came with the prayers of the saints ascended up before God out of the angel's hand.

Q: What is the smoke?

A: Energies carrying prayers and petitions to God.

8:5 - And the angel took the censer, and filled it with fire of the altar, and cast it into the earth: and there were voices, and thunderings, and lightnings, and an earthquake.

Q: "Fire of the altar"?

A: A metaphor for warnings sent from the heavenly abode.

Q: Voices and thunderings, lightning and earthquakes?

A: Metaphors for the sounds of the news broadcasts.

8:6 - And the seven angels which had the seven trumpets prepared themselves to sound.

8:7 - The first angel sounded, and there followed hail and fire mingled with blood, and they were cast upon the earth: and the third part of trees was burnt up, and all green grass was burnt up.

8:8 - And the second angel sounded, and as it were a great mountain burning with fire was cast into the sea: and the third part of the sea became blood;

8:9 - And the third part of the creatures which were in the sea, and had life, died; and the third part of the ships were destroyed.

Q: Is there a special meaning to verses 7, 8 and 9?

A: As we said before, the angels try to warn of impending disasters and to forewarn mankind to prepare for these emergencies. Unfortunately, mankind often does not heed these warnings and thus is subject to the disasters that follow. Statistically, about one third of nature and wildlife can be destroyed.

Q: *Did John write these verses?*

A: Yes, he did. These were his estimates of the disastrous calamities that could occur.

8:10 - And the third angel sounded, and there fell a great star from heaven, burning as it were a lamp, and it fell upon the third part of the rivers, and upon the fountains of waters;

Q: *What is the great star?*

A: The great star is a comet that periodically swings around the solar system. If it comes too close to a planet, it can wreak great havoc.

8:11 - And the name of the star is called Wormwood; and the third part of the waters became wormwood; and many men died of the waters, because they were made bitter.

Q: *What does "wormwood" refer to?*

A: This term means the fallout or residue from a natural disaster—the ashes of fires, plagues, or pollution.

8:12 - And the fourth angel sounded, and the third part of the sun was smitten, and the third part of the moon, and the third part of the stars; so as the third part of them was darkened, and the day shone not for a third part of it, and the night likewise.

Q: *But why only a third?*

A: One-third, of course, is less than a whole, and statistically, one-third of anything is the amount that can be relied on for change in any given moment.

8:13 - And I beheld, and heard an angel flying through the midst of heaven, saying with a loud voice, Woe, woe, woe, to the inhabiters of the earth by reason of the other voices of the trumpet of the three angels, which are yet to sound!

Q: *What is the meaning of "by reason of the other voices of the trumpet of the three angels, which are yet to sound"? Is this a warning of doom?*

A: Not in the spiritual sense, but rather in terms of what can and what has happened when natural calamities strike. You know what happened in Pompeii and Herculaneum when those cities were suddenly covered with lava and ashes. These events have occurred worldwide, but are not a sign of God's wrath. Not heeding warnings is man's fault.

Q: *What about manmade calamities?*

A: These warnings refer to both types, manmade and natural.

Highlights from Chapter 8

— This chapter is thoroughly symbolic, providing a prophetic warning of what could happen to the earth in the ages to come if humankind turns away from God.

— The true spirit of John's prophecy is to warn mankind that it is to blame for destroying the earth and polluting the air and water. Much destructive action is attributed to God or angels in this chapter that should actually be accorded to the effects of human greed and ignorance.

— The seven angels of the trumpets are actually the "angels of nations"(*UB*: 1255) whose work is to influence receptive minds of legislators and heads of state to adjudicate political disagreements peacefully.

— Each "nation angel" supervises a specific area of a nation's activities. (Examples include agriculture, health, finance, medicine, wages, and government.) The nation angels bring together people of like mind to work on specific problems, by influencing those minds where the needed ideas have naturally appeared.

— One key function of angels is to warn of impending disasters and forewarn mankind to prepare for these calamities.

— Meister Eckhart is fascinated by this attempt to decode the Book of Revelation.

9

King James Translation

1 And the fifth angel sounded, and I saw a star fall from heaven unto the earth: and to him was given the key of the bottomless pit.

2 And he opened the bottomless pit; and there arose a smoke out of the pit, as the smoke of a great furnace; and the sun and the air were darkened by reason of the smoke of the pit.

3 And there came out of the smoke locusts upon the earth: and unto them was given power, as the scorpions of the earth have power.

4 And it was commanded them that they should not hurt the grass of the earth, neither any green thing, neither any tree; but only those men which have not the seal of God in their foreheads.

5 And to them it was given that they should not kill them, but that they should be tormented five months: and their torment was as the torment of a scorpion, when he striketh a man.

6 And in those days shall men seek death, and shall not find it; and shall desire to die, and death shall flee from them.

7 And the shapes of the locusts were like unto horses prepared unto battle; and on their heads were as it were crowns like gold, and their faces were as the faces of men.

8 And they had hair as the hair of women, and their teeth were as the teeth of lions.

9 And they had breastplates, as it were breastplates of iron; and the sound of their wings was as the sound of chariots of many horses running to battle.

10 And they had tails like unto scorpions, and there were stings in their tails: and their power was to hurt men five months.

11 And they had a king over them, which is the angel of the bottomless pit, whose name in the Hebrew tongue is Abaddon, but in the Greek tongue hath his name Apollyon.

12 One woe is past; and, behold, there come two woes more hereafter.

13 And the sixth angel sounded, and I heard a voice from the four horns of the golden altar which is before God,

14 Saying to the sixth angel which had the trumpet, Loose the four angels which are bound in the great river Euphrates.

15 And the four angels were loosed, which were prepared for an hour, and a day, and a month, and a year, for to slay the third part of men.

16 And the number of the army of the horsemen were two hundred thousand thousand: and I heard the number of them.

17 And thus I saw the horses in the vision, and them that sat on them, having breastplates of fire, and of jacinth, and brimstone: and the heads of the horses were as the heads of lions; and out of their mouths issued fire and smoke and brimstone.

18 By these three was the third part of men killed, by the fire, and by the smoke, and by the brimstone, which issued out of their mouths.

19 For their power is in their mouth, and in their tails: for their tails were like unto serpents, and had heads, and with them they do hurt.

20 And the rest of the men which were not killed by these plagues yet repented not of the works of their hands, that they should not worship devils, and idols of gold, and silver, and brass, and stone, and of wood: which neither can see, nor hear, nor walk:

21 Neither repented they of their murders, nor of their sorceries, nor of their fornication, nor of their thefts.

9

revised

"And his tail drew a third of the stars of heaven and cast them down in darkness." This is the key image John saw in his famous vision of the great red dragon—the symbol of Lucifer, Satan, and the apostate princes that we read about in those papers in *The Urantia Book* that detail the Lucifer Rebellion (601ff). These crucial passages in the Urantia Revelation should be read alongside this important chapter.

References in code to the "war in heaven" appear in several places in the Book of Revelation. Verse 9:1 says "...a star falls from heaven..."; and 12:4 tells us that "... his tail drew the third part of the stars of heaven, and did cast them to the earth...." Do these verses pertain to the same event? Does the fallen star refer to Satan—the "angel of light" (2 Corinthians 11:14) who had set himself above God, and who fell from grace?

Although *The Urantia Book* clearly states that John understood this symbol of the dragon to refer to Lucifer and his minions (see *UB:*608), I sought confirmation through my many tortuous questionings ranging over several years. On March 23, 1996, during my initial contacts, I asked Corelli for help on chapter 9.

The fifth trumpet

9:1 - And the fifth angel sounded, and I saw a star fall from heaven unto the earth: and to him was given the key of the bottomless pit.

Q: This chapter is more difficult than the others. In a way it seems to tell the story of the Lucifer Rebellion, of some of the characters involved, and the terrible effect the "war in heaven" has had on this world as well as on those who sided with Lucifer. What does the "bottomless pit" mean?

A: The bottomless pit is a symbol of the depths of degradation and disaster that will befall mankind if it turns away from God. But those who are "sealed of God" in their foreheads will not be affected. [See 9:11 for more about the "key" to the pit.]

Much later, on February 13, 1998 I asked: "Corelli, I'm having a terrible time with this chapter. Do you mind my asking more questions?"

A: No, of course not.

Q: Does this chapter refer to the Lucifer Rebellion as I asked previously?

A: Yes, it does. John depicted Lucifer in a symbolic way. His star was crashing, as it were. Lucifer was given a chance to repent but failed to do so; his actions were iniquitous.

I turned to *The Urantia Book* for more information about the latter comment. Here I read that Jesus, in reply to a question of Thomas, made an important distinction among different types of iniquity: "Evil is the unconscious or unintended transgression of the divine law, the Father's will.... Sin is the conscious knowing and deliberate transgression of the divine law.... Iniquity is the willful, determined and persistent transgression of the divine law, the Father's will." (*UB*:1660.)

It seemed to me that Lucifer deliberately and consciously defied divine law. In *The Urantia Book*, Jesus refers to the defiance of divine law by quoting the following proverb: "He who turns away his ear from hearing the divine law, even his prayers shall be an abomination." (1638)

> **9:2** - And he opened the bottomless pit; and there arose a smoke out of the pit, as the smoke of a great furnace; and the sun and the air were darkened by reason of the smoke of the pit.

Q: What does this verse mean?

A: Lucifer influenced a great many cherubim and angels who went to his side and were subsequently lost to eternal life. The despair among those beings was overwhelming. The smoke represents the great turmoil they suffered.

> **9:3** - And there came out of the smoke locusts upon the earth: and unto them was given power, as the scorpions of the earth have power.

Q: And what does this verse mean?

A: Many on earth were also influenced by the Lucifer Rebellion to turn away from God.

> **9:4** - And it was commanded them that they should not hurt the grass of the earth, neither any green thing, neither any tree; but only those men which have not the seal of God in their foreheads.

Q: I can understand the admonition not to damage the environment, but did this apply only to those men who were ungodly?

A: Those who were pure in heart needed no warning. This was a warning to those who had turned towards Lucifer.

> **9:5** - And to them it was given that they should not kill them, but that they should be tormented five months: and their torment was as the torment of a scorpion, when he striketh a man.

Q: What does the five months mean?

A: A figure of speech. All who had followed Lucifer were given time to repent. Some did, and some did not.

9:6 - And in those days shall men seek death, and shall not find it; and shall desire to die, and death shall flee from them.

Q: *Who were those seeking death but unable to find it?*

A: Those who finally realized what had happened sought death due to remorse, but the final death was not granted until they were adjudicated. Many of the rebels absolutely and finally chose not to go on.

9:7 - And the shapes of the locusts were like unto horses prepared unto battle; and on their heads were as it were crowns like gold, and their faces were as the faces of men.

Q: *What is the meaning of "shapes of the locusts were like unto horses..."?*

A: These were guilty men who were prepared to do battle for an unrighteous cause. The Lucifer Rebellion affected them all.

Q: *And the crowns?*

A: Heads of state, kings.

Q: *Specifically, what do locusts symbolize?*

A: A figure of speech that represents the enormity of guilt.

9:8 - And they had hair as the hair of women, and their teeth were as the teeth of lions.

Q: *Hair of women?*

A: Men pretending they did not understand what had happened.

Q: *Teeth as lions?*

A: Those who knew very well what had happened and were defiant.

9:9 - And they had breastplates, as it were breastplates of iron; and the sound of their wings was as the sound of chariots of many horses running to battle.

Q: Breastplates—do they indicate the crusades? And the wings?

A: This is a warning of potential war in the future. The wings represent energies that are deployed uselessly in the pursuit of power over others.

9:10 - And they had tails like unto scorpions, and there were stings in their tails: and their power was to hurt men five months.

Q: Meaning?

A: Again, their influence and "sting" were terrible in its impact.

Q: I notice there are many references to "tail." What does it symbolize?

A: "Tail" means "by their influence you shall know them." Their evil ways influenced many to turn against God. Tail was a figure of speech used in the Old Testament designating sway over others.

9:11 - And they had a king over them, which is the angel of the bottomless pit, whose name in the Hebrew tongue is Abaddon, but in the Greek tongue hath his name Apollyon.

Although I was finally beginning to understand the meaning of this chapter, I was incorrect at one point when I asked Corelli about whether the star in 9:1 could be the symbol for Abaddon, who in 9:11 is designated as the "angel of the bottomless pit."

A: No, 9:1 actually refers to Lucifer. The reference to Abaddon in 9:11 is correct as you have stated.

Abaddon is described in *The Urantia Book* as the chief of staff of Caligastia (i.e., the Planetary Prince of Urantia who followed Lucifer; see especially Paper 67, page 754ff.). Abaddon followed his master into rebellion and became the chief executive of the Urantia rebel angels.

9:12 - One woe is past; and behold, there come two woes more hereafter.

Q: The meaning of this verse?

A: It refers to the compounding of trouble once one turns away from God.

The sixth trumpet

9:13 - And the sixth angel sounded, and I heard a voice from the four horns of the golden altar which is before God.

Q: What do the four horns represent? Are they the four control creatures referenced in 4:5, or are they the power organizers (four angels) in 7:1?

A: They are like the power organizers in 7:1.

9:14 - Saying to the sixth angel which had the trumpet, Loose the four angels which are bound in the great river Euphrates.

Back on March 31, 1996, I asked about the meaning of "Loose the four angels." Corelli replied thus:

A: These are the harbingers of what is to be—something like the "four horsemen" but different. These angels predict—and the horsemen actually bring about—plagues, pestilence, hunger, and war. Such maladies are the result of erring men and can only cease when all mankind works toward the betterment of humanity by doing the will of God.

But on February 18, 1998, I wanted to know more, so I again asked Corelli about this verse.

Q: Why were these four angels bound in the great river Euphrates?

A: The Euphrates River was a figure of speech used commonly in that area symbolizing all good things coming out of the second Eden.

Stella: But I thought nothing good came out of that Eden. According to my reading of The Urantia Book, *Adam and*

Eve worked under appalling conditions to create the second Eden. [See especially Paper 76, page 847ff.]

A: That is true, but nevertheless, they set an example for men and women working together, as they also did in the first garden. But this time, their culture, handiworks, inventions such as the wheel, their spinning, weaving, sound agricultural practices, and training of young people influenced future generations and civilizations throughout the world. The Greeks were one of the many civilizations influenced by the work of the second garden.

The Edenic culture also spread to India, China, and Easter Island, even to South America through Adam's sons, who were the forerunners of the Incas, landing in Peru.

Your planet has suffered greatly because of the Lucifer Rebellion, the so-called Adamic default, and the cruel, untimely death of Jesus. But you have benefited greatly from the influence of Adam and Eve, who built the second garden between the Tigris and Euphrates Rivers.

9:15 - And the four angels were loosed, which were prepared for an hour, and a day, and a month, and a year, for to slay the third part of men.

Q: Were the four angels literally going to slay a third part of man?

A: No. This was an incorrect translation. These angels came to warn and predict, not to slay.

9:16 - And the number of the army of the horsemen were two hundred thousand thousand: and I heard the number of them.

Q: Who were all these horsemen? What were they going to do?

A: These myriads of horsemen represent all those people who can be influenced either to the good or to the bad. The choice is theirs. [Also see 9:14.]

(Note: The Greek translation states "myriads and myriads" rather than two hundred thousand thousand.)

> 9:17 - And thus I saw the horses in the vision, and them that sat on them, having breastplates of fire, and of jacinth, and brimstone: and the heads of the horses were as the heads of lions; and out of their mouths issued fire and smoke and brimstone.

Q: Who are those sitting on the horses?

A: Those are heads of governments and clergy who had cast their lot with the iniquitous Lucifer. Out of their mouths issued blasphemies against a loving God.

> 9:18 - By these three was the third part of men killed, by the fire, and by the smoke, and by the brimstone which issued out of their mouths.

At this point I was becoming increasingly familiar with the nefarious three—Lucifer, Satan and Caligastia—who according to *The Urantia Book* became known, collectively, as the "devil." Also, the dragon became the symbolic representation of all these evil personages: Lucifer, Satan, Caligastia, Beelzebub and Abaddon: "Upon the triumph of Michael [Jesus], 'Gabriel came down from Salvington and bound the dragon (all the rebel leaders) for an age.'" *(UB:602)*

John wrote symbolically of the great red dragon, saying, "And his tail drew a third part of the stars of heaven and cast them down in darkness." In *The Urantia Book* (608), we learn for example that about one-third of the planetary angelic helpers were deceived and were lost, among many other angelic and celestial groups.

To give you a sense of how ruthless these rebels were, see page 531 in the *UB* where we read that they even tried to recruit children living on the mansion worlds. (Those who die young and prematurely always survive into the afterlife. Their souls are held in trust until such time as they can be resurrected and reunited with the first of their surviving parents to arrive in the mansion worlds.)

As I was putting together these thoughts, I asked Corelli:

Q: Corelli, am I interpreting this chapter correctly?

A: Indeed, you have. We are relaying this information to John. He is well pleased with your insight, and wishes you to continue with the rest of the chapters. He will assist in every way he can to get this interpretation written down as correctly as possible. There is so much to be gained by your exposition of the meanings of these symbols. It has puzzled mankind long enough, and now is the time for his true message to be given to the world. Symbols were fine for those times but today you mortals want the facts.

9:19 - For their power is in their mouth, and in their tails: for their tails were like unto serpents, and had heads, and with them they do hurt.

Q: What is the meaning of verse 19?

A: It refers to the power of speech and how it can influence for evil as well as for good. The speech used by Caligastia was intended to corrupt the minds of his followers. [See 9:10 for meaning of "tails."]

9:20 - And the rest of the men which were not killed by these plagues yet repented not of the works of their hands, that they should not worship devils, and idols of gold, and silver, and brass, and stone, and of wood: which neither can see, nor hear, nor walk:

Q: And the meaning of verse 20?

A: Many refused to repent and continued their old forms of worship and the idolizing of material things.

9:21 - Neither repented they of their murders, nor of their sorceries, nor of their fornication, nor of their thefts.

A: The answer is the same as for 9:20.

Thus ended a most difficult and enlightening chapter about the "war in heaven," when Lucifer fell.

Highlights from Chapter 9

— Most of this chapter refers to the Lucifer rebellion and its effects on men and angels.

— The "bottomless pit"(9:1) refers to the depths of degradation, disaster, and depression to which mankind can fall if they turn away from God.

— Evil, sin, and iniquity have different meanings: Evil is the unintended transgression of the divine law; sin is conscious transgression; and iniquity is the willful and persistent transgression of the divine law. Lucifer was wholly iniquitous, and thus was cast down into darkness as described in this chapter.

— Lucifer influenced many angels and other celestial beings who went to his side and were subsequently lost to eternal life; this chapter uses symbols such as "smoke of the pit"(9:2) to depict their anguish upon the realization of their folly. Lucifer's emissaries even tried to corrupt the developing minds of children (*UB*: 531) who had survived into the afterlife. (Children who die prematurely are eventually resurrected upon the arrival after death of the first of their parents.)

— Lucifer's minions also influenced men on the earth. John uses strange symbols at 9:7-8, such as "locusts" (enormity of guilt), "hair of women" (pretense), and "teeth as lions" (defiance) to explain the attitudes of those who went into rebellion.

— Abbadon (9:11) was the chief of staff of Caligastia who went into rebellion with him. The red dragon represents all the evil personages who went into rebellion: Lucifer, Satan, Caligastia, Beelzebub, and Abbadon.

— The "four angels bound in the Euphrates" (9:14) refer to the benefits to mankind arising out of the "second garden of Eden", which was located on this river. (*UB*:847) Despite Adam and Eve's default, civilization has benefited greatly by their influence arising from this period in Mesopotamia. The Edenic culture spread from there to Greece, India, China, Easter Island, and South America.

10

King James Translation

1 And I saw another mighty angel come down from heaven, clothed with a cloud: and a rainbow was upon his head, and his face was as it were the sun, and his feet as pillars of fire:

2 And he had in his hand a little book open: and he set his right foot upon the sea, and his left foot on the earth,

3 And cried with a loud voice, as when a lion roareth: and when he had cried, seven thunders uttered their voices.

4 And when the seven thunders had uttered their voices, I was about to write: and I heard a voice from heaven saying unto me, Seal up those things which the seven thunders uttered, and write them not.

5 And the angel which I saw stand upon the sea and upon the earth lifted up his hand to heaven,

6 And sware by him that liveth for ever and ever, who created heaven, and the things that therein are, and the earth, and the things that therein are, and the sea, and the things which are therein, that there should be time no longer:

7 But in the days of the voice of the seventh angel, when he shall begin to sound, the mystery of God should be finished, as he hath declared to his servants the prophets.

8 And the voice which I heard from heaven spake unto me again, and said, Go and take the little book which is open in the hand of the angel which standeth upon the sea and upon the earth.

9 And I went unto the angel, and said unto him, Give me the little book. And he said unto me, Take it, and eat it up; and it shall make thy belly bitter, but it shall be in thy mouth sweet as honey.

10 And I took the little book out of the angel's hand, and ate it up; and it was in my mouth sweet as honey: and as soon as I had eaten it, my belly was bitter.

11 And he said unto me, Thou must prophesy again before many peoples, and nations, and tongues, and kings.

revised

When I first questioned Corelli about the meaning of "the angel with the little book," who is the key figure in chapter 10, her answer was surprising—to say the least—and certainly not something I could have deduced from reading the chapter. I quote it in full below:

> Corelli: Chapter 10, as a whole, refers to the so-called akashic record of an individual's life: the good, the bad, even the obscene. Eventually, anything not in the will of God will drop from your consciousness as if it had never been. But signs of your previous behavior will not disappear: it will be reflected in the form of your new body after death. In other words, in the afterlife, your new body will reflect how you lived your mortal life. If you are beautiful now, but corrupt in your thinking and action, your new body will reflect those particular traits. If you are now not what may be considered attractive—but are of a loving spirit reflecting the will of God—you will be endowed with a more beautiful form. This applies to all, including those who were born with a disability or received one through no fault of their own. This includes deafness and blindness. All who truly repent will

have further opportunities to regain future bodies of beauty.

Stella: What a beautiful and reassuring message.

On March 24, 1997, I asked for further clarification regarding this chapter. I went through the usual meditation and gave permission to my unseen friends to contact me.

A: Yes, we are here.

Q: Who?

A: Corelli, Aflana, Solonia and Eckhart.

Q: I have a number of questions regarding chapter 10 about things that are puzzling to me. It seems to me when these verses were translated from Aramaic to Greek, and then to English, some of these meanings were obscured. Is this correct?

A: Yes, indeed. Scribes penned these verses. Their handwriting was often difficult to read. Often a space made the difference in the meaning of a message.

The angel with the little book

10:1 - And I saw another mighty angel come down from heaven, clothed with a cloud: and a rainbow was upon his head, and his face was as it were the sun, and his feet as pillars of fire:

10:2 - And he had in his hand a little book open: and he set his right foot upon the sea, and his left foot on the earth.

A. As we said, the "little book" refers to the record of your life.

Q: What does "...set his right foot upon the sea and his left foot on the earth" mean?

A: This mighty angel and other mighty angels have jurisdiction over land and sea, in fact, throughout various universes. They always work for the benefit of humankind on all worlds.

10:3 - And cried with a loud voice, as when a lion roareth: and when he had cried, seven thunders uttered their voices.

A. This angel sent his voice over universal broadcasts as did the other seven "thunders" (angels).

10:4 - And when the seven thunders had uttered their voices, I was about to write: and I heard a voice from heaven saying unto me, Seal up those things which the seven thunders uttered, and write them not.

A: You ask about 10:4. [I had written it on a piece of paper and didn't actually ask. They must have read the question!] In that verse you question if "write them not" meant, "write them out." "Write them out" is correct and means the same as in 10:11 where John is told to go out to prophesy. These two verses, 4 and 11, as written in King James, seem to be contradictory. Both verses should indicate that he was to go out to prophesy—in other words, proclaim this vision to the world. You are correct in questioning this.

Q: But what about the order to "seal up" what was uttered?

A: Instead of "seal," this sentence should read: "Remember those things which the seven thunders uttered, and write them out." Satisfied now?

Stella: Yes, thank you. Now, what about the meaning of the seven thunders?

A: These are seven angels who are utilizing the universal broadcasts. (Same as in 4:3.)

Time shall be no longer

10:5 - And the angel which I saw stand upon the sea and upon the earth lifted up his hand to heaven,

10:6 - And sware by him that liveth forever and ever, who created heaven, and the things that therein are, and the earth, and the things that therein are, and the sea, and the things which are therein, that there should be time no longer.

The King James version reads: "that there should be time no longer." However, the Diaglott translation reads: "that the time shall be no longer delayed." So I questioned Corelli about these interpretations.

A: They mean that John should waste no more time in getting the message out.

On a whim, I asked John mentally if this was correct. "Yes," he answered, "but this applies to you as well." [I think I've reached the point in life where nothing surprises me any more!]

10:7 - But in the days of the voice of the seventh angel, when he shall begin to sound, the mystery of God should be finished, as he hath declared to his servants the prophets.

The Diaglott translation of the "Mystery of God" reads: "the secret of God should be completed as he announced the glad tidings of Himself to his bondservants, the prophets."

Q: Corelli, I don't understand this.

A: This is a convoluted message. But basically it means for all to share the loving message of Michael (Jesus) with the entire world.

The little book is eaten

10:8 - And the voice which I heard from heaven spake unto me again, and said, Go and take the little book which is open in the hand of the angel which standeth upon the sea and upon the earth.

A: John is told to take the record of his own life from the Angel of Resurrection.

10:9 - And I went unto the angel, and said unto him, Give me the little book. And he said unto me, Take it, and eat it up; and it shall make thy belly bitter, but it shall be in thy mouth sweet as honey.

10:10 - And I took the little book out of the angel's hand, and ate it up; and it was in my mouth sweet as honey: and as soon as I had eaten it, my belly was bitter.

Q: In these two verses, why is it that, when John ate the book, it was sweet, but as soon as he swallowed it, it was bitter?

A: Up to this point John thought he had done well. But after "eating" the book of his life, he came to realize the truth—that there were areas in his life where he could have done better. This realization "tasted" bitter.

And this is true of everyone when they come face to face with the reality of how they have lived their lives. John of course was no exception. Although he had lived a long and useful life, there were areas in his life he bitterly regretted. But no matter, for he has been forgiven for what he had perceived as his transgressions and is safely on the mansion worlds.

He just wishes to warn people to live a good life within the will of God, and to realize and accept their shortcomings.

Thank you for questioning this passage.

10:11 - And he said unto me, Thou must prophesy again before many peoples, and nations, and tongues and kings.

A: See 10:4. The message again is to go out and prophesy.

On March 24, 1997, they also added the same request of me: Now your mission will be, subject to your approval, to share this new version of the message with all who will hear.

Q: You mean the Book of Revelation? Me?

A: (Solonia and Eckhart) Yes, your writing or speaking. There is much here that people do not know about although it may now seem familiar to you. Get busy writing. We see you are in earnest. That is good. Many are chosen but few follow through. We are pleased. You are loved.

Highlights from Chapter 10

— Everything about our lives is recorded in the "little book" (10:2), but in the afterlife those things not in accord within the will of God will eventually drop away from consciousness. On the other hand, the form of one's new body in the afterlife will directly reflect everything about how we lived our mortal lives.

— When confronted with the full reality of his mortal life after "eating" (10:10) the book of his life, John came to some bitter realizations about how he had lived his life.

— When our own "book of life" is opened, all of us will have a similar awakening to John's, when we come face to face with the reality of how we had lived our lives on earth.

— John has been forgiven for what he perceived as his transgressions. John also wishes to warn us all to live a good life within the will of God and to realize and accept our shortcomings.

11

King James Translation

1 And there was given me a reed like unto a rod: and the angel stood, saying, Rise, and measure the temple of God, and the altar, and them that worship therein.

2 But the court which is without the temple leave out, and measure it not; for it is given unto the Gentiles: and the holy city shall they tread under foot forty and two months.

3 And I will give power unto my two witnesses, and they shall prophesy a thousand two hundred and threescore days, clothed in sackcloth.

4 These are the two olive trees, and the two candlesticks standing before the God of the earth.

5 And if any man will hurt them, fire proceedeth out of their mouth, and devoureth their enemies: and if any man will hurt them, he must in this manner be killed.

6 These have power to shut heaven, that it rain not in the days of their prophecy: and have power over waters to turn them to blood, and to smite the earth with all plagues, as often as they will.

7 And when they shall have finished their testimony, the beast that ascendeth out of the bottomless pit shall make war against them, and shall overcome them, and kill them.

8 And their dead bodies shall lie in the street of the great city, which spiritually is called Sodom and Egypt, where also our Lord was crucified.

9 And they of the people and kindreds and tongues and nations shall see their dead bodies three days and an half, and shall not suffer their dead bodies to be put in graves.

10 And they that dwell upon the earth shall rejoice over them, and make merry, and shall send gifts one to another; because these two prophets tormented them that dwelt on the earth.

11 And after three days and an half the Spirit of life from God entered into them, and they stood upon their feet; and great fear fell upon them which saw them.

12 And they heard a great voice from heaven saying unto them, Come up hither. And they ascended up to heaven in a cloud; and their enemies beheld them.

13 And the same hour was there a great earthquake, and the tenth part of the city fell, and in the earthquake were slain of men seven thousand: and the remnant were affrighted, and gave glory to the God of heaven.

14 The second woe is past; and, behold, the third woe cometh quickly.

15 And the seventh angel sounded; and there were great voices in heaven, saying, The kingdoms of this world are become the kingdoms of our Lord, and of his Christ; and he shall reign for ever and ever.

16 And the four and twenty elders, which sat before God on their seats, fell upon their faces, and worshipped God,

17 Saying, We give thee thanks, O Lord God Almighty, which art, and wast, and art to come; because thou hast taken to thee thy great power, and hast reigned.

18 And the nations were angry, and thy wrath is come, and the time of the dead, that they should be judged, and that thou shouldest give reward unto thy servants the prophets, and to the saints, and them that fear thy name, small and great; and shouldest destroy them which destroy the earth.

19 And the temple of God was opened in heaven, and there was seen in his temple the ark of his testament: and there were lightnings, and voices, and thunderings, and an earthquake, and great hail.

revised

This chapter contains many more puzzling passages. For example, an angel asks John to measure the temple of God and the altar. Then there are two olive trees who seem to have the power to shut heaven. And what about the reference to "Egypt where our Lord was crucified"? I thought he was crucified at Golgotha in Jerusalem! I needed answers to these questions.

In some ways chapter 11 was the most difficult to understand even after reading it many times over the course of three years. As I indicated previously, when I began my initial questioning early in 1996, I asked only about those items that caught my eye. After that I received a great deal of input. But as a whole this chapter left me baffled. The only thing to do was to go back over my sketchy notes and fill in the gaps with information received as late as February 1998.

Gentiles to be in the holy city forty-two months

11:1 - And there was given me a reed like unto a rod: and the angel stood, saying, Rise, and measure the temple of God, and the altar, and them that worship therein.

11:2 - But the court which is without the temple leave out, and measure it not, for it is given unto the gentiles: and the holy city shall they tread under foot forty and two months.

The original transmission about this chapter, on April 11, 1996, went as follows:

Corelli: Yes, Stella, we were waiting. Glad you are with us today. Your question?

Q: *Can you give me the meaning of this chapter in a nutshell?*

A: We do not know. We wish we did. There has been so much distortion. It's hard to sort through it all. As for what John actually meant, we can only say that the holy city is Jerusalem, and the forty-two months refer to the time it was believed it would take for Jesus' words to spread through the city.

Q: *What does "reed" refer to?*

A: A measuring rod to measure the temple that stood in the center of the city.

Q: *Why was there a need to measure it?*

A: Because so much space in Jerusalem was to be allocated to the Christians and so much to the Jews. There was a sharp line of demarcation.

Q: *Who is the angel?*

A: An angel was sent who told John to measure the territory of Jerusalem.

On March 25, 1997, I probed further.

Q: Corelli, it's hard for me to believe that an angel was sent to Jerusalem to ask John to measure the temple of God and the altar. There must have been some other underlying spiritual purpose for this injunction. Can you clarify?

A: As we said before, this was a means of determining how many people were persuaded to believe in God and in Jesus' teachings. Many were called, but many refused to accept his message. There was no one qualified to spread his teachings, and the angels were concerned about how difficult this task was and what measures could be taken so that the message of Jesus could reach the public. The thinking was that it would take approximately forty-two months for the message to spread throughout the city. This counting was real. John and his assistant Nathan were given the task of counting the gentiles. This was also done with the help of the other apostles, including Peter. We know that measuring the city seems a bit foolish to you; however, in those days it was difficult for news to get around. True, they could speak to small groups, but it was completely different from today when news is flashed from one corner of the world to another in the space of a few seconds. Back then it was a grueling task.

Stella: Thank you.

A: We have been here watching you. You have written correctly even though you feel some doubts.

Prophetic power of the two witnesses

11:3 - And I will give power unto my two witnesses, and they shall prophesy a thousand two hundred and threescore days, clothed in sackcloth.

Q: Does this mean that power was given to John and Peter to prophesy?

A: Yes.

Q: *What about "a thousand two hundred and threescore days"?*

A: A figure of speech meaning an indefinite period of time.

11:4 - These are the two olive trees, and the two candlesticks standing before the God of the earth.

Q: *What are the meanings of the olive trees and the candlesticks?*

A: The two olive trees and the two candlesticks again symbolize the two apostles, John and Peter, who are bringing light to all who would hear.

11:5 - And if any man will hurt them, fire proceedeth out of their mouth, and devoureth their enemies: and if any man will hurt them, he must in this manner be killed.

Q: *What does this verse mean?*

A: This was added by a scribe a long time after John's and Peter's passing. This passage expresses this transcriber's indignation toward anyone who would hurt or kill these two emissaries. John never made such statements.

11:6 - These have power to shut heaven, that it rain not in the days of their prophecy: and have power over waters to turn them to blood, and to smite the earth with all plagues, as often as they will.

Corelli: This same scribe here attributes to John and Peter the power to "shut heaven" and other super-natural vindictive powers. This, of course, is not correct. John's mission was exclusively one of love and mercy.

11:7 - And when they shall have finished their testi-mony, the beast that ascendeth out of the bottomless pit shall make war against them, and shall overcome them, and kill them.

Corelli explained: This statement assumed that when

John and Peter were finished with their mission, the devil, Satan, would make war against them, overcome them, and kill them. The scribes in hindsight figured that the devil was supposedly very powerful, and would kill anyone who preached the gospel of Jesus. Therefore they believed that John and Peter must have been crucified as Jesus had been, and that their dead bodies would lie in the streets of the city [see next verse]. Of course none of this occurred, although Peter was indeed crucified.

11:8 - And their dead bodies shall lie in the street of the great city, which spiritually is called Sodom and Egypt, where also our Lord was crucified.

See 11:7 concerning the reference to dead bodies in the street. Corelli also indicated to me that Sodom and Egypt were symbols of immorality and corruption.

Q: Why is it written here that Jesus was crucified in Egypt?

A: The scribe who wrote this evidently did not know where Jesus was crucified.

11:9 - And they of the people and kindreds and tongues and nations shall see their dead bodies three days and an half, and shall not suffer their dead bodies to be put in graves.

11:10 - And they that dwell upon the earth shall rejoice over them, and make merry, and shall send gifts one to another; because these two prophets tormented them that dwelt on the earth.

Q: The above two verses really puzzle me. What do they mean?

A: The people of those times who did not believe in Jesus' message rejoiced that the prophets John and Peter were killed.

Because I didn't quite get what I had been told, I again asked if these two prophets were Nathan and John. (I was having trouble sorting this out. I wasn't getting a clear transmission.)

A: Let us see. The two prophets were actually Peter and John. Peter was killed, and John lived to a ripe old age. You are wise to question this. It is difficult to figure out what the scribe meant.

A few days later, March 27, 1997, I again questioned Corelli.

Q: *Corelli, I am having difficulty reconciling whether it was John and Nathan or John and Peter who were the two prophets. I would appreciate your clarifying this. I need an actual sequence of the events.*

A: Yes, we understand your confusion. Nathan and John went through the city; however, Peter also accompanied them. John and Peter were the prophets. Nathan was the young man who would later become the scribe to whom John dictated his vision. There is no actual discrepancy. Both John and Nathan were old men at the time of John's vision, and, because Nathan had accompanied Peter and John, he was able to chronicle the events of the time that Jesus was still alive. Nathan actually wrote the Gospel according to John at the behest of John. Does this answer your questions?

Stella: Yes, I guess so.

A: Now, Stella, do you still doubt us after all these months? We have tried to reach you as best we can. Sometimes it is a bit difficult when you still doubt whether you are getting correct information. But, be of good cheer. You are doing an excellent job of transmitting, and we are very pleased.

11:11 - And after three days and an half the spirit of life from God entered into them, and they stood upon their feet; and great fear fell upon them which saw them.

Q: *Did John and Peter return after death?*

A: No, this was a scribe's imagination.

11:12 - And they heard a great voice from heaven saying unto them, Come up hither. And they ascended up to heaven in a cloud; and their enemies beheld them.

A: This is also the scribe's imagination. He had heard of Jesus' ascension and assumed that Peter and John also ascended and that this was witnessed by others.

The great earthquake

11:13 - And the same hour was there a great earthquake, and the tenth part of the city fell, and in the earthquake were slain of men seven thousand: and the remnant were affrighted, and gave glory to the God of heaven.

Q: Was there really an earthquake?

A: There was a great earthquake in which many people were killed. Those who lived through this earthquake praised God for being saved.

11:14 - The second woe is past; and, behold, the third woe cometh quickly.

A: This refers to the chaos after the earthquake.

Vision of the temple of God

11:15 - And the seventh angel sounded, and there were great voices in heaven, saying, the kingdoms of this world are become the kingdoms of our Lord, and of his Christ, and he shall reign for ever and ever.

A: This is John's writing.

11:16 - And the four and twenty elders, which sat before God on their seats, fell upon their faces, and worshipped God.

11:17 - Saying, We give thee thanks, O Lord God Almighty, which art, and wast, and art to come, because thou hast taken to thee thy great power, and hast reigned.

A: These are of course the twenty-four elders. [See 4:4.] They always worship God.

11:18 - And the nations were angry, and thy wrath is come, and the time of the dead, that they should be judged, and that thou shouldest give reward unto thy servants the prophets, and to the saints, and them that fear thy name, small and great; and shouldest destroy them which destroy the earth.

Q: What about 11:18?

A: This verse is so convoluted it is even difficult for us to decipher. We do not know what was in the mind of the transcriber. It is grossly distorted and has little relationship to John's actual vision. As we have seen in earlier chapters, the time of a mass resurrection is also the time of judgment. Eliminate all references to anger, wrath and destruction. They are not in the original.

11:19 - And the temple of God was opened in heaven, and there was seen in his temple the ark of his testament: and there were lightnings, and voices, and thunderings, and an earthquake, and great hail.

A: This is a true account of John's vision when he was allowed to visit the mansion worlds. His visit was extraordinary in that he was privileged to see many things that ordinary mortals rarely see. For example, the "thunderings" are as we have seen universe broadcasts, an extraordinary phenomenon to behold. [See 4:5.]

This vision was humbling to John, who in youth was a rather arrogant man, but he truly believed in Jesus who had made a most profound impression on him. John was never able to forget Jesus' tender love for him, and even though he thought he was the most loved by Jesus, this was not so—Jesus loved everyone equally.

Highlights from Chapter 11

— Much of this chapter consists of convoluted, false, or fear-based verses that were added later by scribes. The few passages that were written by John are not especially significant.

— Immediately after Jesus' death, the angels were concerned about the difficulty of spreading Jesus' teachings in Jerusalem, and it had been estimated that it would take forty-two months (14:2) for Jesus' words to move through the city. John, his assistant Nathan, and Peter were at one time given the task of counting the gentiles to determine the extent of the spread of Jesus' teachings.

— Several passages (11:3-4) refer to "my two witnesses" who are like "candlesticks." These refer to apostles John and Peter, who bring light to all who hear them.

— The chapter ends with a reference to "the temple of God" that "was opened in heaven"(11:19). This is based on a true heavenly vision of John's.

12

King James Translation

1 And there appeared a great wonder in heaven, a woman clothed with the sun, and the moon under her feet, and upon her head a crown of twelve stars.

2 And she being with child cried, travailing in birth, and pained to be delivered.

3 And there appeared another wonder in heaven, and behold a great red dragon, having seven heads and ten horns, and seven crowns upon his heads.

4 And his tail drew the third part of the stars of heaven, and did cast them to the earth: and the dragon stood before the woman which was ready to be delivered, for to devour her child as soon as it was born.

5 And she brought forth a man child, who was to rule all nations with a rod of iron; and her child was caught up unto God, and to his throne.

6 And the woman fled into the wilderness, where she hath a place prepared of God, that they should feed her there a thousand two hundred and threescore days.

7 And there was war in heaven: Michael and his angels fought against the dragon, and the dragon fought his angels.

8 And prevailed not; neither was their place found any more in heaven.

9 And the great dragon was cast out, that old serpent, called the Devil, and Satan, which deceiveth the whole world: he was cast out into the earth, and his angels were cast out with him.

10 And I heard a loud voice saying in heaven, now is come salvation, and strength, and the kingdom of our God, and the power of his Christ: for the accuser of our brethren is cast down, which accused them before our God day and night.

11 And they overcame him by the blood of the lamb, and by the word of their testimony; and they loved not their lives unto the death.

12 Therefore rejoice, ye heavens, and ye that dwell in them. Woe to the inhabiters of the earth and of the sea! For the devil is come down unto you, having great wrath, because he knoweth that he hath but a short time.

13 And when the dragon saw that he was cast unto the earth, he persecuted the woman which brought forth the man-child.

14 And to the woman were given two wings of a great eagle, that she might fly into the wilderness, into her place, where she is nourished for a time, and times, and half a time, from the face of the serpent.

15 And the serpent cast out of his mouth water as a flood after the woman, that he might cause her to be carried away of the flood.

16 And the earth helped the woman, and the earth opened her mouth, and swallowed up the flood which the dragon cast out of his mouth.

17 And the dragon was wroth with the woman, and went to make war with the remnant of her seed, which keep the commandments of God, and have the testimony of Jesus Christ.

revised

If I thought chapter 11 was challenging, this chapter was even more difficult and extraordinary. I could never have imagined that these verses are actually a garbled account of the stories of Eve and Mary juxtaposed into one incomprehensible narrative *and* woven around two different epochal revelations!

This is a chapter of such significance. So please allow me to provide a bit of background concerning the two major epochal revelations to this planet that were lost to history until they were finally re-introduced in the Urantia Revelation. In the process of explaining this, I will touch on the distinction between evolutionary and revelatory religion, and why revelation is periodically necessary.

FROM EVOLUTION TO REVELATION

Generally speaking, religions are either evolutionary or revelatory. Evolutionary religions tend to grow out of the life and teachings of outstanding and charismatic personalities. As the generations pass, the original teachings are inevitably modified. New concepts are added; others are dropped or altered. Over time, the modified belief system comes to be accepted as fact. Eventually, an evolutionary religion tends to stagnate and become a relic of the past, and, as a result, adherents can become imprisoned by outworn traditions and invalid beliefs. Genuine spirituality wanes, and a vital faith in God may become hazy or may even be completely lost.

This is when new revelation becomes necessary. Revelation enters on the stage of religious history to set the record straight, eliminate fixated and outdated beliefs, and provide a fresh new cosmic vision. In the case of Adam and Eve, a revelation can be given to a planet for the purpose of advancing biological evolution as well as cultural and spiritual development. (See Paper 101 in the *UB*, especially page 1110.)

THE FIRST REVELATION AND THE LUCIFER REBELLION

According to *The Urantia Book*, there have been thousands of religious leaders and many religious revelations; however, there have only been five revelations of *epochal* significance. The first of these was the sudden arrival on our planet of an inaugural celestial administration. This great event occurred about 500,000 years ago.

We learn in *The Urantia Book* that when the celestial supervisors of an evolving planet determine that the human inhabitants of a given sphere have evolved sufficiently and there is a readiness for revelation—they will formally inaugurate the process of instituting a planetary administration. This step is the first epochal revelation to a planet: the gift of a "Planetary Prince," accompanied by a well-trained (and visible) staff, who are dispatched from the celestial realm to teach and uplift inhabitants and to establish a planetary headquarters. Around 500,000 years ago, a brilliant being named Caligastia, and a staff of 100 assistants, was sent to our planet to uplift its primitive inhabitants at a point when there were half a billion people on earth. A replete explanation of Caligastia's administration is provided in *The Urantia Book* (730ff.); more than a brief summary of this event is beyond the scope of this chapter.

Suffice it to say that Planetary Prince Caligastia and his staff established a highly effective administration, based in Mesopotamia, that lasted for about 300,000 years.

The history of Urantia is unique in that Caligastia's administration was completely aborted. About 200,000 years ago, Caligastia elected to join the Lucifer Rebellion, which we have discussed briefly earlier in this book. (For details see *The Urantia Book* Papers 53 and 54, beginning on page 601.)

At the time, Lucifer and Satan reigned on Jerusem, the system capital. And it was Satan, Lucifer's first lieutenant, who was sent down to earth, to Urantia, to advocate the cause of Lucifer to Caligastia. And Satan was successful: in short order, Caligastia swung his whole administration over to the cause of Lucifer, arraying himself against the Universal Father and Christ Michael. Lucifer's manifesto appears on page 603 of *The Urantia Book.* There were many terrible charges in Lucifer's contentions; chief among these were the argument that *God does not really exist.*

Satan was able to persuade thousands of angels, midwayers (a specialized type of angel), and many other orders of celestial beings to swing to Lucifer's side. Among these were Caligastia, his chief aid, Daligastia, and Abbadon, the chief of the Midwayers.

It should be noted as well that thirty-six other planets in our local system of planets went over to Lucifer's side. Once the rebel position was fully promulgated, the rebellion planets were severed from the spiritual communication circuits that routinely operate on normal worlds; that meant that our planet, Urantia, was effectively quarantined. It has indeed remained so down to recent times. The long-awaited adjudication of the Lucifer Rebellion was announced with the recent launching of the Teaching Mission. (See glossary.)

The Lucifer Rebellion was so significant that its repercussions are still felt today, eons later. In summary, as a result of his disastrous decision to align his regime with the program of Lucifer and Satan, Caligastia single-handedly plunged the world into a period of darkness that lasted for 200,000 years. The "devil" of Christian lore is actually none other than Caligastia.

ADAM AND EVE: THE SECOND EPOCHAL REVELATION

But about 38,000 years ago, our planet received a second revelation of epochal significance: Adam and Eve were sent to biologically uplift the human race and to ameliorate the effects of the Lucifer Rebellion.

This extraordinary couple materialized on this planet at the first Garden of Eden, which was prepared for them on the eastern side of the Mediterranean. (See *UB*: 821ff.) In those times, previous to the incarnation of Christ Michael as Jesus, Satan was still free to roam the earth; and he was intent on aborting Adam and Eve's mission, much as he had previously subverted the work of Caligastia.

Adam and Eve had been thoroughly briefed as to what they were to do during their dispensation on earth under these unusual conditions and were especially made aware of the dangers they faced. In briefest summary (the complete story in the *UB* begins on page 821), Adam and Even were, according to the divine plan, charged with creating 500,000 descendants before they or their progeny were permitted to intermingle with the genetic pool of the indigenous human races.

Tragically, they defaulted on this plan—just as Caligastia had defaulted previous to them on his charge.

The Bible teaches in mythic terms—and *The Urantia Book*

account explains in detail—just how the wily Satan was able to undo the Adamic regime in the Garden of Eden. Satan interposed himself in such a way as to influence Cano, a leading tribesman in the vicinity of the Garden, to seduce Eve. (Cano was unaware of the sacred promises that Eve had made.) Cano persuaded Eve that the two of them could greatly benefit the human race if they were to initiate an experiment in premature interbreeding. And Cano prevailed with Eve.

It was the angel Solonia (incidentally one of the celestial beings now assisting me with decoding this book), and not "God," who later confronted Adam and Eve in the Garden to inform them that Eve had grievously violated the solemn instructions that had been given them. Adam was devastated when he realized Eve would be banished from the Garden, and, in a laudable but fateful decision to share her fate, went outside the walls of Eden and impregnated countless native women.

But when the surrounding natives learned of this betrayal at the behest of Cano, they went to war. This catastrophic war ended with the destruction of the Garden; Adam and Eve and their remaining party were forced to flee to a new home.

THE STORY OF THE SECOND GARDEN

After much travail, Adam and Eve and their party created a second garden in an area between the Tigris and Euphrates Rivers, now part of Iraq. Legends of this second Garden of Eden are still prevalent in that region.

As the Bible also recounts, Eve gave birth to Cain (son of Cano), who later did slay his younger brother Abel on account of Abel's taunting him about his appearance. (Cain resembled the hairy tribesmen on his father's side, whereas Abel resembled Adam and Eve.) Cain subsequently repented and left to find a wife in the land of Nod, as we read in Genesis. (These were the Nodites, descendants of the first colony established by Daligastia on the Persian Gulf some 500,000 years previous. That city was called Dalamatia, named after Daligastia, the associate of Caligastia. Daligastia was also the chief administrator of the planetary headquarters situated in the Persian Gulf region. The city was eventually engulfed by the sea. Dalmatia has come down to us in legend as "Dilmun.")

The stories of these two epochal revelations—the Caligastia administration and the Adam and Eve dispensation—are indeed complicated. But it is essential to understand these distant events as we continue to decode the Book of Revelation.

The third epochal revelation, the arrival of Melchizedek some 4,000 years ago (see Genesis in the Bible and 1014ff. in *The Urantia Book*) is not mentioned in chapter 12. However, the fourth epochal revelation—the Jesus incarnation—is obviously of paramount import for us. *The Urantia Book* announces itself as the Fifth Epochal Revelation.

A woman clothed with the sun

12:1 - And there appeared a great wonder in heaven a woman clothed with the sun, and the moon under her feet, and upon her head a crown of twelve stars.

Q: Corelli, who is a woman clothed with the sun? Who is the red dragon? What are the seven heads, ten horns, and seven crowns?

Her astounding answers were as follows:

A: The woman clothed with the sun was Eve. This chapter is a garbled version of two incidents: Eve giving birth to Cain, and Mary giving birth to Christ Michael [Jesus]. The red dragon was, of course, the symbol for the nefarious three, Caligastia, Lucifer and Satan.

[Note: My question about ten horns and seven crowns is answered in the next chapter.]

Almost a year later, I belatedly thought to ask about the meaning of the crown with the twelve stars:

A: Yes, Stella, we are here. Glad you are with us again. The twelve stars represent the twelve planets in your solar system.

Q: But we have only ten. [The fifth from the sun became the asteroid belt.]

A: No, there are two more out there. Your astronomers will eventually find them. They swing in a huge orbit and are only visible every 26,000 years.

Stella: That's a long time between swings.

A: This is true. The last swing near your planet was about 25,000 years ago. In another thousand years your astronomers will be able to see them.

Q: Why should these twelve planets be associated with Eve?

A: She and Adam, as members of the Council of Twenty-four, have jurisdiction over all twelve planets in your system.

Q: Wouldn't these planets have their own Adam and Eve? [According to *The Urantia Book*, as noted before, each developing planet receives its own Adam and Eve.]

A: No, those planets will not have their own Adam and Eve until long after life implantation occurs. These planets are being observed to see what forms of life might be most appropriate for their particular physical conditions.

Q: In the image of the "woman clothed with the sun," what is the meaning of the sun?

A: Adam and Eve radiated an aura; in other words, they glowed somewhat like the sun, hence the simile. The aura was like a halo; in fact, this is how the practice of painting a halo around the heads of saints originated.

On the late date of February 26, 1999, it occurred to me to

ask Corelli for the meaning of "moon at her feet." There was a strange silence; no answer was forthcoming. I thought about it for several days, and then decided it probably wasn't that important.

Later it happens that I picked up a copy of the *Bible Dictionary* and came across the figure of Ashtoreth, the principal deity of the Phoenicians who is often considered to be a moon goddess. It turns out that Ashtoreth and Astarte were actually names for Eve. In time these local goddesses evolved into the "Mother Goddess."

The Urantia Book tells us that the Mother Cult, which glorified Eve in the worship of the "Great Mother," reached its apex in Crete. Images of Eve were everywhere in Crete and Asia Minor, right on down to the time of Christ. Eve was later incorporated into the early Christian religion under the guise of the glorification and worship of Mary. (*see* UB:895)

At one point, Solonia and Eckhart told me why John of Patmos chose his particular method of writing the Book of Revelation, and why the two incidents became interwoven. They stated:

A: John of Patmos thought a great deal about how to present his revelation. There was extreme danger in being utterly candid, so he resorted to the symbology of the times. People could read it on several levels, treating it as a lovely tale, or, if they chose, study it for deeper meaning. Subsequent translators could not fully understand his message, so they injected stories that were handed down by word of mouth, consequently distorting the actual sequence of events. *The Urantia Book* provides an excellent account of what actually transpired.

Before proceeding with 12:2, I thought it would be fun to try sorting out those verses that could apply to Eve and those applying to Mary. These guesses were based on information found in *The Urantia Book* and as given above.

My guess was these verses pertained to Eve: 12:1, 2, 3, 4, 6, 13, 14, 15 and 16.

Those belonging to Mary and Jesus: 12:5, 7, 8, 9, 10, 11, 12 and 17.

I congratulated myself on my scholarship, but knew I would need to check these with Corelli. On March 31, 1997, I asked her, and this is what she said:

Q: *Corelli, what do you think of the way I sorted out these verses, dividing those which I think pertain to Eve and those to Mary?*

A: Yes, Stella, you have it substantially correct. There is a point or two you might check, and these are 12:6 and 12:7. Those properly belong with Eve, not Mary.

Stella: Well, I do have 12:6 with Eve, not Mary.

A: For that matter, 12:7 could belong with either. Satan was around Eve so long ago, and he was with Mary too, but the presence of Jesus protected Mary.

Q: *Anything else?*

A: No. You have it about right. As we said before, this chapter is badly garbled, and it's difficult to make sense of some of the wording. *The Urantia Book* provides a complete picture of what actually occurred. This might intrigue people sufficiently so that they might want to read more about these nefarious beings who did so much damage to your world.

[For more complete information on Eve see *The Urantia Book*, Papers 74, 75 and 76, pages 828-854. Those passages pertaining to Mary can be found in *The Urantia Book*, Section IV, "The Life and Teachings of Jesus," beginning with page 1344.]

12:2 - And she being with child cried, travailing in birth, and pained to be delivered.

A: Eve gives birth to Cain, son of Cano, a local tribesman.

The red dragon

12:3 - And there appeared another wonder in heaven, and behold a great red dragon, having seven heads and ten horns, and seven crowns upon his heads.

A: This refers to Satan who arrived to abort Adam and Eve's mission to uplift the human races.

12:4 - And his tail drew the third part of the stars of heaven, and did cast them to the earth: and the dragon stood before the woman which was ready to be delivered, for to devour her child as soon as it was born.

A: This refers to Satan's literal presence at the birth of Jesus.

Birth of Christ

12:5 - And she brought forth a man child, who was to rule all nations with a rod of iron; and her child was caught up unto God, and to his throne.

A: This refers to Mary who gives birth to Christ Jesus, known as Michael of Nebadon, creator and ruler of 10,000 systems of inhabited worlds, containing 10,000,000 inhabitable planets.

Q: *Regarding this child, is this also Christ Jesus who after his resurrection "was caught up unto God"?*

A: Yes, that is correct.

12:6 - And the woman fled into the wilderness, where she hath a place prepared of God, that they should feed her there a thousand two hundred and threescore days.

A: Now we switch back to Eve again. This refers to her flight with Adam to the Second Garden.

War in heaven

12:7 - And there was war in heaven: Michael and his

angels fought against the dragon, and the dragon fought his angels.

Corelli explained that the war in heaven affected both women as well as all humanity. This was a real war for the souls of men and women. *The Urantia Book* presents a quote from a different translation of this verse, and adds more detail:

> "There was war in heaven; Michael's commander [Gabriel] and his angels fought against the dragon (Lucifer, Satan, and the apostate princes); and the dragon and his rebellious angels fought but prevailed not." This "war in heaven" was not a physical battle...but...was very terrible and very real...this conflict was far more deadly; material life is in jeopardy in material combat, but the war in heaven was fought in terms of life eternal. (606)

We also read that Lucifer and Satan were free to roam the rebellious planets until the completion of Christ Michael's mission on Urantia. They were last together for a final assault upon the Son of Man during their notorious confrontation with Jesus during his 40 days in the wilderness after his baptism. When Jesus vanquished the nefarious ones once and for all (See *UB*:605, and the various Gospel accounts), they had no power to corrupt humankind. This event terminated the Lucifer Rebellion, but as we have seen its final resolution occurred only recently with the adjudication of this case in the celestial courts.

In an interesting commentary in the Anchor Bible (pp. 193-4), the writer expresses bewilderment as to why the Old Testament indicates that the Archangel Michael fought against the dragon while it was Jesus, the Messiah, who had confronted Satan. But now we know that Jesus and Archangel Michael are one and the same. I made it a special point to ask Corelli if the Archangel Michael was really Jesus. She said, "Yes, indeed, he is the creator of 10,000,000 worlds, and Urantia was the home of his birth and death." (Obviously John was privy to this information when he wrote 12:7. The writers of the Old Testament had no way of knowing that the Archangel Michael would eventually incarnate as the baby Jesus.)

12:8 - And prevailed not; neither was their place found any more in heaven.

Jesus overcame Satan when he said, "Get thee behind me Satan." (See 12:7.)

Satan is cast out of heaven

12:9 - And the great dragon was cast out, that old serpent, called the Devil, and Satan, which deceiveth the whole world: he was cast out into the earth, and his angels were cast out with him.

This of course refers to the fall of Satan, Lucifer, and the rebel angels—"... the archrebels were dethroned and shorn of all governing powers..."—as we read in *The Urantia Book* (609).

12:10 - And I heard a loud voice saying in heaven, now is come salvation, and strength, and the kingdom of our God, and the power of his Christ: for the accuser of our brethren is cast down, which accused them before our God day and night.

A voice from heaven proclaims that the evil ones have lost their influence.

The word "accuser" is an interesting one and appears in many sections of the Bible as well as in the Book of Revelation. Its meaning appears to have changed throughout the ages. We think of the accused as someone charged with wrongdoing. The Greek word for accuser is diabolos, which means to separate, accuse or slander. It is also used as a name for Satan in the sense of one who separates, accuses, slanders, seduces.

12:11 - And they overcame him by the blood of the lamb, and by the word of their testimony; and they loved not their lives unto the death.

Q: What is the meaning of "and they loved not their lives unto the death"?

A: The men who persecuted Jesus were unaware that with their actions, they jeopardized the possibility of eternal life.

12:12 - Therefore rejoice, ye heavens, and ye that dwell in them. Woe to the inhabiters of the earth and of the sea! For the devil is come down unto you, having great wrath, because he knoweth that he hath but a short time.

Here Satan realizes that he is about to be defeated.

Satan wars with the earth

12:13 - And when the dragon saw that he was cast unto the earth, he persecuted the woman which brought forth the man-child.

As we have noted, Satan was loose on the earth at the time of Eve. He successfully aborted her mission by insidiously urging Cano to persuade Eve to intermingle human genes with hers. This action was against the divine plan.

On March 1, 1998, I felt I had to confirm with Corelli whether this "man-child" was Jesus or Cain.

A: In this case, Cain.

Q: What was the manner of this persecution?

A: Satan was successful in that the First Garden was destroyed, and Eve was forced to flee.

12:14 - And to the woman were given two wings of a great eagle, that she might fly into the wilderness, into her place, where she is nourished for a time, and times, and half a time, from the face of the serpent.

The extraordinary explanation for this passage can be found only in *The Urantia Book*. Adam and Eve had available for their use a giant bird, the fandor, now long extinct. They were able to fly great distances. (See *The Urantia Book:*831.)

12:15 - And the serpent cast out of his mouth water as a flood after the woman, that he might cause her to be carried away of the flood.

Q: What is the meaning of the serpent casting forth water from his mouth? Why did he want her [Eve] to be carried away by a flood?

A: A figure of speech. He was spewing hate and wanted to destroy Eve. He had induced Eve to go against the plan of God. But when Eve realized what she had done, she would have nothing further to do with anyone who would take her away from her chosen path. Satan's anger was great when he realized he could no longer influence her through others.

As a side note, isn't it an irony that while theologians justify the subordination of women as being ordained by God, they are actually propagating Satan's hatred of Eve? His insidious influence is still being picked up by the receptive minds of men who hate women. Many religious leaders throughout the ages used religious teachings as a justification for denigrating and enslaving women. Even today certain churches find it difficult to ordain women as ministers because Jesus supposedly only appointed twelve male apostles.

JESUS AND THE LIBERATION OF WOMEN

According to *The Urantia Book* (1679)—but left out of the Bible—Jesus commissioned twelve women as deaconesses to go out to preach the gospel and minister to the sick, a shocking and unprecedented action for those times. This act on his part was "an emancipation proclamation which set free all women for all time."

These women were: Susanna, the daughter of the former chazan of the Nazareth synagogue; Joanna, the wife of Chuza, the steward of Herod Antipas; Elizabeth, the daughter of a wealthy Jew of Tiberias and Sepphoris; Martha, the elder sister of Andrew and Peter; Rachel, the sister-in-law of Jude, the Master's brother in the flesh; Nasanta, the daughter of Elman, the Syrian physician; Milcha, a cousin of the Apostle Thomas; Ruth, the eldest daughter of Matthew Levi; Celta, the daughter of a Roman centurion; and Agaman, a widow of Damascus... Mary Magdalene and Rebecca, the daughter of Joseph of Arimathea....and this liberation of women ...was practiced by the apostles immediately after the Master's departure, albeit they fell back to the olden customs in subsequent generations....Paul...conceded all this in theory...[but] found it difficult to carry out in practice.

Q: But why, Corelli, were these women left out of the Bible?

A: The scribes and priests could not allow this information to go out to the public. Their scorn for women was imbedded too deeply, and subsequent generations carried on these disgraceful traditions.

12:16 - And the earth helped the woman, and the earth opened her mouth, and swallowed up the flood which the dragon cast out of his mouth.

Q: How exactly did the earth help Eve?

A: Adam and Eve were forced to toil in the Second Garden. Tilling the soil was a therapeutic way of working off their sorrow over what they perceived would be their eternal doom. In the days of the first Garden, when Adam and Eve had access to the fruit of the tree of life, they could have lived on indefinitely. But once they transgressed they no longer had this ability and were forced to live as earthly mortals. [Adam lived to the age of 530 and Eve died 19 years before him. See *UB*:852]

12:17 - And the dragon was wroth with the woman, and went to make war with the remnant of her seed, which keep the commandments of God, and have the testimony of Jesus Christ.

Q: How did Satan make war with the remnant of Mary's seed?

A: One way was by the persecution of the early Christians by godless men who wanted to stop the spread of Christ's teachings. However, note that only those who wanted to be influenced could carry out Satan's nefarious plans. Ever since Pentecost no one can be influenced unless he consciously chooses to embrace godless methods.

Thus ended a most informative and intriguing chapter.

Highlights from Chapter 12

— This chapter is a garbled narrative which switches back and forth between the stories of Eve and Mary and Christ Michael as they struggle with the "red dragon" (12:3). To fully understand it, one must review *The Urantia Book's* account of the first and second epochal revelations and the Lucifer Rebellion (which are summarized in the first part of this chapter).

— Eve is the woman "clothed with the sun" (12:1), with the moon at her feet. She had been known as the "moon goddess" in early cult worship; the Great Mother cult of the pre-Christian Mediterranean was later incorporated into Christianity in the guise of veneration of the Virgin Mary.

— Satan tries to abort Adam and Eve's mission to uplift the human race. Under Satan's influence, Eve was persuaded by Cano to intermingle her genes with his in the First Garden. She gives birth to Cain, "travailing in birth"(12:2).

— As a result, Adam and Eve "flee into the wilderness" (12:6) as they are expelled from the First Garden after a devastating war with surrounding tribes. (UB:821ff.)

— After she repents, Satan is "wroth" with Eve (12:17) and, by extension, with all women, thus contributing to their subordination throughout the ages.

— The fact that Jesus had commissioned twelve female deaconesses (UB:1679) was intentionally left out of the Bible.

— Satan inspired the persecution of the early Christians. (12:17)

— Jesus (who is identified as "Archangel Michael" in Old Testament accounts) vanquishes Satan in a deadly "war in heaven"(12:7-9) fought in terms of life eternal. The *UB* reveals that this Michael is one and the same as Christ Jesus. Jesus is Michael of Nebadon and is creator of our local universe of 10 million worlds.

13

King James Translation

1 And I stood upon the sand of the sea, and saw a beast rise up out of the sea, having seven heads and ten horns, and upon his horns ten crowns, and upon his heads the name of blasphemy.

2 And the beast which I saw was like unto a leopard, and his feet were as the feet of a bear, and his mouth as the mouth of a lion: and the dragon gave him his power, and his seat, and great authority.

3 And I saw one of his heads as it were wounded to death; and his deadly wound was healed: and all the world wondered after the beast.

4 And they worshipped the dragon which gave power unto the beast: and they worshipped the beast, saying, Who is like unto the beast? who is able to make war with him?

5 And there was given unto him a mouth speaking great things and blasphemies; and power was given unto him to continue forty and two months.

6 And he opened his mouth in blasphemy against God, to blaspheme his name, and his tabernacle, and them that dwell in heaven.

7 And it was given unto him to make war with the saints, and to overcome them: and power was given him over all kindreds, and tongues, and nations.

8 And all that dwell upon the earth shall worship him, whose names are not written in the book of life of the Lamb slain from the foundation of the world.

9 If any man have an ear, let him hear.

10 He that leadeth into captivity shall go into captivity: he that killeth with the sword must be killed with the sword. Here is the patience and the faith of the saints.

11 And I beheld another beast coming up out of the earth; and he had two horns like a lamb, and he spake as a dragon.

12 And he exerciseth all the power of the first beast before him, and causeth the earth and them which dwell therein to worship the first beast, whose deadly wound was healed.

13 And he doeth great wonders, so that he maketh fire come down from heaven on the earth in the sight of men,

14 And deceiveth them that dwell on the earth by the means of those miracles which he had power to do in the sight of the beast; saying to them that dwell on the earth, that they should make an image to the beast, which had the wound by a sword, and did live.

15 And he had power to give life unto the image of the beast, that the image of the beast should both speak, and cause that as many as would not worship the image of the beast should be killed.

16 And he causeth all, both small and great, rich and poor, free and bond, to receive a mark in their right hand, or in their foreheads.

17 And that no man might buy or sell, save he that had the mark, or the name of the beast, or the number of his name.

18 Here is wisdom. Let him that hath understanding count the number of the beast: for it is the number of a man; and his number is Six hundred threescore and six.

13
revised

This chapter, perhaps more than the others, has been a source of much speculation regarding the meaning of certain images, such as the seven heads, the ten horns, the beast rising out of the sea, the second beast rising from the earth, and the meaning of "666." Perhaps most important, who is this fearsome beast, and how does he relate to the number 666? If he is not the dreaded Antichrist—as many Christians believe—then who is he? As usual, my celestial friends and *The Urantia Book* give a factual and an almost down-to-earth interpretation of these images and of the obscure historical events of long ago which John tried to explain symbolically. John's vision, as reported in this chapter, took him back more than 200,000 years to events that are clearly described for the first time in *The Urantia Book*.

But how could anyone reading this chapter deduce that the "seven heads" (13:1) refers to seven nations that existed over 200 millennia ago? This is quite impossible when you take into account that the earliest known recorded history goes back about 25,000 years. Could there be any physical evidence of such nations existing? In my naiveté I thought this was something I could verify. After all, new archaeological findings are continually pushing back recorded time; and carbon dating techniques might confirm the existence of such ancient communities. Perhaps future archaeologists will one day uncover many of these prehistoric dates and places about which the Urantia Revelation gives many useful clues.

Whatever the case, the *UB*'s claim of civilizations existing 200,000 years is just as mind-boggling as is its account of the events of 500,000 years ago (the time of Caligastia's arrival in the Persian Gulf). Genesis hints at these distant events, but, of course, no dates are given. Numerous cultures also allude to these ultra-ancient transactions in their oral traditions and myth. Books by Zechariah Sitchin and others also offer modern interpretations. But the clearest exposition of the time sequence of these events is, I believe, found in *The Urantia Book*.

The following are the astounding answers I received on May 2, 1996, when I questioned Corelli about 13:1.

The rise of the beast and the false prophet

13:1 - And I stood upon the sand of the sea, and saw a beast rise up out of the sea, having seven heads and ten horns, and upon his horns ten crowns, and upon his heads the name of blasphemy.

Q: *Who was the beast who rose out of the sea? Why seven heads and ten horns? Ten crowns?*

A: Good morning, Stella. We are glad to be with you again. We see you are puzzled about the continued reference to the seven heads, ten horns, and ten crowns. In this case, the seven heads refer to the seven nations that existed at that very far-distant time: Syria, Damascus, Lithia, Chronus, Pythagia,

Hermania and Almyra. These nations were aligned with Pythagia, which was considered the leader of this federation of nations. Almyra was the home of Satan [I clarify this statement later on] who rose out of the sea of iniquity to join forces with Caligastia and Daligastia—"serpents" in their own right—to oppose the divine plan. When they arose out of this symbolic sea of evil, they were admonished to mend their ways or the repercussions of their iniquity would be felt by the seven nations.

I tried to verify the existence of these nations, but had difficulty finding any references. So a year later, on April 9, 1997, I questioned Corelli and Aflana:

Q: *Did John go back in time to see what happened during the Lucifer Rebellion, and to these seven nations that existed at that time? I have checked out these names but cannot find any references to Lithia, Chronus, Pythagia, Hermania and Almyra. I found names that sound something like them. Can you clarify? And why was Almyra the home of Satan when presumably he had no earthly home?*

A: We understand your confusion. Almyra was a figure of speech meaning the bloody conquest from which Satan arose symbolically. His path was one of destruction. As we have seen, Caligastia, the Planetary Prince, cast his lot with the nefarious Satan, who in turn was influenced by Lucifer. All three were notorious for their calumny against God.

The names of the other nations were indeed the names of nations that existed 200,000 years ago. These names have changed considerably over time. Lithia became Lycia; Chronus is no more but faded from the world scene thousands of years ago. Pythagia became Phrygia; Hermania became Germany. These nations, or more accurately tribes, had a wide scope of activity. Volunteers from these outposts migrated to the original Garden of Eden to absorb its culture and to become educated in physical and religious matters. These people then returned to their original homes to spread what they had learned in the garden.

Does this make sense to you?

Stella: I suppose so. I can't really prove what you say, but must take your word for it.

Since my initial conversations with Corelli and Aflana, I continued my sleuthing, determined to find a record indicating that such nations existed. I found a record of Lithia (Lycia) on, of all places, a map of Paul's travels in the King James Bible. Pythagia (Phrygia) was on an old map in the Thomas Jefferson Bible. I found nothing on Chronus, which exists no more; and nothing on Almyra. Hermania is now Germany, as was indicated; Syria and Damascus are, of course, still in existence.

My celestial friends appear to be correct. I continued asking questions:

Q: *What were the ten horns?*
A: The ten horns were ten kings who ruled through several generations. Ten crowns mean the same as ten horns.

Q: *Was John literally able to see what happened so long ago?*
A: Yes, he was given a vision of what actually happened so he could report about what he had seen.

On April 5, 1997, I spoke to Corelli, and told her that this chapter is very difficult for me to understand. (As if the others were not!)

Q: *Could you possibly answer more questions on this chapter?*
A: We will try.

13:2 - And the beast which I saw was like unto a leopard, and his feet were as the feet of a bear, and his mouth as the mouth of a lion: and the dragon gave him his power, and his seat, and great authority.

Q: *Is this beast Satan or a head of state? It sounds as if an actual head of state were given power and great authority.*

A: Yes, it is a head of state, the king of Pythagia, the leader of the federation of seven nations. He was inclined to follow all manner of corruption, so he was a ripe candidate for the blandishments of the devil. He had great authority in these times.

13:3 - And I saw one of his heads as it were wounded to death; and his deadly wound was healed: and all the world wondered after the beast.

Q: Was the king wounded somehow?

A: This king was severely wounded in battle. This was a great opportunity for him to have a change of heart and repent. However, greed and corruption were too deeply imbedded in his mind; he continued to do things against the will of God. He was a deeply troubled man, and he could not change his evil ways. His name was Omar.

I was still puzzled about 13:2 and 13:3, so again asked:

Q: In 13:2, is the beast Satan? And was he given power by the dragon, the nefarious three?

A: Yes. [This discrepancy is clarified below.]

Q: Regarding 13:3, was "one of his heads" a king who fell?

A: Yes.

Q: Why was his deadly wound healed?

A: He repented of his misdeeds, and all in his domain wondered what happened to the man that he so completely changed. [This is clarified in the questions below.]

In typing this on February 28, 1998, I noted two discrepancies and asked:

Q: Regarding 13:2: Corelli, in May of 1996, you said that the beast was the king of Pythagia. Yet in 13:2, April 9, 1997, you said it was Satan. Which is correct?

A: We are reading this verse. The beast was the king, and the dragon was Satan who was influencing the king. Does this clear it up?

Stella: I guess so. It's still confusing to me.

A: We are sorry.

Q: Regarding 13:3, you said this king could not change his evil ways. Yet in April of 1997, you said he did. So which is correct in this verse?

A: Don't forget a lot has happened in 200,000 years! In life this man could not repent, but after death he had ample opportunity. John saw the transformation that occurred. Those who followed him in death, those of his nation, marveled at how he had changed.

13:4 - And they worshipped the dragon which gave power unto the beast: and they worshipped the beast, saying, Who is like unto the beast? Who is able to make war with him?

Q: Did this nation worship the dragon? And this beast, was he the same king as before?

A: This answer is the same as before.

13:5 - And there was given unto him a mouth speaking great things and blasphemies; and power was given unto him to continue forty and two months.

Q: Who spoke great things? And what does forty-two months mean?

A: The devil spoke through others who tried to influence this king, and he was influenced by promises of greater conquests and greater gains. Forty-two months was a figure of speech.

Q: Did "forty-two months" mean an indefinite period of time?

A: Yes, in reality the influence continued on and on.

13:6 - And he opened his mouth in blasphemy against God, to blaspheme his name, and his tabernacle, and them that dwell in heaven.

Q: Who is doing this, Satan or the ruler? It seems as if this is switching back and forth from Satan to the king.

A: Yes, we can see your confusion. Lucifer and Satan are behind all of this. But there were many humans who went along with Satan's plan of subverting the influence of God.

13:7 - And it was given unto him to make war with the saints, and to overcome them: and power was given him over all kindreds, and tongues, and nations.

Q: *Who was given power, and by whom?*

A: We are not quite sure what this meant. Satan was given authority, by Caligastia, to use his influence as best he could to persuade nations and rulers to go against God and to side with the three.

13:8 - And all that dwell upon the earth shall worship him, whose names are not written in the book of life of the Lamb slain from the foundation of the world.

Q: *It seems as if all who are not godly worship the devil.*

A: That is exactly right.

Q: *In verse 8, all those who did not believe in God or "whose names are not written in the book of life of the Lamb" worshipped the devil? Did I interpret this correctly?*

A: Yes, you have interpreted this correctly. It is very difficult reading. The verses are convoluted so it is difficult to make logical sense out of them. But, yes, it is the story of Lucifer's influence on all those who have tendencies to do evil.

13:9 - If any man have an ear, let him hear.

13:10 - He that leadeth into captivity shall go into captivity: he that killeth with the sword must be killed with the sword. Here is the patience and the faith of the saints.

Q: *Is this retribution if one sins?*

A: Yes, indeed. No one escapes the results of their own deeds or misdeeds. Justice may be slow, but it is certain.

The beast out of the land, and the number 666

13:11 - And I beheld another beast coming up out of the earth; and he had two horns like a lamb, and he spake as a dragon.

Q: Who is the second beast?

A: The second beast is Satan, and the first beast was actually Lucifer who gave power to Satan.

13:12 - And he exerciseth all the power of the first beast before him, and causeth the earth and them which dwell therein to worship the first beast, whose deadly wound was healed.

Q: Meaning?

A: The same as above.

13:13 - And he doeth great wonders, so that he maketh fire come down from heaven on the earth in the sight of men.

Q: Why would he do great wonders, and who is he?

A: Satan was given great power to do great works, but he did this only initially to tantalize mortals who would fall for these blandishments.

13:14 - And deceiveth them that dwell on the earth by the means of those miracles which he had power to do in the sight of the beast; saying to them that dwell on the earth, that they should make an image to the beast, which had the wound by a sword, and did live.

Q: Who was the beast who was wounded by a sword and lived?

A: This refers to Satan. When Christ won the "war of the heavens," Satan "did live" but was wounded in the sense that he was cast into the prison worlds. As you know, the Lucifer Rebellion has been recently adjudicated, and the nefarious three live no more.

13:15 - And he had power to give life unto the image of the beast, that the image of the beast should both speak, and cause that as many as would not worship the image of the beast should be killed.

Q: Who had power to "give life unto the image of the beast"?

A: Lucifer and Satan had the power to give life unto the "image," to all the cults who deliberately worshipped Baal and idolatrous images.

13:16 - And he causeth all, both small and great, rich and poor, free and bond, to receive a mark in their right hand, or in their foreheads.

13:17 - And that no man might buy or sell, save he that had the mark, or the name of the beast, or the number of his name.

Q: Who caused all to have a mark on their foreheads? And why could only those who had the mark buy and sell?

A: The mark of the beast designates all those who do not believe in God, and are therefore concerned with worldly things. At the time of John's vision, only those who were not Christians could buy and sell in the market places; Christians were despised and frowned upon.

I wondered how the mark of the beast could be eradicated. Regarding this, *The Urantia Book* alludes to this ancient Biblical phrase when it describes the processes undergone in the worlds inhabited after death: "Here you will be purged of all the remnants of unfortunate heredity, unwholesome environment, and unspiritual planetary tendencies. The last remnants of the 'mark of the beast' are here eradicated." (538)

13:18 - Here is wisdom. Let him that hath understanding count the number of the beast: for it is the number of a man; and his number is Six hundred threescore and six.

Q: What does 666 really mean?

A: (Solonia and Eckhart) Let us clear up some of this

confusion. The number of your planet in your local system of approximately 1,000 inhabitable planets is 606. This number should not be confused with Satan's number that was 13666. That is one reason why the number 13 has been considered to be bad luck. The notorious number 666 came about as a result of a simple confusion in writen figures. The number 666 should have been 606.

We see you are tired. We will continue on another day. We love you. Be of good cheer.

And so ended a difficult and challenging chapter. The mystery of the two beasts and the meaning of 666 is solved.

Highlights from Chapter 13

- John in his vision was literally able to go back in time to see nations that existed 200,000 years ago that were directly influenced by Satan, Lucifer and their followers. Their evil influence on those "whose lives were not written in the book of life of the Lamb" (13:8) was considerable and long-standing.

- "Seven heads" (13:1) actually refer to these seven ancient nations that existed long before Adam and Eve. A few of these still exist, at least by name.

- With the approval of Caligastia, Satan was given authority and power by Lucifer to persuade these nations to go against the divine plan.

- The king of the leading nation in this federation was like a "beast" in that he was very powerful. This man, named Omar, was especially influenced by the "dragon [who] gave him power" (13:2). But he repented in the afterlife.

- When Christ won the war in heaven, Satan continued "did live" (13:14) but had a "wound by the sword". In other words, he was shorn of most of his power, but was still able to visit the earth and appears in chapter 13 as the second beast "coming up out of the earth" (13:11). This beast is Satan, and interpretations which identify this beast as the "Antichrist" are therefore incorrect.

- In the times immediately after Christ, Christians were not permitted to "buy and sell" (13:17) in the market-place.

- As individuals progress on their eternal journey, the "mark" (13:6-7), which in *The Urantia Book's* account refers to human frailties linked with our animal origins (UB: 538), will eventually be eradicated.

- Out of 1,000 inhabitable planets in our local system of planets, 606 is the literal number of our planet. Satan's actual number is 13666, which is the origin of the reference to 666 in 13:18.

14

King James Translation

1 And I looked, and, lo, a Lamb stood on the mount Sion, and with him an hundred forty and four thousand, having his Father's name written in their foreheads.

2 And I heard a voice from heaven, as the voice of many waters, and as the voice of a great thunder: and I heard the voice of harpers harping with their harps:

3 And they sung as it were a new song before the throne, and before the four beasts, and the elders: and no man could learn that song but the hundred and forty and four thousand, which were redeemed from the earth.

4 These are they which were not defiled with women; for they are virgins. These are they which follow the Lamb whithersoever he goeth. These were redeemed from among men, being the first fruits unto God and to the Lamb.

5 And in their mouth was found no guile: for they are without fault before the throne of God.

6 And I saw another angel fly in the midst of heaven, having the everlasting gospel to preach unto them that dwell on the earth, and to every nation, and kindred, and tongue, and people,

7 Saying with a loud voice, Fear God, and give glory to him; for the hour of his judgment is come: and worship him that made heaven, and earth, and the sea, and the fountains of waters.

8 And there followed another angel, saying, Babylon is fallen, is fallen, that great city, because she made all nations drink of the wine of the wrath of her fornication.

9 And the third angel followed them, saying with a loud voice, If any man worship the beast and his image, and receive his mark in his forehead, or in his hand,

10 The same shall drink of the wine of the wrath of God, which is poured out without mixture into the cup of his indignation; and he shall be tormented with fire and brimstone in the presence of the holy angels, and in the presence of the Lamb:

11 And the smoke of their torment ascendeth up for ever and ever: and they have no rest day nor night, who worship the beast and his image, and whosoever receiveth the mark of his name.

12 Here is the patience of the saints: here are they that keep the commandments of God, and the faith of Jesus.

13 And I heard a voice from heaven saying unto me, Write, Blessed are the dead which die in the Lord from henceforth: Yea, saith the Spirit, that they may rest from their labours; and their works do follow them.

14 And I looked, and behold a white cloud, and upon the cloud one sat like unto the Son of man, having on his head a golden crown, and in his hand a sharp sickle.

15 And another angel came out of the temple, crying with a loud voice to him that sat on the cloud, Thrust in thy sickle, and reap: for the time is come for thee to reap; for the harvest of the earth is ripe.

16 And he that sat on the cloud thrust in his sickle on the earth; and the earth was reaped.

17 And another angel came out of the temple which is in heaven, he also having a sharp sickle.

18 And another angel came out from the altar, which had power over fire; and cried with a loud cry to him that had the sharp sickle, saying, Thrust in thy sharp sickle, and gather the clusters of the vine of the earth; for her grapes are fully ripe.

19 And the angel thrust in his sickle into the earth, and gathered the vine of the earth, and cast it into the great winepress of the wrath of God.

20 And the winepress was trodden without the city, and blood came out of the winepress, even unto the horse bridles, by the space of a thousand and six hundred furlongs.

revised

John begins this chapter with a vision of all those survivors of death, the so-called 144,000, who have overcome their animal natures (the "mark of the beast") on their way to stand in triumph before the throne of God in "the first heaven." After their long journey of heavenly ascent, they have—according to the account in the Urantia Revelation on page 539—finally arrived in Jerusem, the system capital of our local system of over 600 inhabited planets (1,000 is the eventual total). The celestial hosts and the myriads of survivors of past ages who have preceded these ascenders are there to greet them; it is a stupendous and joyous occasion. The four "beasts" are there as well as the Council of Twenty-four and innumerable other beings—but you'll note that this scene in the Book of Revelation contains *no women*. A disturbing verse 4 reads: "These are they which were not defiled with women; for they are virgins."

This statement has been and still is a terrible travesty on the value of women. What are women to think of their exclusion from this grand event in heaven? Are women to be victimized here on earth and in heaven? It appears that way if we accept that only men not defiled by women are granted access to the heavenly abode.

Statements such as this, among others in the Bible, have been used as a justification to exclude women from participation in ministerial life and in many other areas of human endeavor. God supposedly authorized this inferior status and had it set into the Bible and, therefore, it is not to be questioned.

HOW JESUS REGARDED WOMEN

But Jesus never taught such misogynist doctrines. *The Urantia Book* proclaims that Jesus raised women to absolute equality with men:

> The most astonishing and the most revolutionary feature of Michael's mission on earth was his attitude toward women. In a day and generation when a man was not supposed to salute even his own wife in a public place, Jesus dared to take women along as teachers of the gospel in connection with his third tour of Galilee. And he had the consummate courage to do this in the face of the rabbinic teaching which declared that it was "better that the words of the law should be burned than delivered to women."

> In one generation Jesus lifted women out of the disrespectful oblivion and the slavish drudgery of the ages. And it is the one shameful thing about the religion that presumed to take Jesus' name that it lacked the moral courage to follow this noble example in its subsequent attitude toward women. (1671)

Christianity is not alone in relegating women to an inferior status. Other religions are equally to blame, perhaps even more so. Despite their many differences, most traditional religions seem to be united in one respect: a mutual belief in the inferiority of women and the need to suppress whatever abilities they might bring to the affairs of men. With indignation at the injustices suffered by women by supposedly "holy" teachings, I continued my work on this chapter.

The lamb on Mount Zion

14:1 - And I looked, and, lo, a Lamb stood on the mount Sion, and with him an hundred forty and four thousand, having his father's name written in their foreheads.

The Lamb is of course a metaphor for Christ. As we have noted before, ritual animal sacrifices were customary; therefore, it was natural to refer to Christ as a sacrificial lamb. According to Corelli, the reference to 144,000 is a figure of speech that refers to all those who were fused with their indwelling spirit (the so-called "Thought Adjusters" or fragment of God) at the time of John's vision, an event which occurs in the afterlife.

The Urantia Book teaching on the fragment of God within—and our sacred goal of fusion with this indwelling spirit of God—is set forth on pages 1215-1224 and was introduced in chapter 3. The technical term for it is "Thought Adjuster," and the following is a brief review of this key concept:

There are two special forces at work within the minds of mortals: first, men and women ascending upwards in their deeply personal search for God, and second, God the Father descending to each of us by bestowing a pre-personal fragment of himself. This so-called God-fragment seeks fusion with the aspiring creature personality, which in a sense is its host. During a lifetime, the human mind and this God-spirit slowly come to synchronize their work—thereby creating the immortal soul, which will always be unique.

Either on this planet or on a future mansion world in heaven, there is final and total attunement of the mortal will and the will of God (as it is expressed to the human mind by the impulses coming from the Thought Adjuster). At this moment in the future, the two will become one. If this grand event occurs on this planet, the mortal is immediately taken up in a swirl of radiant energies; the body is instantly immolated, and the soul flashes over to the next world. (This is, as we have seen, what happened to Enoch of Biblical fame, the first human to fuse with his thought adjuster; what John saw in 14:1 were ascenders who had fused in the afterlife.) In fusion, the pre-personal God-fragment achieves personality, and the human achieves a permanent spiritual state.

> 14:2 - And I heard a voice from heaven, as the voice of many waters, and as the voice of a great thunder: and I heard the voice of harpers harping with their harps.

Q: Corelli, who is the voice in heaven?

A: The voice is an angel of God in charge of the assembly gathered to greet those ascenders who after countless centuries have fused and have arrived on Jerusem. You, too, in that far distant future, will have that honor.

Q: Are these voices of thunder and music of harps interplanetary broadcasts telling the news that these ascendant beings have arrived?

A: Indeed, yes. There is great rejoicing throughout the planetary systems that these new arrivals have completed this phase of their long journey of ascension.

> 14:3 - And they sung as it were a new song before the throne, and before the four beasts, and the elders: and no man could learn that song but the hundred and forty and four thousand, which were redeemed from the earth.

As noted earlier, *The Urantia Book* explains in detail what happens when ascending mortals finally reach the "first heaven" of Jerusem. Note that this passage paraphrases the Book of Revelation:

> The reception of a new class of mansion world graduates is the signal for all Jerusem to assemble as a committee

of welcome.... for those who have run the planetary race and finished the mansion world progression....

John the Revelator saw a vision of the arrival of a class of advancing mortals from the seventh mansion world to their first heaven, the glories of Jerusem. He recorded: "And I saw as it were a sea of glass mingled with fire and those who had gained the victory of the beast that was originally in them and over the image that persisted through the mansion worlds and finally over the last mark and trace, standing on the sea of glass, having the harps of God [the heavenly communication instrument; [see 5:8] and singing the song of deliverance from mortal fear and death...."

Paul also had a view of the ascendant-citizen corps of perfection mortals on Jerusem, for he wrote: "But you have come to Mount Zion and to the city of the living God, the heavenly Jerusem, and to an innumerable company of angels, to the grand assembly of Michael [Jesus] and to the spirit of just men being made perfect." (539)

On March 20, 1998, Corelli further elaborated on this subject:

Corelli: Those who arrive on Jerusem are greeted joyously by those who had once traversed the same path. They eagerly watch for those they had known and who had lagged behind for an age or so. These new arrivals will be helped and taught by those who greet them.

14:4 - These are they which were not defiled with women; for they are virgins. These are they which follow the lamb whithersoever he goeth. These were redeemed from among men, being the first fruits unto God and to the Lamb.

On May 6, 1996, I asked for the meaning of "they not defiled with women." (I was somewhat mollified by her answer but still indignant about the oppression under which women have been forced to live.)

A: This paragraph was inserted by a man who had revulsion towards women and could not conceive of God bestowing grace on any man who had sex with a woman. He had absorbed the beliefs of the time that women were inferior creatures who had no souls. Of course this is completely erroneous and does a terrible disservice to women.

Q: *When was verse 14:4 inserted?*

A: (Solonia) It was inserted long after the death of John and Nathan and just before the onset of the dark ages in Europe.

14:5 - And in their mouth was found no guile: for they are without fault before the throne of god.

A: Okay as written.

An angel with the everlasting gospel

14:6 - And I saw another angel fly in the midst of heaven, having the everlasting gospel to preach unto them that dwell on the earth, and to every nation, and kindred, and tongue, and people.

14:7 - Saying with a loud voice, Fear God, and give glory to him; for the hour of his judgment is come: and worship him that made heaven, and earth, and the sea, and the fountains of water.

Q: *Do we literally have to fear God?*

A: No, of course not—rather fear the results of your own actions. A scribe inserted this reference to the fear of God.

Fall of Babylon

14:8 - And there followed another angel, saying, Babylon is fallen, is fallen, that great city, because she made all nations drink of the wine of the wrath of her fornication.

Q: What is meant by the "fall of Babylon"?

A: It means that evil has fallen away from those who turned to God. Babylon is a figure of speech denoting corruption.

On May 6, 2000, I asked for clarification of this confusing interpretation.

Q: Regarding 14:8, your statement that the "fall of Babylon" means that evil has fallen away from those who turned to God seems to directly contradict this verse in that it seems to indicate that the city has fallen because of its corruption. Can you clarify?

A: Yes. While the verse seems to refer to Babylon as having fallen because of corruption, John meant to say that evil falls away from those who turned to God.

Fate of the worshippers of the beast

14:9 - And the third angel followed them, saying with a loud voice, If any man worship the beast and his image, and receive his mark in his forehead, or in his hand,

14:10 - The same shall drink of the wine of the wrath of God, which is poured out without mixture into the cup of his indignation; and he shall be tormented with fire and brimstone in the presence of the holy angels, and in the presence of the lamb.

14:11 - And the smoke of their torment ascendeth up for ever and ever: and they have no rest day nor night, who worship the beast and his image, and whosoever receiveth the mark of his name.

Q: What do the above three verses mean?

A: It means all those who realize they have lived wrongly will bitterly regret the path they chose to follow in life. "Fire and brimstone" should not be taken literally, of course. It symbolizes all-consuming regret.

14:12 - Here is the patience of the saints: here are they that keep the commandments of God, and the faith of Jesus.

This verse is okay. The saints and angels in charge of your welfare are very patient with erring mankind. They try to instill righteous actions in keeping with the will of God. There are holy former humans, who literally weep when they see that people have turned away from God.

Vision of the Son of man

14:13 - And I heard a voice from heaven saying unto me, Write, Blessed are the dead which die in the Lord from henceforth: Yea, saith the Spirit, that they may rest from their labours; and their works do follow them.

A: John is told to write what he has seen, that death is not to be feared—and that good deeds will be recognized in the afterlife. But you mortals must gather your most intense experiences here on earth. That is very important. Only on your world will you be able to experience certain trials and tribulations as well as certain joys which are never to be repeated.

14:14 - And I looked, and behold a white cloud, and upon the cloud one sat like unto the Son of man, having on his head a golden crown, and in his hand a sharp sickle.

A: This is Christ Michael appearing as the Son of Man in this guise.

Harvest of the earth

14:15 - And another angel came out of the temple, crying with a loud voice to him that sat on the cloud, Thrust in thy sickle, and reap: for the time is come for thee to reap; for the harvest of the earth is ripe.

This refers to the mass resurrection of the sleeping survivors, an event which is described in *The Urantia Book* on page 341.

Note that the Greek translation defines "ripe" as "dry," whereas the King James version reads "ripe."

On March 21, 1998, I tried to clarify this verse by asking Corelli:

Q: *Can you say more about his use of the sickle?*

A: Yes, in those days it was used to cut out or to remove that which is dry from that which is ripe. In this verse it meant all those who have followed God's will are the "ripe" ones; the "dry" ones are those who are not eligible for spiritual ascension at the present time.

14:16 - And he that sat on the cloud thrust in his sickle on the earth; and the earth was reaped.

14:17 - And another angel came out of the temple which is in heaven, he also having a sharp sickle.

A: These verses refer again to resurrection. After an epochal or dispensational resurrection (which are described in *The Urantia Book* on pages 568 and 2024), each person will be asked to choose whether they will continue in the heavenly ascent. You are given sufficient time to make this decision, but as we have seen in earlier chapters, many choose not to go on—a sad fact to note.

14:18 - And another angel came out from the altar, which had power over fire; and cried with a loud cry to him that had the sharp sickle, saying, thrust in thy sharp sickle, and gather the clusters of the vine of the earth; for her grapes are fully ripe.

A: The clusters of vines and grapes refer to mortals who are ready for harvest.

14:19 - And the angel thrust in his sickle into the earth, and gathered the vine of the earth, and cast it into the great winepress of the wrath of God.

A: Leave out "and cast it into the great winepress of the wrath of God." It has no place in John's original message.

14:20 - And the winepress was trodden without the city, and blood came out of the winepress, even unto the horse bridles, by the space of a thousand and six hundred furlongs.

A: This means that all those who forsake God will suffer great torment in their souls. Yet all will have one chance to repent.

This is all for tonight. Thank you, Stella, for your persistence.

Stella: The thanks are mine for your assistance.

Sometimes as I receive follow-up information, I'm as puzzled as I was when I first asked the question, so eventually I ask again. On March 23, 1998, I decided to try to get more information on 14:20.

Q: What does "blood came out of the winepress" mean?

A: Only those who have turned to God will be resurrected immediately—that is, three days after death; this has been the case since the coming of Christ. The rest are known as "the sleeping survivors"; they must await the next mass resurrection, which comes at the end of an age or epoch of time.

Q: Is this a resurrection of the physical body, or is it a spiritual body?

A: Only a spiritual or "morontial" body. Once the physical body dies, it returns to ashes. No physical resurrection is possible, but the spiritual body goes on and on through a variety of transmutations once a person chooses eternal life.

Q: What does "space of a thousand and six hundred furlongs" mean?

A: Merely a figure of speech. What this really means is a worldwide resurrection.

Stella: Thank you very much.

A: You are welcome.

On February 4, 2000, I asked:

Q: Why did John write in metaphors that are so difficult to understand?

A: We really do not know why he chose these symbols. We will ask him. [Pause] John says he chose these symbols because the people of those times understood what grapes and winepresses meant. These were words with which the people were familiar. People in your time find it difficult to relate to their terminology. Does this help?

Stella: I suppose.

A: Now, Stella. We know you still doubt us. We are trying very hard to reach you. This is the best we can do.

Stella: Thank you.

Highlights from Chapter 14

— The 144,000 with the "father's name written on their foreheads" (14:1) is a figure of speech referring to those men and women who in the afterlife have fused with their indwelling spirit (or "thought adjuster"). They have completed the long ascent through the mansion worlds and are now arrived on Jerusem as "graduates"(*UB*: 539). In John's vision they are now singing "a new song before the throne"(14:3).

— A scribe inserted a passage at 14:4 indicating that only celibate men "not defiled by women" can attain this status on high. This egregious forgery flies in the face of the fact that Jesus raised women into absolute equality with men. Unfortunately, Paul and others reverted to the age-old beliefs of the inferiority of women (*UB*:1671).

— The city of Babylon is used as a figure of speech denoting worldly corruption, a place of worshippers of the beast who will come to regret their actions, which is symbolized by "fire and brimstone" and "smoke of torment" (14:9-11).

— When "the harvest of the earth is ripe" (14:15), there is a mass, worldwide resurrection known as a dispensational resurrection. But "the great winepress" (14:19) selects as it were those who will be resurrected individually and immediately because of their devotion to God.

15

King James Translation

1 And I saw another sign in heaven, great and marvellous, seven angels having the seven last plagues; for in them is filled up the wrath of God.

2 And I saw as it were a sea of glass mingled with fire: and them that had gotten the victory over the beast, and over his image, and over his mark, and over the number of his name, stand on the sea of glass, having the harps of God.

3 And they sing the song of Moses the servant of God, and the song of the Lamb, saying, Great and marvellous are thy works, Lord God Almighty; just and true are thy ways, thou King of saints.

4 Who shall not fear thee, O Lord, and glorify thy name? for thou only art holy: for all nations shall come and worship before thee; for thy judgments are made manifest.

5 And after that I looked, and, behold, the temple of the tabernacle of the testimony in heaven was opened:

6 And the seven angels came out of the temple, having the seven plagues, clothed in pure and white linen, and having their breasts girded with golden girdles.

7 And one of the four beasts gave unto the seven angels seven golden vials full of the wrath of God, who liveth for ever and ever.

8 And the temple was filled with smoke from the glory of God, and from his power; and no man was able to enter into the temple, till the seven plagues of the seven angels were fulfilled.

revised

Most of the symbols in this chapter had been explained in previous chapters and were by now becoming increasingly clear to me. However, I was becoming more observant of areas that I hadn't really questioned before. For example, there was the very pleasant subject of angels. I had come to realize that the Book of Revelation mentions many orders of angels who seem to have different functions.

THE PLANETARY ANGELS

To verify John's teaching on angels, I turned to *The Urantia Book* and discovered that here are twelve corps of specialized planetary angels operating on Urantia, with each corps having a specialized function. Quoting here directly from the *UB*, these divisions are as follows:

1) The epochal angels;
2) The progress angels;
3) The religious guardians [at 3:1 in the Book of Revelation they are called the "angels of the churches"];

4) The angels of nation life [these are the "angels of the trumpets" referred to in chapter 8 who are directors of the political performances of national life];

5) The angels of the races;

6) The angels of the future;

7) The angels of enlightenment;

8) The angels of health;

9) The home seraphim;

10) The angels of industry;

11) The angels of diversion; and

12) The angels of superhuman industry. (1255-1256)

Judging from the information on our "earth angels" provided *The Urantia Book* as well as the Book of Revelation, it appears that we are surrounded by the gracious acts of a myriad of angels who are trying to help humanity in just about every area of life.

The seven last plagues

15:1 - And I saw another sign in heaven, great and marvellous, seven angels having the seven last plagues; for in them is filled up the wrath of God.

On April 11, 1997, I questioned Corelli as follows:

Q: What is the meaning of "seven angels having the seven last plagues; for in them is filled up the wrath of God"? I thought angels were loving and kind and unable to do such things as cast plagues upon the people of the earth.

A: Of course it is not really the angels who cast plagues; rather, people bring these consequences upon themselves. These were real warnings that John saw and heard. John, unfortunately, had to work with the primitive thinking of the time that attributed everything to God. To get his message across, he used the threat of God's displeasure to warn and wake up the people. Now he regrets using this symbolism, and he is glad you are trying to get the true meaning out to your people.

Q: *Are you sure this is the correct explanation?* [What temerity on my part to question their veracity!]

A: Unfortunately, yes.

Q: *I thought perhaps it was some scribe who wrote this.*

A: No, this was John's dictation to Nathan. The two did discuss whether they should word it in this fashion, and, between them, they decided to do so. They did not wish to offend the authorities. Regarding the rest of the chapter, you have the meanings of the symbols from the previous chapters.

> **15:2** - And I saw as it were a sea of glass mingled with fire: and them that had gotten the victory over the beast, and over his image, and over his mark, and over the number of his name, stand on the sea of glass, having the harps of God.

Here are some definitions of terms used in this important and famous verse that we have encountered before:

Sea of glass – covered at 4:6 and in *The Urantia Book* at 487. This is John's term for the celestial landing and transporting field on Jerusem, the capital of our local system of planets. In appearance, the sea of glass is a real crystal; it is circular in shape, and is 30 miles in depth, and about 100 miles in circumference. This verse indicates that a victorious group of ascenders are gathering on this landing field.

Victory over the beast – the overcoming of man's animal nature. (*UB*: 538)

Mark of the beast – see 13:17, and the reference to man's animal nature just above.

Harps of God – see 5:8 and 14:2; these are instruments of communication used by celestial beings.

Song of Moses

15:3 - And they sing the song of Moses the servant of God, and the song of the Lamb, saying, Great and marvellous are thy works, Lord God Almighty; just and true are thy ways, thou King of saints.

Moses' role in the Book of Revelation is greater than we have so far acknowledged, and therefore a brief overview of Moses' role in religious history might be helpful here.

ROLE OF MOSES IN JOHN'S VISION

The song of Moses referred to in 15:3 can be interpreted as a paean of praise to the matchless Moses, the founder of the Jewish religion. Moses vastly enlarged his people's concept of Yahweh, the Jewish tribal god of old. He declared that Yahweh was over and above all. But he had difficulty presenting his new and higher idea of deity to the ignorant band of former slaves who were these early Hebrews. We learn in *The Urantia Book* (1052-76), in its crucial sections on Hebrew history, that Moses would not have succeeded had it not been for the violent eruption of Mt. Horeb when "...the whole mountain quaked greatly." He was then able to impress the teaching that their God was "mighty, terrible, a devouring fire, fearful, and all powerful." Moses told his followers that Yahweh was a "jealous God" but also a loving God, "just and righteous in all his ways." With their limited understanding it was necessary to speak of God as being in man's image—subject to fits of anger, wrath and severity. They had difficulty comprehending that God was just and loving.

According to *The Urantia Book* (see 1014ff.), Moses was the greatest teacher between the times of a man named Melchizedek—an incarnate divine being, we are told, who lived in Palestine 4,000 years ago—and Jesus of 2,000 years ago. Moses' beliefs were in fact based directly on the teachings of Melchizedek to Abraham and his contemporaries. (Cryptic references to the mysterious but important figure of Melchizedek can be found in the Bible at Genesis 14:18, Psalms 110:4, and in Hebrews.)

As *The Urantia Book* explains, the purpose of Melchizedek's incarnation was to foster a religion of one God in order to prepare the way for the coming of a Son of that one God; Moses did his best to transmit this teaching to the Hebrews. (See especially 1052-1059.) Moses' own teachings influenced almost one half of the world, laying the basis for Judaism, Christianity and Islam. As noted before, he is now a member of the Council of Twenty-four Elders.

When John of Patmos wrote about his vision, he decided to adopt the style of Moses to some extent, using images of a vengeful God who would punish humankind with calamities if it turned away from belief in him. As explained above, John regrets writing in this manner. Also, as has been noted many times by my celestial guides, many such statements were added later by others who were far less enlightened than John.

The "Song of the Lamb" in verse 15:3 indicates that there was great rejoicing that the Word of God through Jesus was being felt by people everywhere.

15:4 - Who shall not fear thee, O Lord, and glorify thy name? for thou only art holy: for all nations shall come and worship before thee; for thy judgments are made manifest.

A: Can remain as written.

Seven vials full of the wrath Of God

15:5 - And after that I looked, and, behold, the temple of the tabernacle of the testimony in heaven was opened:

A: This temple refers to the heavenly assembly hall for welcoming ascenders. See 14:2-3.

15:6 - And the seven angels came out of the temple, having the seven plagues, clothed in pure and white linen, and having their breasts girded with golden girdles.

Refers back to warnings from the seven angels that was covered in 15:1.

15:7 - And one of the four beasts gave unto the seven angels seven golden vials full of the wrath of God, who liveth for ever and ever.

These are the four beasts plus another erroneous reference to the "wrath of God" that we have encountered before.

15:8 - And the temple was filled with smoke from the glory of God, and from his power; and no man was able to enter into the temple, till the seven plagues of the seven angels were fulfilled.

A: This verse indicates that no one may enter the temple until they have overcome their animal natures, i.e., the mark of the beast.

Again it should be stated that it is unfortunate that John, through Nathan, portrayed angels as casting plagues upon the earth and equating these so-called plagues as the wrath of God. As stated, John now regrets his decision as to how this chapter was written; these angels in reality are mankind's benefactors in that they were issuing warnings of what may occur if people turn away from God. John's new and positive interpretation of a loving God and helpful angels, as presented here, will hopefully go far to alleviate the inordinate fears of an end-time and an Armageddon; such events are not a part of God's plan for the human race.

Highlights from Chapter 15

— There are twelve corps of "planetary angels" (*UB*:1255) ministering on the earth, each corps having a specialized function to aid humanity. Two of these twelves orders are mentioned by John: the angels of the churches (3:1) and the angels of the trumpets (chapter 8).

— The "seven angels"(15:1) issued real warnings to John, but it is the action of humans—and not the angels—who are responsible for the consequences of the "seven plagues."

— Moses' methods had a strong influence on John. Moses had great difficulty presenting a higher idea of deity to his followers (*UB*:1052ff.). In order to get through to them, he had to resort to the event of the eruption of Mt. Horeb as a metaphor for teaching that God was subject to fits of wrath and severity.

— John used the style of Moses in depicting God and his angels as wrathful. But John now regrets using threats of God's displeasure to wake up the people.

— An end-time or so-called Armageddon is not a part of God's plan for the human race.

16

King James Translation

1 And I heard a great voice out of the temple saying to the seven angels, Go your ways, and pour out the vials of the wrath of God upon the earth.

2 And the first went, and poured out his vial upon the earth; and there fell a noisome and grievous sore upon the men which had the mark of the beast, and upon them which worshipped his image.

3 And the second angel poured out his vial upon the sea; and it became as the blood of a dead man: and every living soul died in the sea.

4 And the third angel poured out his vial upon the rivers and fountains of waters; and they became blood.

5 And I heard the angel of the waters say, Thou art righteous, O Lord, which art, and wast, and shalt be, because thou hast judged thus.

6 For they have shed the blood of saints and prophets, and thou hast given them blood to drink; for they are worthy.

7 And I heard another out of the altar say, Even so, Lord God Almighty, true and righteous are thy judgments.

8 And the fourth angel poured out his vial upon the sun; and power was given unto him to scorch men with fire.

9 And men were scorched with great heat, and blasphemed the name of God, which hath power over these plagues: and they repented not to give him glory.

10 And the fifth angel poured out his vial upon the seat of the beast; and his kingdom was full of darkness; and they gnawed their tongues for pain,

11 And blasphemed the God of heaven because of their pains and their sores, and repented not of their deeds.

12 And the sixth angel poured out his vial upon the great river Euphrates; and the water thereof was dried up, that the way of the kings of the east might be prepared.

13 And I saw three unclean spirits like frogs come out of the mouth of the dragon, and out of the mouth of the beast, and out of the mouth of the false prophet.

14 For they are the spirits of devils, working miracles, which go forth unto the kings of the earth and of the whole world, to gather them to the battle of that great day of God Almighty.

15 Behold, I come as a thief. Blessed is he that watcheth, and keepeth his garments, lest he walk naked, and they see his shame.

16 And he gathered them together into a place called in the Hebrew tongue Armageddon.

17 And the seventh angel poured out his vial into the air; and there came a great voice out of the temple of heaven, from the throne, saying, It is done.

18 And there were voices, and thunders, and lightnings; and there was a great earthquake, such as was not since men were upon the earth, so mighty an earthquake, and so great.

19 And the great city was divided into three parts, and the cities of the nations fell: and great Babylon came in remembrance before God, to give unto her the cup of the wine of the fierceness of his wrath.

20 And every island fled away, and the mountains were not found.

21 And there fell upon men a great hail out of heaven, every stone about the weight of a talent: and men blasphemed God because of the plague of the hail; for the plague thereof was exceeding great.

revised

Seven angels instructed to pour out more of God's wrath upon humanity? Am I reading this correctly? This was certainly not my understanding of a loving God. I was in utter despair as I contemplated the message of this chapter. How am I going to get through this one?

At first, I had only a brief one-page note from Corelli dated May 15, 1996—and that didn't even begin to answer my questions. I had asked about the meaning of the wrath of God, and Solonia and Eckhart had replied to me that there is no such thing as divine wrath.

By this time I was getting tired, as you might imagine, and I even wondered whether they would continue to answer my questions. Should I just stop all this? But I realized I could not stop now. I had to continue my contacts despite the fact that some people will be offended that these answers to my questions contradict the holy writ of the Bible.

The information about angels in the previous chapter was a comfort to me. It is uplifting to know about the orders of angels who have specialized responsibilities in the care of humans. It was especially reassuring to confirm that angels do not cause plagues and all kinds of disasters. These calamities (other than naturally occurring earth changes) are generally caused by humans themselves and are never caused by God.

So I pressed on. The following are answers to questions I have asked Corelli at various times since May 15, 1996:

Seven angels pour out their vials

16:1 - And I heard a great voice out of the temple saying to the seven angels, Go your ways, and pour out the vials of the wrath of God upon the earth.

Q: Is an angel of God now telling the seven angels to send out their warnings?

A: Yes, indeed.

Q: Regarding the upcoming verses 16:2-14, are these tribulations that can happen if men turn away from God and continue to ravish the earth and wage wars? Is it correct to say that these people blamed God for these calamities, but not themselves?

A: Yes, also correct.

I needed more detailed information, so on March 29, 1998, I asked Corelli the following:

Q: Corelli, to what category do these seven angels belong?

A: As we have noted before, there are many angels who act in the affairs of men. In this instance, these verses refer to the angels of tribulation, health, the future and others. They all work in coordination to bring enlightenment to the various areas of human endeavor.

ANGELIC INFLUENCE

The Urantia Book teaches that angels cannot compel humans, but they do try to influence them with the aid of that fragment of God that indwells every normal human mind:

The urge to pray...very often arises as the result of seraphic influence. The guardian seraphim is constantly manipulating the mortal environment for the purpose of augmenting the cosmic insight of the human ascender to the end that such a survival candidate may acquire enhanced realization of the presence of the indwelling Adjuster [i.e., God fragment]. (*UB*:1245)

Q: But Corelli, regarding the angels of tribulation that you mention, isn't this in contradiction to what was said previously, that angels do not send tribulation?

A: No again. Humans are often placed in situations by these angels so that they can better learn how to cope. But through all of this, they are sustained by God's presence, that fragment within the mind; they can always call upon this divine aid by going within.

16:2 - And the first went, and poured out his vial upon the earth; and there fell a noisome and grievous sore upon the men which had the mark of the beast, and upon them which worshipped his image.

Q: What kind of a disease was the "grievous sore"?

A: Sexual diseases of a particularly virulent kind.

16:3 - And the second angel poured out his vial upon the sea; and it became as the blood of a dead man: and every living soul died in the sea.

Q: What is this warning about the sea becoming bloody and every living soul in the sea dying?

A: Stop the pollution of your seas!

This of course was a long-range prophecy; it is only now that the seas are so polluted that those eating fish could die of the poisons ingested.

16:4 - And the third angel poured out his vial upon the rivers and fountains of waters; and they became blood.

A: These warnings apply to your rivers and sources of water as well.

16:5 - And I heard the angel of the waters say, Thou art righteous, O Lord, which art, and wast, and shalt be, because thou hast judged thus.

16:6 - For they have shed the blood of saints and prophets, and thou hast given them blood to drink; for they are worthy.

It's curious. The Greek translation reads "they are worthy" as does the King James version; however, the Diaglott translation of the Greek states, "they deserve it." So I questioned:

Q: *Which is correct, "they are worthy" or they "deserve it"?*

A: "They deserve it" is correct. The Diaglott translation is correct.

Q: *Who are "they" who poured out the blood of saints?*

A: All those who persecuted the innocent and saintly.

Q: *Blood—is this word a symbol for warning?*

A: Yes, in a sense it is.

16:7 - And I heard another out of the altar say, Even so, Lord God Almighty, true and righteous are thy judgments.

A: Praise to God for his unerring judgment in settling the affairs of men.

16:8 - And the fourth angel poured out his vial upon the sun; and power was given unto him to scorch men with fire.

16:9 - And men were scorched with great heat, and blasphemed the name of God, which hath power over these plagues: and they repented not to give him glory.

Q: *Regarding the above two verses, how and why were the men burned with fire?*

A: Again, this is a long-term warning: Do not destroy your ozone layer or you will suffer the consequences of great heat. Remember, John was given great prophecies concerning the distant future. It was almost impossible for the people of those times to compre-hend what he had been told. Only now are you beginning to understand that these prophecies were pointing to problems that must be solved by today's people.

16:10 - And the fifth angel poured out his vial upon the seat of the beast; and his kingdom was full of darkness; and they gnawed their tongues for pain,

Q: To whom and what does this refer?

A: This is properly addressed to Lucifer and his co-horts. They were warned of the consequences of what would happen if they placed themselves above the plan of God; but they refused to repent. Gnawing their tongues with pain is a metaphor for no longer being allowed to use their tongues to try to influence people against belief in God.

16:11 - And blasphemed the God of heaven because of their pains and their sores, and repented not of their deeds.

A: Same as 16:10, but now includes humans who had turned to the side of Lucifer and Satan.

16:12 - And the sixth angel poured out his vial upon the great river Euphrates; and the water thereof was dried up, that the way of the kings of the east might be prepared.

Q: This one is a puzzle. Why would the river Euphrates be dried up to make way for the kings of the east?

A: We do not know what is meant by this verse—John did not write it. This verse looks as if some writer may have been thinking of the three kings who came out of the East at the time of Jesus' birth, but we cannot say.

Frogs come out of the mouth of the dragon

16:13 - And I saw three unclean spirits like frogs come out of the mouth of the dragon, and out of the mouth of the beast, and out of the mouth of the false prophet.

Q: Who are these three unclean spirits?

A: They are of course the nefarious three, Caligastia, Lucifer and Satan—still trying to work on the minds of credulous people.

Q: And who is the false prophet?

A: A man at that time who claimed to be the Messiah. He is no more; he could not repent of his blasphemy.

16:14 - For they are the spirits of devils, working miracles, which go forth unto the kings of the earth and of the whole world, to gather them to the battle of that great day of God Almighty.

Q: What is the meaning of this verse?

A: This refers to those people who were still under the influence of the nefarious three and were endeavoring to corrupt the minds of the leaders of the world. The residue of that influence is still here—but has lost its power since the advent of Jesus.

Christ comes as a thief

16:15 - Behold, I come as a thief. Blessed is he that watcheth, and keepeth his garments, lest he walk naked, and they see his shame.

Stella: Corelli, I don't like the idea of Christ coming as a thief. What an unfortunate metaphor.

A: We agree. As we also noted in chapter 3, this image should never have been equated with Christ. Apparently, in those times they could only think of Christ as sneaking up to catch them in error. Of course, this is not true; Christ would never stoop to such degrading behavior. This was written into the text by a scribe to warn people to be on their best behavior always.

Of course it is true that you cannot hide from God. He knows your intent and your deeds. As we noted earlier, you will be judged in that far distant future when you literally stand before Christ and the Eternal Son. Until that day you are accountable for your actions.

16:16 - And he gathered them together into a place called in the Hebrew tongue Armageddon.

Q: Why gather them in Armageddon?

A: Armageddon is a historic location in Israel where followers of Yahweh gathered for safety. The Christian writers assumed that since the Jews had once gathered there, the Christians would also gather there. Incorrect, of course.

Armageddon has taken on the connotation of a place of punishment equated with the end-times where the final struggle between good and evil will take place. The struggle between good and evil usually takes place within you, so in a sense Armageddon is a symbol for that. Of course, nations may and have waged wars based on this same concept. Only love and understanding can end these evil wars.

Q: Corelli, I don't understand what you mean that nations often launch wars based on this same concept. What same concept?

A: We will try to explain. In your history, nations often launched wars to prove that they are powerful, and therefore must be obeyed by those they have conquered. Each side invokes the name of God for victory. Such a plea cannot be granted. A struggle between good or evil or "Armageddon" does indeed occur between nations or within individuals. But there will be no set time for a final battle between good and evil. Such battles take place anywhere or at any time that men continue their aggressive ways. Good sense will prevail eventually.

The seventh angel pours out his vial

16:17 - And the seventh angel poured out his vial into the air; and there came a great voice out of the temple of heaven, from the throne, saying, It is done.

Q: What does "it is done" mean?

A:. It simply means that the series of warnings have now been put forth. However, the warnings still stand. The question remains: What will you do to your earth? The answers are up to you.

16:18 - And there were voices, and thunders, and lightnings; and there was a great earthquake, such as was not since men were upon the earth, so mighty an earthquake, and so great.

As previously stated, the voices, thunder and lightning represent the broadcasts emanating from the celestial worlds.

Q: Was this a real earthquake?

A: Yes, it was, but of course God did not cause it, although the people thought it was a punishment for their misdeeds. As long as a world is in its infancy, so to speak, earthquakes will continue to occur. Some day, in the far distant future, earthquakes will cease once the tectonic plates are firmly settled. The world's continents will be much different than they are now.

16:19 - And the great city was divided into three parts, and the cities of the nations fell: and great Babylon came in remembrance before God, to give unto her the cup of the wine of the fierceness of his wrath.

Corelli continued: John saw a vision of the earthquake and the devastation it caused. But 16:18 and 16:19 should be reversed in sequence. This earthquake was not caused by God's wrath, but the people thought it was. It could also be thought of as symbolic of that great upheaval which occurs when one is faced with one's failures.

16:20 - And every island fled away, and the mountains were not found.

16:21 - And there fell upon men a great hail out of heaven, every stone about the weight of a talent: and men blasphemed God because of the plague of the hail; for the plague thereof was exceeding great.

A: This last verse deals with the reality of the aftermath of a giant quake and the eruption of a volcano that rained ashes and stones upon a great city. Again, sickness resulted in its wake. Instead of turning to God, the people blamed him for their misery.

Q: *What was the great hail?*

A: The fallout: volcanic ash and large stones fell that demolished the countryside, causing great suffering. Disease and hunger were prevalent.

And thus ended another chapter with more reassurance that God is not the cause of calamities, and neither are angels. Instead they work together to help suffering humanity master its problems through contact with that small voice within.

Highlights from Chapter 16

— Neither God nor the angels cause plagues and other kinds of disasters. There really is no such thing as the pouring of "the wrath of God on the earth" (16:1). This chapter is a warning to those who "worship his image" (16:2), who bring these calamities upon themselves.

— Angels are able to influence receptive human minds by working with that portion of God indwelling a normal mind. (*UB*:1245)

— Angels of tribulation place humans in certain situations to enable them to learn how to cope and grow spiritually.

— John's visions in this chapter were in particular a warning to protect the environment from the ravages of pollution. For example, "men were scorched with great heat" (16:9) refers to the destruction of the ozone layer in our present generation. These warnings were incomprehensible in his time, but were pointing to dangers facing us in the current age. John's prophetic warnings, if rightly interpreted, still stand.

— As indicated in chapter 3, the image of Christ coming upon us secretly "as a thief" (16:15) is totally incorrect. But it is true that God is aware of our intentions and our deeds, and that we are accountable for our behavior in the afterlife.

— There will be no final battle between good and evil— no literal "gathering into a place called... Armageddon"(16:16). Christian writers incorrectly assumed that since the Jews gathered at Megiddo (thought to be the Biblical Armageddon) for safety, Christians would also gather there for the final battle between good and evil. But it is true that epic struggles between good and evil can occur at any time between groups or within individuals.

17

King James Translation

1 And there came one of the seven angels which had the seven vials, and talked with me, saying unto me, Come hither; I will shew unto thee the judgment of the great whore that sitteth upon many waters:

2 With whom the kings of the earth have committed fornication, and the inhabitants of the earth have been made drunk with the wine of her fornication.

3 So he carried me away in the spirit into the wilderness: and I saw a woman sit upon a scarlet coloured beast, full of names of blasphemy, having seven heads and ten horns.

4 And the woman was arrayed in purple and scarlet colour, and decked with gold and precious stones and pearls, having a golden cup in her hand full of abominations and filthiness of her fornication:

5 And upon her forehead was a name written, MYSTERY, BABYLON THE GREAT, THE MOTHER OF HARLOTS AND ABOMINATIONS OF THE EARTH.

6 And I saw the woman drunken with the blood of the saints, and with the blood of the martyrs of Jesus: and when I saw her, I wondered with great admiration.

7 And the angel said unto me, Wherefore didst thou marvel? I will tell thee the mystery of the woman, and

of the beast that carrieth her, which hath the seven heads and ten horns.

8 The beast that thou sawest was, and is not; and shall ascend out of the bottomless pit, and go into perdition: and they that dwell on the earth shall wonder, whose names were not written in the book of life from the foundation of the world, when they behold the beast that was, and is not, and yet is.

9 And here is the mind which hath wisdom. The seven heads are seven mountains, on which the woman sitteth.

10 And there are seven kings: five are fallen, and one is, and the other is not yet come; and when he cometh, he must continue a short space.

11 And the beast that was, and is not, even he is the eighth, and is of the seven, and goeth into perdition.

12 And the ten horns which thou sawest are ten kings, which have received no kingdom as yet; but receive power as kings one hour with the beast.

13 These have one mind, and shall give their power and strength unto the beast.

14 These shall make war with the Lamb, and the Lamb shall overcome them: for he is Lord of lords, and King of kings: and they that are with him are called, and chosen, and faithful.

15 And he saith unto me, The waters which thou sawest, where the whore sitteth, are peoples, and multitudes, and nations, and tongues.

16 And the ten horns which thou sawest upon the beast, these shall hate the whore, and shall make her desolate and naked, and shall eat her flesh, and burn her with fire.

17 For God hath put in their hearts to fulfil his will, and to agree, and give their kingdom unto the beast, until the words of God shall be fulfilled.

18 And the woman which thou sawest is that great city, which reigneth over the kings of the earth.

17

revised

Surely of all the chapters in the Book of Revelation this one is the most puzzling and contradictory. For example, in 17:1 John is called by an angel and told he would be shown the judgment upon the whore of Babylon with whom the kings and people of the area had committed "fornication." Then, as despicable as she is and what she stands for, John in 17:6 looks upon her with great admiration. And this is just one example of the many difficulties of this strange chapter. My celestial teachers were a great help in clearing most of these up.

The woman called Babylon

17:1 - And there came one of the seven angels which had the seven vials, and talked with me, saying unto me, Come hither; I will shew unto thee the judgment of the great whore that sitteth upon many waters:

Early in my transmitting, on May 15, 1996, when I was going randomly through the Book of Revelation, I asked for the meaning of the woman of Babylon. Solonia replied:

A: The woman of Babylon is merely a metaphor for the cause of disasters—and in those days she was considered an agent of God in creating them. Women were routinely blamed for men's misdeeds and difficulties. Fortunately, this, too, is passing, and women will eventually take their rightful place on an equal footing with men.

Babylon was a great city but filled with many vices of varying degrees, and as a result was doomed to failure. Its demise resulted from a great earthquake, which again was attributed to God's wrath, but was in fact due to naturally occurring tectonic plate slippage.

Cities usually rise and fall due to economic reasons and only occasionally due to earthquakes; but if citizens do not have funds laid aside, rebuilding cannot occur.

Solonia's early statement regarding women being blamed for evil continued to concern me. Why would John, who was having a revelatory experience, write verses equating women with all manner of evil and corruption?

My puzzled questioning continued, and she replied:

A: John used this symbol as it was one commonly in use at that time. He is sorry now, for it did a grave injustice to women.

Q: *On April 4, 1998, I asked: Is the angel in 17:1 asking John to go with him to show him the judgment of the great whore? Does this judgment refer to the city of Babylon itself? And what does "many waters" mean?*

A: The whore, metaphorically speaking, is being judged for all the evil that is collectively present in all of mankind. Again, there is retribution, yes, but these results are all of mankind's doing. The "waters" simply refer to the fact that all continents are surrounded by water. The point is that an individual or a nation cannot escape the results of its actions. Does this answer your questions?

Stella: Yes, thank you.

17:2 - With whom the kings of the earth have committed fornication, and the inhabitants of the earth have been made drunk with the wine of her fornication.

See the notes above.

17:3 - So he carried me away in the spirit into the wilderness: and I saw a woman sit upon a scarlet coloured beast, full of names of blasphemy, having seven heads and ten horns.

Q: Who is the scarlet beast?

A: It represents the influence of evil thinking on the leaders of those times—the "seven heads" and "ten kings" that we learned about earlier.

17:4 - And the woman was arrayed in purple and scarlet colour, and decked with gold and precious stones and pearls, having a golden cup in her hand full of abominations and filthiness of her fornication:

A: This image applies to the cities or nations as the case may be. Material possessions are of no use as spiritual accomplishments. However, if used for the greatest good, they are accepted in the eyes of God.

17:5 - And upon her forehead was a name written, MYSTERY, BABYLON THE GREAT, THE MOTHER OF HARLOTS AND ABOMINATIONS OF THE EARTH.

17:6 - And I saw the woman drunken with the blood of the saints, and with the blood of the martyrs of Jesus: and when I saw her, I wondered with great admiration.

Q: Why would John look at this woman with admiration?

A: He did not; this was added later. Delete that portion.

Out of curiosity I checked the Greek translation to see how it was worded. Rather than "I wondered with great admiration," it reads: "I wondered with great wonder." This is obviously a key difference in meaning.

17:7 - And the angel said unto me, Wherefore didst thou marvel? I will tell thee the mystery of the woman, and of the beast that carrieth her, which hath the seven heads and ten horns.

A: John marvels at the corruption he sees which was the basis for this evil. This was partially Lucifer's influence but mostly due to man's greed and lust for power.

Meaning of the scarlet beast

17:8 - The beast that thou sawest was, and is not; and shall ascend out of the bottomless pit, and go into perdition: and they that dwell on the earth shall wonder, whose names were not written in the book of life from the foundation of the world, when they behold the beast that was, and is not, and yet is.

Q: *Who was the beast that was and is not?*

A: Again, this refers to the belief that although you could not see Satan (i.e., "is not," as the verse indicates), he was able to do horrible things.

17:9 - And here is the mind which hath wisdom. The seven heads are seven mountains, on which the woman sitteth.

Q: *What does this verse mean? Who is "the mind which hath wisdom" and "the seven heads on the seven mountains"?*

A: The seven heads are the seven kings, heads of their particular territories. The mind of wisdom in this case represents he who discerns the wickedness and turns away in disgust.

17:10 - And there are seven kings: five are fallen, and one is, and the other is not yet come; and when he cometh, he must continue a short space.

See 17:9. But I did also ask whether this was a prophecy of kings to come?

A: Yes.

17:11 - And the beast that was, and is not, even he is the eighth, and is of the seven, and goeth into perdition.

Q: To whom does this refer?

A: The beast of course represents satanic influences. The eighth beast is a descendant not yet born of the seven kings. Evil as well as good influences can pass from generation to generation.

As we have noted, your planet is still suffering from the Caligastia betrayal of God's plan. These evil influences are still with you if you are receptive to them. Therefore, it is extremely important that children be loved and nurtured in loving ways so that evil cannot be perpetuated. Those that practice evil will eventually self-destruct.

17:12 - And the ten horns which thou sawest are ten kings, which have received no kingdom as yet; but receive power as kings one hour with the beast.

Q: This seems to be a prophecy of ten kings who are not in power yet. But what does "one hour with the beast" mean?

A: That hour of temptation when they wrestle with the decision as to which way will they go.

17:13 - These have one mind, and shall give their power and strength unto the beast.

Q: I suppose all these kings gave their will to the beast within themselves. Is this interpretation correct?

A: Yes, it is, and further, you know the adage of Jesus, "Do unto others as you would have done unto yourself." These people assumed others would act and do evil just as they would do themselves. As a consequence, cunning and evil developed among them rather than loving their neighbor as Christ taught.

Victory of the lamb

17:14 - These shall make war with the Lamb, and the Lamb shall overcome them: for he is Lord of lords, and

King of kings: and they that are with him are called, and chosen, and faithful.

A: Those kings will rail against the teachings of Christ. Yet, nevertheless, the teachings of Christ will prevail in the long run.

17:15 - And he saith unto me, The waters which thou sawest, where the whore sitteth, are peoples, and multitudes, and nations, and tongues.

This is a confirmation of my question in 17:1 as to the meaning of "waters." It means people of all tongues and nations.

17:16 - And the ten horns which thou sawest upon the beast, these shall hate the whore, and shall make her desolate and naked, and shall eat her flesh, and burn her with fire.

Q: So eventually even the kings and people will repent?

A: Yes, most of them. That fragment of God within everyone's mind will gently lead them inward and upwards to a true belief in a loving God and to say: "It is my will that your will be done."

I continued my questioning on April 4, 1998, regarding this verse:

Q: These ten horns, are they also the symbol for kings?

A: Yes.

Q: I'm puzzled. If these ten kings were corrupt themselves, why would they hate the whore [Babylon] if they created the despair and desolation in the first place?

A: They threw the blame for their actions on the people. They refused to accept the blame, and they hated what they created.

17:17 - For God hath put in their hearts to fulfil his will, and to agree, and give their kingdom unto the beast, until the words of God shall be fulfilled.

Q: If God inclined their hearts to do his purpose [Greek translation is "will"], why would he give their kingdom to the beast, until the words of God shall be completed?

A: God allows all men the choice of doing his will, even to those who would do evil.

But evil should be exposed. Such exposure will enable people to discern and eventually turn to doing God's will—thus allowing good to overcome evil. It sometimes seems that good happens to evil people. But eventually these people reap what they have sown. On the other hand, good does come out of evil, but only to those to whom the evil has been done.

This was getting to be difficult. I decided to check *The Urantia Book* to see what it had to say about evil:

The moral will creatures of the evolutionary worlds are always bothered with the unthinking question as to why the all-wise Creators permit evil and sin. They fail to comprehend that both are inevitable if the creature is to be truly free.... Man's ability to choose good or evil is a universe reality....

Although conscious and wholehearted identification with evil (sin) is the equivalent of nonexistence (annihilation), there must always intervene between the time of such personal identification with sin and the execution of the penalty—the automatic result of such a willful embrace of evil—a period of time of sufficient length to allow for such an adjudication of such an individual's universe status as will prove entirely satisfactory to all related universe personalities, and which will be so fair and just as to win the approval of the sinner himself. (615)

17:18 - And the woman which thou sawest is that great city, which reigneth over the kings of the earth.

Q: This verse seems a strange way to end a chapter, especially after the profound message of 17:17.

A: Yes, we agree. This was an afterthought on the part of a writer who merely wanted to recapitulate the message about Babylon, and to reinforce the notion that somehow women were a cause of the evil pervading the city.

Stella: Thank you for clearing up so much.

A: You are welcome. We are glad to be of service.

Q: Who is with me?

A: This time Corelli, Aflana, Meister Eckhart and many others who are watching to see how you are doing. We are all delighted with your progress.

I was pleased that my many questions regarding the whore of Babylon had been answered, and, particularly, that John did not look upon the whore with admiration. This is a good example of how incorrect translations can completely change the meaning of a text.

Highlights from Chapter 17

— The "whore of Babylon" was a metaphor for vice, evil and corruption. John applied this lurid image to women; he now regrets using that symbol for it has done a grave injustice to women.

— In this chapter, the whore, metaphorically speaking, is being judged for the evil that is collectively present in all of mankind. There is indeed retribution for collective evil, but only in the sense that these repercussions are the lawful and inevitable result of human actions.

— The so-called "beast" (17:11) represents satanic influences resulting from the fact that we are still suffering from the Caligastia betrayal of God's plan for our planet . These evil influences are still with us if we are receptive to them and can be passed from generation to generation. Therefore, it is extremely important that children be nurtured in loving ways so that this residual evil cannot be perpetuated.

18

King James Translation

1 And after these things I saw another angel come down from heaven, having great power; and the earth was lightened with his glory.

2 And he cried mightily with a strong voice, saying, Babylon the great is fallen, is fallen, and is become the habitation of devils, and the hold of every foul spirit, and a cage of every unclean and hateful bird.

3 For all nations have drunk of the wine of the wrath of her fornication, and the kings of the earth have committed fornication with her, and the merchants of the earth are waxed rich through the abundance of her delicacies.

4 And I heard another voice from heaven, saying, Come out of her, my people, that ye be not partakers of her sins, and that ye receive not of her plagues.

5 For her sins have reached unto heaven, and God hath remembered her iniquities.

6 Reward her even as she rewarded you, and double unto her double according to her works: in the cup which she hath filled fill to her double.

7 How much she hath glorified herself, and lived deliciously, so much torment and sorrow give her: for she saith in her heart, I sit a queen, and am no widow, and shall see no sorrow.

8 Therefore shall her plagues come in one day, death, and mourning, and famine; and she shall be utterly burned with fire: for strong is the Lord God who judgeth her.

9 And the kings of the earth, who have committed fornication and lived deliciously with her, shall bewail her, and lament for her, when they shall see the smoke of her burning,

10 Standing afar off for the fear of her torment, saying, Alas, alas, that great city Babylon, that mighty city! for in one hour is thy judgment come.

11 And the merchants of the earth shall weep and mourn over her; for no man buyeth their merchandise any more:

12 The merchandise of gold, and silver, and precious stones, and of pearls, and fine linen, and purple, and silk, and scarlet, and all thyine wood, and all manner vessels of ivory, and all manner vessels of most precious wood, and of brass, and iron, and marble,

13 And cinnamon, and odours, and ointments, and frankincense, and wine, and oil, and fine flour, and wheat, and beasts, and sheep, and horses, and chariots, and slaves, and souls of men.

14 And the fruits that thy soul lusted after are departed from thee, and all things which were dainty and goodly are departed from thee, and thou shalt find them no more at all.

15 The merchants of these things, which were made rich by her, shall stand afar off for the fear of her torment, weeping and wailing,

16 And saying, Alas, alas, that great city, that was clothed in fine linen, and purple, and scarlet, and decked with gold, and precious stones, and pearls!

17 For in one hour so great riches is come to nought. And every shipmaster, and all the company in ships, and sailors, and as many as trade by sea, stood afar off,

18 And cried when they saw the smoke of her burning, saying, What city is like unto this great city!

19 And they cast dust on their heads, and cried, weeping and wailing, saying, Alas, alas, that great city, wherein were made rich all that had ships in the sea by reason of her costliness! for in one hour is she made desolate.

20 Rejoice over her, thou heaven, and ye holy apostles and prophets; for God hath avenged you on her.

21 And a mighty angel took up a stone like a great millstone, and cast it into the sea, saying, Thus with violence shall that great city Babylon be thrown down, and shall be found no more at all.

22 And the voice of harpers, and musicians, and of pipers, and trumpeters, shall be heard no more at all in thee; and no craftsman, of whatsoever craft he be, shall be found any more in thee; and the sound of a millstone shall be heard no more at all in thee;

23 And the light of a candle shall shine no more at all in thee; and the voice of the bridegroom and of the bride shall be heard no more at all in thee: for thy merchants were the great men of the earth; for by thy sorceries were all nations deceived.

24 And in her was found the blood of prophets, and of saints, and of all that were slain upon the earth.

18

revised

This chapter seems to be a continuation of chapter 17—and appears to be referring to the aftermath of the great earthquake and its effect on Babylon. On April 17, 1997, I asked Corelli:

Q: Was John writing about an actual earthquake that occurred in his lifetime or were these statements added later? Is he using the fall of Babylon in an earthquake as a metaphor to demonstrate that treasures mean nothing when one turns away from God?

A: John was writing about an actual earthquake, but he did use the metaphor of an earthquake as well. Much of this chapter was inserted at a later date by writers looking back and trying to make sense out of this great upheaval wherein more than a third of the city was destroyed. As we stated earlier, they attributed all of this to the judgment of God, which, of course, it was not.

Babylon Falls

18:1 - And after these things I saw another angel come down from heaven, having great power; and the earth was lightened with his glory.

18:2 - And he cried mightily with a strong voice, saying, Babylon the great is fallen, is fallen, and is become the habitation of devils, and the hold of every foul spirit, and a cage of every unclean and hateful bird.

Q: Corelli, did the angel actually say all the rest of the verses in this chapter?

A: No. All were filled in by writers who wanted to make a point to the people that riches such as gold, jewels, spices and other material possessions are of no value if one turns away from God's word.

18:3 - For all nations have drunk of the wine of the wrath of her fornication, and the kings of the earth have committed fornication with her, and the merchants of the earth are waxed rich through the abundance of her delicacies.

Q: This verse seems to apply to everyone, high and low. Are all people guilty of greed and materialism?

A: Yes, to a certain degree.

18:4 - And I heard another voice from heaven, saying, Come out of her, my people, that ye be not partakers of her sins, and that ye receive not of her plagues.

Q: Is this other voice also calling people to turn away from sin and evil so that they can partake of God's blessings?

A: Yes.

18:5 - For her sins have reached unto heaven, and God hath remembered her iniquities.

Corelli continued: As stated before, there is an accounting to be made of whatever you do. Choose wisely; eternal life is the goal.

John did not actually write the verses 18:2 to 18:19, according to Corelli. They all seem to be lamentations over the terrible tragedy that had befallen Babylon. But note below that I went through a moment of doubt about this when I got to 18:8.

> 18:6 - Reward her even as she rewarded you, and double unto her double according to her works: in the cup which she hath filled fill to her double.

> 18:7 - How much she hath glorified herself, and lived deliciously, so much torment and sorrow give her: for she saith in her heart, I sit a queen, and am no widow, and shall see no sorrow.

> 18:8 - Therefore shall her plagues come in one day, death, and mourning, and famine; and she shall be utterly burned with fire: for strong is the Lord God who judgeth her.

I was always surprised when I was told John hadn't written certain passages, so I asked:

Q: *Are you sure John didn't write this?*

A: Yes, we are. Stella, Stella, you still doubt?

Stella: Sorry.

From here, verses 18:9 through 18:19 stand with no commentary.

Saints rejoice over the fall of Babylon

> 18:20 - Rejoice over her, thou heaven, and ye holy apostles and prophets; for God hath avenged you on her.

On April 17, 1997, I asked Corelli: Why would the saints rejoice over the fall of Babylon?

> A: These writers assumed that the saints would react as men do, feeling satisfaction when others get what is coming to them. Actually, the angels weep when foolish men go against the will of God.

As we told you before, you are safe when you disregard the negative aspects of this revelation. It is not complete and far from what John wrote. We are happy you are trying to correct these negative writings.

18:21 - And a mighty angel took up a stone like a great millstone, and cast it into the sea, saying, Thus with violence shall that great city Babylon be thrown down, and shall be found no more at all.

Q: What is this great stone?

A: Merely a symbol for the force that caused the earthquake. Certainly not caused by the angel.

18:22 - And the voice of harpers, and musicians, and of pipers, and trumpeters, shall be heard no more at all in thee; and no craftsman, of whatsoever craft he be, shall be found any more in thee; and the sound of a millstone shall be heard no more at all in thee;

Q: To me this sounds that: If you disregard God's promptings you will not have the privilege of eventually standing before the assembly on Jerusem. In other words, you will deny yourself the journey of eternal life.

A: Yes, as we have said several times, you have the option of choosing eternal life or rejecting it. It is sad that many turn it down. But those who do not know about eternal life will be given one additional opportunity to choose it. And if they turn away, they will experience the second death, which is final.

18:23 - And the light of a candle shall shine no more at all in thee; and the voice of the bridegroom and of the bride shall be heard no more at all in thee: for thy merchants were the great men of the earth; for by thy sorceries were all nations deceived.

Q: What is the symbolism of the bride and bridegroom?

A: The bride was a symbol of innocence coming to the bridegroom trustingly as a child worshipping the Father. In this case, the bridegroom signifies God or Jesus. The union would signify the beginning of heaven on earth—the initiation of the era of Light and Life in the hearts of men and women. [See "The Spheres of Light and Life", in *The Urantia Book,* 621ff.]

Q: What does "thy merchants were the great men of the earth: for by thy sorceries were all nations deceived" mean?

A: These are the men of old who placed their faith in Lucifer at the time of the rebellion 200,000 years ago. Their misguided influence has haunted this planet ever since. The results of their misguided thinking have caused many unjust wars, greed and famine from that time to this date.

Only by a collective act of turning to God and loving one's fellows will humankind overcome these three unfortunate incidents: the Lucifer rebellion, the default of Adam and Eve, and the death of Jesus Christ on the cross. Your planet has been heavily burdened ever since these catastrophes, but we are encouraged by the current renaissance in spiritual thinking on your planet.

18:24 - And in her was found the blood of prophets, and of saints, and of all that were slain upon the earth.

Corelli continued: Many innocent people on your planet have perished through iniquity. But they will rejoice once they discovered that they have not lived in vain and when they find themselves being rewarded with the glories of heaven and eternal life.

This chapter is yet another example of material that was not written by John—providing more evidence of how subsequent writers distorted his prophetic message of hope and the need for humankind to turn to a spiritual path of living.

Highlights of Chapter 18

— Subsequent writers inserted verses 18:2 through 18:19 in an attempt to make sense out of an historic earthquake by attributing it to wrathful divine judgment.

— John himself used the event of the earthquake as a metaphor to show the futility of storing up one's treasures on earth.

— We are again advised to disregard the negative aspects of the Book of Revelation as being later additions. An example is the passage at 18:20 advising "apostles and prophets" to rejoice that "God has avenged you" by the destruction of Babylon.

— "Her sins hath reached into heaven, and God hath remembered her iniquities"(18:5) points to the genuine truth that there is an accounting in the afterlife for every choice we make in this life.

— The men of old, "by [whose] sorceries were all nations deceived" (18:23), are those followed Lucifer and have caused many earthly problems and calamities.

— According to Corelli: "Only by a collective act of turning to God and loving one's fellows will humankind overcome the calamities of the Lucifer rebellion, the default of Adam and Eve and the death of Jesus Christ on the cross."

— Many innocent people have perished unjustly, but they will rejoice when they find they have not lived in vain and are rewarded with the glories of heaven and eternal life.

19

King James Translation

1 And after these things I heard a great voice of much people in heaven, saying, Alleluia; Salvation, and glory, and honour, and power, unto the Lord our God:

2 For true and righteous are his judgments: for he hath judged the great whore, which did corrupt the earth with her fornication, and hath avenged the blood of his servants at her hand.

3 And again they said, Alleluia. And her smoke rose up for ever and ever.

4 And the four and twenty elders and the four beasts fell down and worshipped God that sat on the throne, saying, Amen; Alleluia.

5 And a voice came out of the throne, saying, Praise our God, all ye his servants, and ye that fear him, both small and great.

6 And I heard as it were the voice of a great multitude, and as the voice of many waters, and as the voice of mighty thunderings, saying, Alleluia: for the Lord God omnipotent reigneth.

7 Let us be glad and rejoice, and give honour to him: for the marriage of the Lamb is come, and his wife hath made herself ready.

8 And to her was granted that she should be arrayed in fine linen, clean and white: for the fine linen is the righteousness of saints.

9 And he saith unto me, Write, Blessed are they which are called unto the marriage supper of the Lamb. And he saith unto me, These are the true sayings of God.

10 And I fell at his feet to worship him. And he said unto me, See thou do it not: I am thy fellowservant, and of thy brethren that have the testimony of Jesus: worship God: for the testimony of Jesus is the spirit of prophecy.

11 And I saw heaven opened, and behold a white horse; and he that sat upon him was called Faithful and True, and in righteousness he doth judge and make war.

12 His eyes were as a flame of fire, and on his head were many crowns; and he had a name written, that no man knew, but he himself.

13 And he was clothed with a vesture dipped in blood: and his name is called The Word of God.

14 And the armies which were in heaven followed him upon white horses, clothed in fine linen, white and clean.

15 And out of his mouth goeth a sharp sword, that with it he should smite the nations: and he shall rule them with a rod of iron: and he treadeth the winepress of the fierceness and wrath of Almighty God.

16 And he hath on his vesture and on his thigh a name written, KING OF KINGS, AND LORD OF LORDS.

17 And I saw an angel standing in the sun; and he cried with a loud voice, saying to all the fowls that fly

in the midst of heaven, Come and gather yourselves together unto the supper of the great God;

18 That ye may eat the flesh of kings, and the flesh of captains, and the flesh of mighty men, and the flesh of horses, and of them that sit on them, and the flesh of all men, both free and bond, both small and great.

19 And I saw the beast, and the kings of the earth, and their armies, gathered together to make war against him that sat on the horse, and against his army.

20 And the beast was taken, and with him the false prophet that wrought miracles before him, with which he deceived them that had received the mark of the beast, and them that worshipped his image. These both were cast alive into a lake of fire burning with brimstone.

21 And the remnant were slain with the sword of him that sat upon the horse, which sword proceeded out of his mouth: and all the fowls were filled with their flesh.

19
revised

*Dear Corelli: I am having trouble with this chapter, too.
Do you have any idea how I can begin chapter 19?*

A: Dear Stella, why don't you start with this? Maybe
it will help you:

This chapter is a paean to our Lord Christ Michael. He
is the beginning and the end, the Alpha and Omega.
Without him nothing was—and from him everything
came into being. He, along with the Mother Spirit, is
the creator of this particular universe, the creator of
you and me.

Q: Creator of you too?

A: Yes, creator of me and of the star system from
which I came. Our men of old had heard about the
existence of our Creator Son. On my home planet,
rumors and tales about him were handed down to us
by word of mouth, and then finally written down.
When I arrived on the morontia worlds thousands of
years ago, I was of course told all about Michael, the
Creator of us all. Therefore, we were all greatly

interested in what was happening on your world when he incarnated there.

CORELLI ON THE FATE OF THE EARTH

We watched with horror and amazement when Christ Michael, your Jesus, was crucified and died on the cross. How could this happen to such a marvelous Father-Son who chose to come to your planet to right the terrible wrongs perpetrated by the nefarious three? His sole mission was to elevate the human race from the bondage that seemed to be holding your people down in perpetuity. His cruel death was the most shameful event that had ever occurred in all of Nebadon.

The only comfort we were able to glean from this incredible tragedy was that with his death, Jesus was able to release the Spirit of Truth upon all of humanity. This proved more than ever the magnanimity of Jesus and his incredible love for all souls willing to do God's will. By releasing the Spirit of Truth at Pentecost, he gave even those who chose not to do his will another chance.

You are more blessed than you realize. Without his incarnation, your world would have fallen into utter chaos and degradation. You may say: "But we are in a mess with our wars and the despoliation of our environment." That is true, but it would have been worse. Michael's loving gesture was sufficient to save your planet and direct all men and women to a clearer realization of the need to be loving to one another and to all of humankind.

As I have said before, the present chaos is the lingering residue of the Lucifer Rebellion and the Adam and Eve default. But now we have inaugurated the Correcting Time. Michael would never allow the planet of his mortal birth to be destroyed. There are now thousands of people who are willing to work together to bring about peace and love to all.

With the advent of the Teaching Mission—authorized by Christ Michael along with *The Urantia Book*—Urantia is on its way to an age of Light and Life. Nothing, I say nothing, will stop this process. From your future vantage point, once you have arrived here on the other side, you will witness great changes occurring on your planet. Urantia will take its place among the more civilized worlds in this great system of planets. Be not discouraged with what you see at the moment. What God wills, is. We love you. Goodbye for now.

Stella: Thank you, Corelli. This is what I needed.

Corelli: We are glad you were able to take this down.

After such a message, going back to my earlier notes seemed almost anti-climactic. I wrote the above in shorthand as it was dictated to me. It was certainly more than I expected, and I was and am deeply grateful.

Praise of God

19:1 - And after these things I heard a great voice of much people in heaven, saying, Alleluia; Salvation, and glory, and honour, and power, unto the Lord our God:

Q: Are these the angelic hosts greeting ascenders?

A: In this case they are rejoicing that Christ had finished his mission on Urantia despite his shameful death on the cross.

All the universes watched the dreadful scene unfolding when Jesus died. They could hardly believe that anyone would kill the creator of their universe—and for that matter, the creator of themselves.

19:2 - For true and righteous are his judgments: for he hath judged the great whore, which did corrupt the earth with her fornication, and hath avenged the blood of his servants at her hand.

Q: Is this verse what John really wrote?

A: Delete the whole sentence beginning with "for he hath judged..." and ending with "her hand." It had no place in the original.

19:3 - And again they said, Alleluia. And her smoke rose up for ever and ever.

19:4 - And the four and twenty elders and the four beasts fell down and worshipped God that sat on the throne, saying, Amen; Alleluia.

A: This refers again to the Twenty-four Elders, the former Urantians appointed by Christ Michael, and the four beasts, who we have discussed before.

19:5 - And a voice came out of the throne, saying, Praise our God, all ye his servants, and ye that fear him, both small and great.

The voice of an angel of God

19:6 - And I heard as it were the voice of a great multitude, and as the voice of many waters, and as the voice of mighty thunderings, saying, Alleluia: for the Lord God omnipotent reigneth.

I offer here this lovely quote from *The Urantia Book*, which alludes to this passage: "All the universes know that 'the Lord God omnipotent reigns.' The affairs of this world and of other worlds are divinely supervised." Vast legions of angels works out the eternal purpose of the Universal Father, proceeding in harmony and order and in keeping with his all-wise plan. (See *UB*, Papers 26, 27 and 28; this section begins on page 285.)

Marriage of the lamb

19:7 - Let us be glad and rejoice, and give honour to him: for the marriage of the Lamb is come, and his wife hath made herself ready.

19:8 - And to her was granted that she should be arrayed in fine linen, clean and white: for the fine linen is the righteousness of saints.

19:9 - And he saith unto me, Write, Blessed are they which are called unto the marriage supper of the Lamb. And he saith unto me, These are the true sayings of God.

See 18:23 for background on the above three verses. We can also say that the union of the bride and bridegroom signify the beginning of heaven on earth, the beginning of Light and Life in the hearts of men and women.

19:10 - And I fell at his feet to worship him. And he said unto me, See thou do it not: I am thy fellowservant, and of thy brethren that have the testimony of Jesus: worship God: for the testimony of Jesus is the spirit of prophecy.

Q: Who is "he" and who is "thy fellowservant?"

A: The "fellowservant" refers to an angel of God. The "he" is also this same angel.

Q: But I thought all angels were female.

A: They generally work in pairs, one negative and one positive, so in a sense, one can be considered male, as the case can be.

19:11 - And I saw heaven opened, and behold a white horse; and he that sat upon him was called Faithful and True, and in righteousness he doth judge and make war.

19:12 - His eyes were as a flame of fire, and on his head were many crowns; and he had a name written, that no man knew, but he himself.

19:13 - And he was clothed with a vesture dipped in blood: and his name is called The Word of God.

Q: Who is "clothed with a vesture dipped in blood," and why the blood?

A: The blood is supposedly that blood shed for our sins. This image should be deleted. "He was clothed with the vesture..." is, of course, Jesus Christ, one of the divine sons. Divine sons are indeed the "Word of God." Jesus was such a Son—the "Alpha and Omega, the beginning and the end, the first and the last," the Ruler of the Universe, the Lord God of all creation, the Holy One of Israel, the Universe Mind of this creation, the One in whom are hid all treasures of wisdom and knowledge, the Giver of Eternal life and many other appellations. Jesus only objected to one title: When he was once called Immanuel, he merely replied, "Not I, that is my elder brother."

19:14 - And the armies which were in heaven followed him upon white horses, clothed in fine linen, white and clean.

Q: What exactly does "the armies" refer to here?

A: Gabriel of Salvington is the chief executive of the universe of Nebadon and is responsible for the execution of superuniverse mandates relating to non-personal affairs in the local universe. He is the commander-in-chief of "the armies of heaven"—the celestial hosts. [For more on Gabriel, see *UB*: 369-70.]

19:15 - And out of his mouth goeth a sharp sword, that with it he should smite the nations: and he shall rule them with a rod of iron: and he treadeth the winepress of the fierceness and wrath of Almighty God.

Q: Is this verse also not in keeping with John's original?

A: You are becoming adept as to what probably does not belong. Yes, delete it. It again deals with wrath of God, which is incorrect.

19:16 - And he hath on his vesture and on his thigh a name written, KING OF KINGS, AND LORD OF LORDS.

This verse seems self-evident, but I wondered if I could find more. *The Urantia Book* alludes to this same title on page 240 in explaining the basis of Christ Michael's sovereignty over this universe as it was acquired by his incarnation here on our planet.

> 19:17 - And I saw an angel standing in the sun; and he cried with a loud voice, saying to all the fowls that fly in the midst of heaven, Come and gather yourselves together unto the supper of the great God;

Q: Why is the angel calling all the fowls to the supper of the great God?

A: These fowls or birds represent souls who will arrive on the mansion worlds—but who are still uncertain as to which way to go: whether to follow the teachings of the nefarious three or to turn to the true worship of God. These souls are being invited to eat of the bread of life.

> 19:18 - That ye may eat the flesh of kings, and the flesh of captains, and the flesh of mighty men, and the flesh of horses, and of them that sit on them, and the flesh of all men, both free and bond, both small and great.

Q: Why would these souls be invited to eat of the flesh of kings, captains, mighty men, horses, etc.?

A: Again, this is a twist on the original meaning. These souls are not invited to eat in this way, but rather not to eat of them. Again, a reversal of meaning.

Destruction of the beast and false prophet

> 19:19 - And I saw the beast, and the kings of the earth, and their armies, gathered together to make war against him that sat on the horse, and against his army.

Q: Is this really what John saw?

A: John foresaw the terrible effects that would befall the world when people followed the depraved teachings of Caligastia, Satan and Lucifer rather than following in the footsteps of Jesus.

19:20 - And the beast was taken, and with him the false prophet that wrought miracles before him, with which he deceived them that had received the mark of the beast, and them that worshipped his image. These both were cast alive into a lake of fire burning with brimstone.

Q: What is the identity of the false prophet?

A: This refers to the residue of the false teachings of the nefarious three.

But on April 27, 1998, I wanted more information:

Q: What does this verse really mean?

A: John sees the time when the influences of the nefarious three end, when earth enters the age of Light and Life. The false prophets are all those who extol personal freedom at the expense of others. They use wile and cunning to turn people away from a belief in an all-loving and compassionate God. The lake of fire is merely a symbol of their eventual self-destruction.

A year later, I again questioned:

Q: What is this continual reference to the false prophet. Who is he?

A: In this case it is Caligastia, the deposed Planetary Prince of Urantia. He is no more, since he refused to repent. His ego was too strong to allow him to repent; Caligastia could never admit that there was error in his thinking.

Q: Corelli, when John had this vision, was he shown the history of this planet, from the Caligastia betrayal, to Adam and Eve, and the events around the time of Jesus' death? Did he also see the confinement and quarantine of Caligastia, Lucifer and Satan?

A: Yes to all your questions. He was given the great privilege of seeing the origin of your present problems, the impact that the default of Adam and Eve had on contemporary life, and to see what Jesus' death would mean for those times as well as for the present time. He tried to faithfully dictate to Nathan what he saw and heard, but wrote in code. He now considers that an unfortunate decision, but, again unfortunately, necessary at that time. He knew about the confinement of the nefarious three. He refers to them many times in the Revelation as "the beast."

Q: So this beast is Caligastia or Lucifer?

A: Sometimes it is one or the other depending on the verse or in what context.

Q: In 19:20, when the beast was taken, who was the false prophet taken with him?

A: In this case it was Lucifer who was the spokesman for Caligastia. Lucifer was still free to roam the earth, but was confined at Jesus' death.

Q: Corelli, once again tell me, did John have this vision on Patmos?

A: Yes, when he was 99. Nathan had two years to write down John's recollections of Jesus as he remembered it. As I noted before, John also dictated the Gospel of John to Nathan.

Q: Nathan wasn't the Apostle Nathaniel, was he?

A: No, two different people.

19:21 - And the remnant were slain with the sword of him that sat upon the horse, which sword proceeded out of his mouth: and all the fowls were filled with their flesh.

Q: What does this last verse mean?

A: Those who refused to repent suffered the last death. They chose not to continue the eternal journey so they were no more. This is obscure phraseology.

THE ASSETS OF ETERNAL LIFE

In regard to those who refuse to repent, I wondered about what exactly happens to a person's mind, his dreams and his aspirations, if he or she actually chooses extinction, or the second death. *The Urantia Book* reveals that all of the accomplishments of every individual—every valuable experience—becomes an organic part of evolutionary deity—the ever-evolving "God the Supreme." (For more on these teachings on God as an evolutionary deity—an attribute that exists alongside his eternity— see the papers on the Supreme Being, page 1260ff.)

In a sense, each person becomes a co-creator with God by using his or her unique talents. Nothing is wasted since whatever is brought into creation can be assigned to another human being if the original human being chooses not to continue.(See 1198-99.) Perhaps this explains the sudden appearance of genius or talent in a family without that genetic trait. The gifted individual may be reaping the benefit of humans who declined the choice of going on to eternal life.

However, according to Corelli, genes can also carry stored memories. These memories or talents sometimes reappear in subsequent generations.

Considering the great store of memories, abilities, and knowledge in an individual's mind, isn't it far greater to choose eternal life rather than letting these assets become a part of another?

Highlights from Chapter 19

— Michael chose to be incarnated on our planet as Jesus to right the terrible wrongs perpetrated by the nefarious three—Caligastia, Lucifer and Satan.

— Celestial beings watched with horror and amazement as they saw the creator of our universe being crucified on the cross. According to Corelli, this event was the most shameful event in all of our local universe.

— Jesus' central mission was to elevate the human race from the bondage of the planet's tragic history. Without his coming, our world would have been plunged into chaos and degradation.One of the few comforts that the watching universe gleaned from the tragedy of Jesus' death was the release of the Spirit of Truth upon all humanity after his resurrection.

— Michael (Jesus) would never allow his creation to be destroyed. Urantia will take its place among the more civilized worlds. To this end Christ Michael has recently authorized new contacts by celestial beings, called the Teaching Mission, as a follow-up to the revelations of *The Urantia Book.*

— The union of bride and bridegroom at the "marriage supper of the Lamb" (19:9) signify the beginning of heaven on earth, the inauguration of the age of Light and Life.

— Gabriel is the commander-in-chief of the "armies of heaven" (19:14).

— With his death, Michael could rule the local universe in his own right and name as "KING OF KINGS AND LORD OF LORDS"(19:16).

— The "lake of fire" (19:20) is a symbol for the eventual self-destruction of the nefarious three and their followers.

— John was shown the entire pre-history of this planet and how these past events will have an impact on the present day. He also was able to witness our world settled in Light and Life in the distant future.

— No talents are wasted since whatever is brought into creation can be assigned to another human being if the original human being chooses not to continue.

— The "false prophet" (19:20) is he who extols personal freedom at the expense of others.

20

King James Translation

1 And I saw an angel come down from heaven, having the key of the bottomless pit and a great chain in his hand.

2 And he laid hold on the dragon, that old serpent, which is the Devil, and Satan, and bound him a thousand years,

3 And cast him into the bottomless pit, and shut him up, and set a seal upon him, that he should deceive the nations no more, till the thousand years should be fulfilled: and after that he must be loosed a little season.

4 And I saw thrones, and they sat upon them, and judgment was given unto them: and I saw the souls of them that were beheaded for the witness of Jesus, and for the word of God, and which had not worshipped the beast, neither his image, neither had received his mark upon their foreheads, or in their hands; and they lived and reigned with Christ a thousand years.

5 But the rest of the dead lived not again until the thousand years were finished. This is the first resurrection.

6 Blessed and holy is he that hath part in the first resurrection: on such the second death hath no power, but they shall be priests of God and of Christ, and shall reign with him a thousand years.

7 And when the thousand years are expired, Satan shall be loosed out of his prison,

8 And shall go out to deceive the nations which are in the four quarters of the earth, Gog and Magog, to gather them together to battle: the number of whom is as the sand of the sea.

9 And they went up on the breadth of the earth, and compassed the camp of the saints about, and the beloved city: and fire came down from God out of heaven, and devoured them.

10 And the devil that deceived them was cast into the lake of fire and brimstone, where the beast and the false prophet are, and shall be tormented day and night for ever and ever.

11 And I saw a great white throne, and him that sat on it, from whose face the earth and the heaven fled away; and there was found no place for them.

12 And I saw the dead, small and great, stand before God; and the books were opened: and another book was opened, which is the book of life: and the dead were judged out of those things which were written in the books, according to their works.

13 And the sea gave up the dead which were in it; and death and hell delivered up the dead which were in them: and they were judged every man according to their works.

14 And death and hell were cast into the lake of fire. This is the second death.

15 And whosoever was not found written in the book of life was cast into the lake of fire.

20

revised

As I progressed through these chapters, the symbols were becoming easier to understand. Many had been repeated several times, and by now I could almost follow the story that was being told. I had become aware of the various angels and their functions, as well as the "four beasts," the "dragon," and the "devil." I had learned about the throne of judgment and the first and last death, and the meaning of the "seven seals." I now understood that the plagues were actually symbols of prophetic warnings. In addition I had learned about the role of the Twenty-four Elders, the default of Adam and Eve, and much more.

THE THREE LEVELS OF JOHN'S REVELATION

It now became clear that John's revelation is a story on at least three levels. In one aspect, John is telling the history of our planet beginning with the Lucifer Rebellion over 200 millennia ago. This of course includes the story of Satan—the fallen angel of Biblical lore—who was Lucifer's assistant sent to our planet to advocate for the cause of Lucifer, right on down to the time of Jesus' death.

The second level is an almost fantastic story of bizarre creatures, prophetic events and threats of God's supposed wrath that can be translated into real warnings about future challenges to humankind that John foresaw.

But also woven throughout the entire revelation is the story of Michael of Nebadon, our Jesus, and his central role as revealer of God's love and of the divine plan for eternal life once we vanquish the "mark of the beast"—our unlovely animal natures.

This vision of John's was, indeed, a remarkable message, albeit distorted and incomplete. But once it was decoded, I was confirmed in my intuitive belief that there will be no mass destruction in the future.

I was learning that Armageddon can be a useful symbol for the ultimate battle within ourselves. This battle is in reality a personal choice between good and evil—your and my decision to follow God's plan of lovingkindness, rather than the false teachings which are the residue of the evil of Lucifer's rebellion against the plan of God.

But there were still many questions I needed to resolve. At this point I went back to my notes of May 1996, when I first haphazardly asked Corelli the following question. (As it turned out, this question was out of sequence and properly belonged to verse 20:2.)

Q: *Why would Satan be bound for a thousand years and then be released?*

A: It was believed that they had better release Satan for a while. If they didn't, he might create more havoc. [I should have asked who "they" were. But as I have indicated before, I really did not know at that time what to ask, or, for that matter, even how to ask.] A thousand years seemed like a long time in the future. In the meantime they would have peace on earth. It did not concern them what would happen in the future.

Q: So did John write this section?

A: No, it was not he but rather a scribe whose sole task was to transcribe John's writings into some sort of cohesion. The scribe merely added the thousand years to comfort his friends of that time. This passage was written a long time after John's death. The scribe took fragments of myths and legends and wound them into what he thought were correct sequences. Of course, these events do not match the account given in *The Urantia Book.*

Still not satisfied with this answer, I turned to *The Urantia Book.* On page 611, I read that the Ancient of Days allowed Satan to continue to visit with the apostate Planetary Princes until the time of the completion of the presentation of The Urantia Papers in 1934, after which he was "unqualifiedly detained on the Jerusem prison worlds" in connection with the opening of the case of Gabriel vs. Lucifer. The facts are that Satan was allowed to roam freely for over 200,000 years until this time.[1]

Q: Why exactly did the Ancient of Days allow Satan to stay free? Does chapter 20 refer to this situation?

A: He was allowed to roam so that more souls who had gone over to Lucifer's side would have an increased opportunity to repent—once they more fully realized the treachery of these nefarious beings. Two hundred thousand years may seem like a long time to you, but in reality, it is a mere second in universe time. Actually, the effect of this decision was that many souls were redeemed; and in the end, the good from this terrible event far exceeded the bad.

This repentance of many souls was felt by many worlds besides your own. As of the time The Urantia Papers were presented, Satan was arrested but he refused to repent. Now he no longer exists. The evil you see today cannot be attributed to him. If an individual is fascinated by evil, then he or she is only reactivating the lingering effects of the rebellion. But in reality, they are acting on their own.

In answer to your question, yes, the account in chapter 20 refers to this story. The King James version is a garbled report of what actually happened.

Satan bound for a thousand years

I continued my research in *The Urantia Book* for help in understanding the following verses:

> 20:1 - And I saw an angel come down from heaven, having the key of the bottomless pit and a great chain in his hand.

This is how *The Urantia Book* recasts this famous line: "Upon the triumph of Michael, Gabriel came down from Salvington and bound the dragon [all the rebel leaders] for an age." (See 602).

> 20:2 - And he laid hold on the dragon, that old serpent, which is the Devil, and Satan, and bound him a thousand years,

The "devil" is, as we have seen, Caligastia, the deposed Planetary Prince of Urantia. In rereading 20:2 and in checking the Greek translation, I noted a considerable difference in the wording from the King James version, so I am quoting below the original Greek:

"And he seized the dragon, the old serpent, who is an accuser and an adversary, and he bound him a thousand years."

The Diaglott translation reads:

"And he seized the dragon—the old serpent, who is an enemy and the adversary and bound him a thousand years."

> 20:3 - And cast him into the bottomless pit, and shut him up, and set a seal upon him, that he should deceive the nations no more, till the thousand years should be fulfilled: and after that he must be loosed a little season.

When Michael (Christ) became the settled head of the local universe of Nebadon just after his resurrection, *The Urantia Book* indicates that Lucifer was taken into custody and consigned to one of the celestial prison worlds. This prison is represented by the bottomless pit.

We read in *The Urantia Book* that "Paul knew of the status of these rebellious leaders, for he wrote of Caligastia's chiefs as 'spiritual hosts of wickedness in the heavenly places.'" (611)

The first resurrection

20:4 - And I saw thrones, and they sat upon them, and judgment was given unto them: and I saw the souls of them that were beheaded for the witness of Jesus, and for the word of God, and which had not worshipped the beast, neither his image, neither had received his mark upon their foreheads, or in their hands; and they lived and reigned with Christ a thousand years.

A: John sees the resurrection halls, the judges and those ascenders who were translated into the afterlife immediately after death. These were former mortals who had mastered the mark of the beast (their animal natures).

20:5 - But the rest of the dead lived not again until the thousand years were finished. This is the first resurrection.

RESURRECTION AND THE AFTERLIFE

As we have noted previously, there are two types of resurrections of the dead. Those who are spiritually advanced are immediately resurrected in "three days," one at a time, as individuals who have overcome the "mark of the beast"; for all others a mass resurrection occurs at certain epochal stages, and these all graduate to the afterlife together. For example, the last mass resurrection occurred at the time of Jesus' death. The next will occur upon either the return of Jesus or upon the arrival of some other celestial being, even possibly Adam and Eve.

A mass resurrection did also occur at the time of Adam and Eve, some 38,000 years ago. Between the time of Adam and Eve and Jesus, 36,000 years elapsed. Those who died during those years slumbered until Jesus' arrival.

Whenever a mass resurrection occurs, the sleeping survivors awake and then are ushered into the Halls of Judgment as indicated in 20:4. They are asked to choose whether they wish to continue their eternal journey or not. This is their "first resurrection."

Physical bodies as such are never resurrected. We translate over to the afterlife only in the morontia form, as *The Urantia Book* calls it. This morontia body is still somewhat like the physical body, but finer. (We also learned previously that the form of this new body reflects a person's actual "inner beauty.") As you ascend through increasingly higher planes of existence on your eternal journey, your body will become increasingly spiritualized, eventually becoming pure spirit.

When Christ resurrected after his death, it was in the morontia form. (See the glorious section on the resurrection and morontia appearances of Jesus in the *UB*, 2020ff.) He was somewhat recognizable in this form—especially after he spoke to the Apostles.

> 20:6 - Blessed and holy is he that hath part in the first resurrection: on such the second death hath no power, but they shall be priests of God and of Christ, and shall reign with him a thousand years.

Q: Corelli, is this the "second death" that we talked about earlier?

A: Yes, these are those people who have chosen eternal life. Therefore, they are not candidates for the second or final death, which as we have seen means annihilation.

Satan loosed and destroyed

20:7 - And when the thousand years are expired, Satan shall be loosed out of his prison,

A: This verse seems to be a repeat of 20:3.

20:8 - And shall go out to deceive the nations which are in the four quarters of the earth, Gog and Magog, to gather them together to battle: the number of whom is as the sand of the sea.

Q: *In this verse, did Satan literally deceive the nations?*

A: He tried, but did not fully succeed. His power was curtailed by Christ Michael when he was on earth and finally terminated by the recent adjudication of the Lucifer Rebellion in the celestial courts.

Q: *In researching Gog and Magog, I found that some sources say the Magog were ancient people, descended from Japheth, Noah's son. Figuratively, the expressions, Gog and Magog, represent the nations which Satan would mobilize for the final attack on the forces of the Messiah. Is this interpretation correct?*

A: Only to this degree: True, there were real ancient people called by this name, but Satan was not and will not be able to muster these forces against the Messiah. Again, Satan has today been completely immobilized.

20:9 - And they went up on the breadth of the earth, and compassed the camp of the saints about, and the beloved city: and fire came down from God out of heaven, and devoured them.

A: Gog and Magog continued to use their influence, but were defeated in their attempts.

20:10 - And the devil that deceived them was cast into the lake of fire and brimstone, where the beast and the false prophet are, and shall be tormented day and night for ever and ever.

A: Satan, who attempted to deceive them, is shorn of

his power. In this passage he is confined in the prison worlds. Delete "and shall be tormented day and night forever and ever." This was never part of John's original message.

Q: Who is the false prophet?

A: It is Caligastia.

THE MEANING OF HELL

Q: What is this "lake of fire"?

A: The lake of fire refers to the superstition that all who go against God's will are thrown into hell. This simply is not true. Men of those times knew how terrible fire can be so naturally assumed that this is the worst possible punishment that God would impose. As we have stated, "hell" is mostly of one's own making, or it may symbolize the general suffering that results from certain conditions caused by man's inhumanity to man.

Let us emphasize: God is loving and just and would never countenance a death of this sort.

It should also be noted that there are accidents in time, often catastrophic events of no one's fault, but these memories are soon forgotten if death should occur.

God, in his infinite wisdom, allowed the Lucifer Rebellion to run its course so that even those beings who sided with Lucifer would have sufficient time to repent. With the exception of Satan, they were all consigned to the prison worlds. When they refused to repent, in the recent adjudication, they were judged guilty and are no more.

However, many of those who initially believed Lucifer realized what he had become, i.e., conceited and arrogant with his power, have repented, and have been forgiven. (See *UB*: 610-11.)

On May 8, 2000, I again asked for an explanation of 20:10. The answer was almost the same but with a bit more information. The communication came not from Corelli this time, but from Aflana.

Q: *Many people believe that hell is a place where you burn forever and ever. Can you, please, explain this in some depth?*

A: Yes, I can. The idea of a hell where you burn throughout eternity is completely preposterous. A loving God would never consign a single mortal to such a cruel fate. As we have said, and as *The Urantia Book* indicates, the beast and the false prophet were confined in the prison worlds. Fire and brimstone refer to the anguish some people feel when they realize how they have wronged others. But some people do not regret their misdeeds and, if they do not repent, are eventually annihilated. But, no, there is no hell. Remove the references to fire and brimstone. It should read: "And the devil that deceived them was cast into prison with the beast and the false prophet." And remove "and shall be tormented day and night for ever and ever." Not John's writing.

20:11 - And I saw a great white throne, and him that sat on it, from whose face the earth and the heaven fled away; and there was found no place for them.

Q: *Who is on the white throne?*

A: Jesus, of course. All must pass before his judgment before they can continue on their eternal journey.

General resurrection

20:12 - And I saw the dead, small and great, stand before God; and the books were opened: and another book was opened, which is the book of life: and the dead were judged out of those things which were written in the books, according to their works.

Corelli continued: John sees all those ascenders who

stand before Christ Michael and the celestial court and who are being judged.

20:13 - And the sea gave up the dead which were in it; and death and hell delivered up the dead which were in them: and they were judged every man according to their works.

A: This refers again to the mass resurrection and judgment that occurred after Jesus' death and resurrection.

20:14 - And death and hell were cast into the lake of fire. This is the second death.

A: Leave out "and death and hell were cast into the lake of fire." This verse should really have been a description of what a second death means. As we have explained, everyone has opportunity to go on or not—even after the first resurrection.

20:15 - And whosoever was not found written in the book of life was cast into the lake of fire.

A: Again a garbled version. If your life was one of evil, you are given a choice to go on with eternal life or oblivion through final death. See above for meaning of "lake of fire."

Q: Who is speaking?

A: Solonia, with Eckhart standing by.

FOOTNOTE

[1]As we have seen, three Ancients of Days rule each of the seven superuniverses. To paraphrase the Urantia Revelation on this point, we can say the following: The Ancients of Days are the most powerful and mighty of any of the direct rulers of the time-space creations, and they are the arbiters of the final extinction of all will creatures. Michael (Jesus) petitioned the Ancients of Days for authority to intern all per-

sonalities concerned in the Lucifer Rebellion. The Ancients of Days granted Michael's petition with one exception: Satan was allowed to make periodic visits to the apostate planetary princes until a Son of God should be incarnate or until such time as the courts of Uversa (the superuniverse capital) should begin the adjudication of the case of *Gabriel vs. Lucifer*. (See 209-210 and 611.)

Highlights from Chapter 20

— Binding Satan for "a thousand years" (20:2) then releasing him for another thousand years is a garbled way to say that Satan was allowed to roam for 200,000 years until the presentation of the Urantia papers, circa 1934.

— Satan was allowed to roam free so that souls who sided with Lucifer would see his true colors and repent.

— When Michael became the settled head of the local universe of Nebadon after his resurrection, Lucifer was taken into custody and consigned to one of the prison worlds (the "bottomless pit" at 20:1) where he remained until his recent annihilation.

— Since Satan, Lucifer and many other of the rebels refused to repent, they were recently judged and exist no more.

— There are two types of resurrection following bodily death: immediate individual resurrection and mass resurrections of "the rest of the dead" (20:5) at the time of the arrival of a high celestial being or some other epochal event. There were mass resurrections at the time of the advent of Adam and Eve and of Christ Michael. John was permitted to actually witness a mass resurrection.

— Physical bodies are never resurrected. We resurrect only in the so-called morontia form, which is still somewhat like the physical body, but finer.

— There is no such place as hell; this is a preposterous and superstitious idea. God is loving and just and would never countenance a place of death of this sort.

21

King James Translation

1 And I saw a new heaven and a new earth: for the first heaven and the first earth were passed away; and there was no more sea.

2 And I John saw the holy city, new Jerusalem, coming down from God out of heaven, prepared as a bride adorned for her husband.

3 And I heard a great voice out of heaven saying, Behold, the tabernacle of God is with men, and he will dwell with them, and they shall be his people, and God himself shall be with them, and be their God.

4 And God shall wipe away all tears from their eyes; and there shall be no more death, neither sorrow, nor crying, neither shall there be any more pain: for the former things are passed away.

5 And he that sat upon the throne said, Behold, I make all things new. And he said unto me, Write: for these words are true and faithful.

6 And he said unto me, It is done. I am Alpha and Omega, the beginning and the end. I will give unto him that is athirst of the fountain of the water of life freely.

7 He that overcometh shall inherit all things; and I will be his God, and he shall be my son.

8 But the fearful, and unbelieving, and the abominable, and murderers, and whoremongers, and sorcerers, and idolaters, and all liars, shall have their part in the lake which burneth with fire and brimstone: which is the second death.

9 And there came unto me one of the seven angels which had the seven vials full of the seven last plagues, and talked with me, saying, Come hither, I will shew thee the bride, the Lamb's wife.

10 And he carried me away in the spirit to a great and high mountain, and shewed me that great city, the holy Jerusalem, descending out of heaven from God,

11 Having the glory of God: and her light was like unto a stone most precious, even like a jasper stone, clear as crystal;

12 And had a wall great and high, and had twelve gates, and at the gates twelve angels, and names written thereon, which are the names of the twelve tribes of the children of Israel:

13 On the east three gates; on the north three gates; on the south three gates; and on the west three gates.

14 And the wall of the city had twelve foundations, and in them the names of the twelve apostles of the Lamb.

15 And he that talked with me had a golden reed to measure the city, and the gates thereof, and the wall thereof.

16 And the city lieth foursquare, and the length is as large as the breadth: and he measured the city with the reed, twelve thousand furlongs. The length and the breadth and the height of it are equal.

17 And he measured the wall thereof, an hundred and forty and four cubits, according to the measure of a man, that is, of the angel.

18 And the building of the wall of it was of jasper: and the city was pure gold, like unto clear glass.

19 And the foundations of the wall of the city were garnished with all manner of precious stones. The first foundation was jasper; the second, sapphire; the third, a chalcedony; the fourth, an emerald;

20 The fifth, sardonyx; the sixth, sardius; the seventh, chrysolite; the eighth, beryl; the ninth, a topaz; the tenth, a chrysoprasus; the eleventh, a jacinth; the twelfth, an amethyst.

21 And the twelve gates were twelve pearls; every several gate was of one pearl: and the street of the city was pure gold, as it were transparent glass.

22 And I saw no temple therein: for the Lord God Almighty and the Lamb are the temple of it.

23 And the city had no need of the sun, neither of the moon, to shine in it: for the glory of God did lighten it, and the Lamb is the light thereof.

24 And the nations of them which are saved shall walk in the light of it: and the kings of the earth do bring their glory and honour into it.

25 And the gates of it shall not be shut at all by day: for there shall be no night there.

26 And they shall bring the glory and honour of the nations into it.

27 And there shall in no wise enter into it any thing that defileth, neither whatsoever worketh abomination, or maketh a lie: but they which are written in the Lamb's book of life.

21

revised

Of all the chapters in John's awesome revelation, chapters 21 and 22 are by far the most sublime. Except for some negative passages added by others such as 21:8, John gives us a detailed description of what he saw in his vision of the higher worlds. He describes what he sees and hears before the throne of God, as well as his vision of Jesus, and most importantly, of the "Lamb's wife" (21:9)—the "bride" of Christ who represents the new epoch that will some day be inaugurated on earth. He also presents us with a picture of the beautiful heavenly city that we will all see once we too arrive on the mansion worlds.

In addition, John also has a vision of the "New Jerusalem" itself, which will sometime be established here on our planet, and which is represented on the cover of this book.

As usual, I wondered how to begin this chapter. How could I do justice to this extraordinary message? The previous chapters seemed to deal with prophecies of death and destruction, which are a diversion from the origial message that John tried to convey. This chapter and the next are far more hopeful. I decided once again to call upon my unseen friends for advice as to how to proceed. This is what they dictated to me on May 4, 1998:

JOHN'S VISION OF THE FUTURE

These passages are from the original revelation of John as compiled in 103 A.D. This chapter is a true account of what John saw in his vision of the mansion worlds; these were his own thoughts as he dictated to Nathan. Subsequently, various scribes mistranslated some of it, but basically, it is a true account.

John was also told a true account of what happens in the coming Age of Light and Life[1] when the "New Jerusalem" will be brought to earth. These plans have long been in the making, and it is a glorious vision of what is to be. It will be a long time in the future, many millennia from now, but it will happen.

Your planet has been one of bloody conquests, but the next task for humanity will be the battle against the evil within. But that too will pass. There will be other conflicts and wars, but no wholesale destruction of the planet. You humans are on the way to a more loving and compassionate way of life, more in keeping with Christ's admonition to do the Father's will.

What you have been writing so far, Stella, has mostly been a story of the past. These last two chapters are in a sense a prophecy of things to come—a bright new future of hope and good cheer for all humanity. Be not dismayed by what appears to be retrogression. Overall it is not so. Be of good cheer. We love you and applaud your efforts.

Q: Who is speaking?
A: Solonia. Corelli, Aflana and Eckhart are standing by.

Q: Thank you very much.
A: You are more than welcome.

A new heaven and a new earth

21:1 - And I saw a new heaven and a new earth: for the first heaven and the first earth were passed away; and there was no more sea.

21:2 - And I John saw the holy city, new Jerusalem, coming down from God out of heaven, prepared as a bride adorned for her husband.

21:3 - And I heard a great voice out of heaven saying, Behold, the tabernacle of God is with men, and he will dwell with them, and they shall be his people, and God himself shall be with them, and be their God.

THE DESCENT OF THE TEMPLE

As I understand it, John in these passages foresees the day when our world will be settled in Light and Life. That will be at the time of the inauguration of an epoch in planetary history when the "tabernacle of God is with men" (21:3). Corelli indicated to me that John did see a literal temple or tabernacle of unparalleled beauty.

In reality, the descent of the the holy city and the temple "out of heaven" does not literally mean that materials come down from heaven. Instead, the architecture is worked out in miniature on the system capital on Jerusem, and these approved plans are brought to earth and the temple built here. These temples seat about 300,000 spectators and are used for worship, play, receiving broadcasts, and special ceremonies. (See *UB*: 622.) This temple will figuratively permit God to "dwell with them" (21:3).

21:4 - And God shall wipe away all tears from their eyes; and there shall be no more death, neither sorrow, nor crying, neither shall there be any more pain: for the former things are passed away.

This lovely passage is alluded to in *The Urantia Book* (299) in connection with the last "transit sleep" when you awaken on the shore of Paradise, after the long, long ascent to the central universe. Our arrival on Paradise is the climax of our eternal career in the afterlife, and occurs millions and millions of years in the future after our survival of mortal death.

> 21:5 - And he that sat upon the throne said, Behold, I make all things new. And he said unto me, Write: for these words are true and faithful.

As you ascend and are translated from life to life you become increasingly spiritualized and "old things are passing away; behold all things are becoming new." On 631, the *UB* quotes this famous passage in explaining life in the distant future when more than half of the inhabitants of our planet will be so advanced that they translate directly to the morontia state "from among the living" (i.e., they skip the ordeal of physical death, as did Enoch and Elijah of Old Testament fame).

> 21:6 - And he said unto me, It is done. I am Alpha and Omega, the beginning and the end. I will give unto him that is athirst of the fountain of the water of life freely.

Christ, of course, is the beginning and the end of all things. (See 1:8.) He gives spiritual sustenance to all.

> 21:7 - He that overcometh shall inherit all things; and I will be his God, and he shall be my son.

Those who overcome their animal nature shall inherit eternal life.

> 21:8 - But the fearful, and unbelieving, and the abominable, and murderers, and whoremongers, and sorcerers, and idolaters, and all liars, shall have their part in the lake which burneth with fire and brimstone: which is the second death.

I pondered over this verse which seemed so negative and wondered if this belonged in this chapter. Apparently Corelli saw me writing the question, "Was this John's writing?" I quickly received the answer:

> A: No, it was not. Leave it out. It was a total fabrication and another attempt to frighten the readers. Even those who do terrible things have a chance to repent or rather to change their thinking.

The New Jerusalem

21:9 - And there came unto me one of the seven angels which had the seven vials full of the seven last plagues, and talked with me, saying, Come hither, I will shew thee the bride, the Lamb's wife.

Q: Does the bride refer to Christ's consort, or is it a symbol of the new world coming down from heaven, the New Jerusalem?

A: In this case, it is a symbol for the coming new age.

Q: But what I cannot understand is how you can equate the New Jerusalem with the bride of the lamb?

A: This is a metaphorical meaning. The bride is equated with newness [that's how I heard it]. Of course, it is not literally the bride of Jesus, but rather refers to Jesus' plan for a New Jerusalem that will eventually be built on earth in a far distant future. Does this answer your question?

Q: I suppose so. Thank you.

A: You sound doubtful.

Q: Well, I am sort of, but I will let it stand as you say.

21:10 - And he carried me away in the spirit to a great and high mountain, and shewed me that great city, the holy Jerusalem, descending out of heaven from God,

Q: Is this the mountain The Urantia Book *(521) refers to that is called Mt. Seraph, the highest elevation on Jerusem, almost 15,000 feet high? [The book also states that the mountain is the point of departure for transport seraphim. These transports arrive on the crystal sea of glass.]*

A: That is a correct reference. John saw this mountain in his vision and was greatly astonished at its beauty as well as that of the terrain surrounding the mountain.

21:11 - Having the glory of God: and her light was like unto a stone most precious, even like a jasper stone, clear as crystal;

Q: *What about these descriptions in verses 21:11 through 21:21?*

A: This is a rather confused description of two phenomena. John sees the coming of the new age, but the jewel descriptions are of Jerusem, the system capital.

21:12 - And had a wall great and high, and had twelve gates, and at the gates twelve angels, and names written thereon, which are the names of the twelve tribes of the children of Israel:

Q: *What about these twelve gates?*

A: The scribe who wrote this portion assumed that the names of the twelve tribes of Israel would have their names engraved on the portals, as was the custom in Rome to write names on edifices. This was not so. Delete beginning with "which are the names of the twelve tribes of the children of Israel."

21:13 - On the east three gates; on the north three gates; on the south three gates; and on the west three gates.

21:14 - And the wall of the city had twelve foundations, and in them the names of the twelve apostles of the Lamb.

21:15 - And he that talked with me had a golden reed to measure the city, and the gates thereof, and the wall thereof.

21:16 - And the city lieth foursquare, and the length is as large as the breadth: and he measured the city with the reed, twelve thousand furlongs. The length and the breadth and the height of it are equal.

21:17 - And he measured the wall thereof, an hundred and forty and four cubits, according to the measure of a man, that is, of the angel.

21:18 - And the building of the wall of it was of jasper: and the city was pure gold, like unto clear glass.

21:19 - And the foundations of the wall of the city were garnished with all manner of precious stones. The first foundation was jasper; the second, sapphire; the third, a chalcedony; the fourth, an emerald;

21:20 - The fifth, sardonyx; the sixth, sardius; the seventh, chrysolite; the eighth, beryl; the ninth, a topaz; the tenth, a chrysoprasus; the eleventh, a jacinth; the twelfth, an amethyst.

21:21 - And the twelve gates were twelve pearls; every several gate was of one pearl: and the street of the city was pure gold, as it were transparent glass.

A: These verses are almost an accurate description of Jerusem's residential and administrative areas. The buildings are all exquisitely beautiful.

Those interested should be sure to read about the physical aspects of our local system headquarters, as described in *The Urantia Book* (519-529): "Jerusem...is truly the heaven visualized by the majority of twentieth-century religious believers."

Q: I remember my father joking about the pearly gates. Do they really exist?

A: Yes, indeed. They are pearly gates somewhat like alabaster with an iridescent hue.

21:22 - And I saw no temple therein: for the Lord God Almighty and the Lamb are the temple of it.

Q: Why would there be no temple to the Father and the Lamb?

A: There is no need for a temple when the Father and the Lamb's presences are felt by all.

21:23 - And the city had no need of the sun, neither of the moon, to shine in it: for the glory of God did lighten it, and the Lamb is the light thereof.

A: This refers to the lighting system of Jerusem. "The

energy of Jerusem is superbly controlled...[the] light [is] of about the intensity of Urantia sunlight when the sun is shining overhead at 10 o'clock in the morning." (*UB*: 519-520)

21:24 - And the nations of them which are saved shall walk in the light of it: and the kings of the earth do bring their glory and honour into it.

A: All those who have made the ascension journey will be welcomed there.

21:25 - And the gates of it shall not be shut at all by day: for there shall be no night there.

A: This provides a further description of Jerusem and its lighting system.

21:26 - And they shall bring the glory and honour of the nations into it.

21:27 - And there shall in no wise enter into it any thing that defileth, neither whatsoever worketh abomination, or maketh a lie: but they which are written in the Lamb's book of life.

A: Only those who have lived exemplary lives will be admitted. Others may have chosen to drop out long ago.

Thus ended a basically true—and truly glorious— account of John's vision.

FOOTNOTE

[1]*The Urantia Book*'s definition of the Age of Light And Life is as follows:

"The age of light and life is the final evolutionary attainment of a world of time and space...The presence of a morontia temple at the capital of an inhabited world is the certificate of admission of such a sphere to the settled ages of light and life...This age is marked by one language, one religion, and on a normal world one race...Disease has not been entirely vanquished. There are still hospitals and homes for the sick and elderly. But you would consider it...'a heaven on earth.' (621)

Highlights from Chapter 21

- Chapter 21 is basically an accurate account of the many glorious things that John saw in his vision.

- John is in particular given a vision of the coming age of Light and Life on our planet.

- The famous passage that begins "God shall wipe away all tears from their eyes..." refers to our arrival on Paradise at the climax of our eternal career in the afterlife.

- In part of his vision, John is told that the "holy temple" will be brought to earth to inaugurate the new era. He is also shown a "high and great mountain" which is an actual mountain on Jerusem (our system capital). He confuses this mountain with his vision of the New Jerusalem which will sometime appear on earth.

- Much of this chapter gives descriptions of what John actually saw on Jerusem, including "pearly gates"— which actually do exist there—and even the lighting system of this heavenly sphere.

22

King James Translation

1 And he shewed me a pure river of water of life, clear as crystal, proceeding out of the throne of God and of the Lamb.

2 In the midst of the street of it, and on either side of the river, was there the tree of life, which bare twelve manner of fruits, and yielded her fruit every month: and the leaves of the tree were for the healing of the nations.

3 And there shall be no more curse: but the throne of God and of the Lamb shall be in it; and his servants shall serve him:

4 And they shall see his face; and his name shall be in their foreheads.

5 And there shall be no night there; and they need no candle, neither light of the sun; for the Lord God giveth them light: and they shall reign for ever and ever.

6 And he said unto me, These sayings are faithful and true: and the Lord God of the holy prophets sent his angel to shew unto his servants the things which must shortly be done.

7 Behold, I come quickly: blessed is he that keepeth the sayings of the prophecy of this book.

8 And I John saw these things, and heard them. And when I had heard and seen, I fell down to worship before the feet of the angel which shewed me these things.

9 Then saith he unto me, See thou do it not: for I am thy fellowservant, and of thy brethren the prophets, and of them which keep the sayings of this book: worship God.

10 And he saith unto me, Seal not the sayings of the prophecy of this book: for the time is at hand.

11 He that is unjust, let him be unjust still: and he which is filthy, let him be filthy still: and he that is righteous, let him be righteous still: and he that is holy, let him be holy still.

12 And, behold, I come quickly; and my reward is with me, to give every man according as his work shall be.

13 I am Alpha and Omega, the beginning and the end, the first and the last.

14 Blessed are they that do his commandments, that they may have right to the tree of life, and may enter in through the gates into the city.

15 For without are dogs, and sorcerers, and whoremongers, and murderers, and idolaters, and whosoever loveth and maketh a lie.

16 I Jesus have sent mine angel to testify unto you these things in the churches. I am the root and the offspring of David, and the bright and morning star.

17 And the Spirit and the bride say, Come. And let

him that heareth say, Come. And let him that is athirst come. And whosoever will, let him take the water of life freely.

18 For I testify unto every man that heareth the words of the prophecy of this book, If any man shall add unto these things, God shall add unto him the plagues that are written in this book:

19 And if any man shall take away from the words of the book of this prophecy, God shall take away his part out of the book of life, and out of the holy city, and from the things which are written in this book.

20 He which testifieth these things saith, Surely I come quickly. Amen. Even so, come, Lord Jesus.

21 The grace of our Lord Jesus Christ be with you all. Amen.

revised

At 22:10 we read: "Seal not the sayings of the prophecy of this book for the time is at hand." Such was the mandate given to John almost 2,000 years ago—to share his extraordinary vision with the entire world. But, sad to say, the original message was written in code, and as we now abundantly see, this code was greatly distorted by subsequent scribes. The resulting text has caused endless confusion down through the Christian era.

As I approached this final chapter, I decided to just sit quietly, meditate and think how best to render the material. Then, as if in answer to my silent prayer, the following information was dictated to me by Solonia. This was how she told me to begin this chapter:

> John is overwhelmed by what he sees. He falls on his knees to worship the angel, but is told sharply not to do so; only God should receive such obeisance. John is told to convey the good news of eternal life if all will live a morally clean life today. This chapter is not a

rebuke to John but rather a warning to convey the necessity of living a spiritual life. Nothing less will do if you are at all spiritually inclined. John endeavors to follow the edict of Jesus to go out to the world to preach, but, as you know, his message was sorely distorted. He now regrets that he was forced to write in code. Today's believers need facts about what John really saw in his vision and its true meaning.

After receiving this message I went back to my notes of May 3, 1997, and gave permission for my teachers to contact me.

A: Yes, we are here.

Q: Who?

A: Corelli, Solonia, Aflana and Meister Eckhart. We are glad you are with us again. We see you are nearly finished with your task

Stella: Yes, you can see that, and I thank you for your help. I do have some questions.

River of the water of life

22:1 - And he shewed me a pure river of water of life, clear as crystal, proceeding out of the throne of God and of the Lamb.

Q: What exactly is the "river of the water of life"?

A: It is God's spiritual blessings being beamed to all if they will but listen and hear. These blessings are free to one and all. There is a steady stream of this incredible energy being sent to everyone. It refreshes, energizes and renews. The river of life also refers to the Spirit of Truth that is always being poured out onto all mankind through Jesus, the Son of God.

The tree of life

22:2 - In the midst of the street of it, and on either side of the river, was there the tree of life, which bare

twelve manner of fruits, and yielded her fruit every month: and the leaves of the tree were for the healing of the nations.

Q: It sounds like John is being shown the tree of life in its original state. The Urantia Book *(825-826) says that the tree of life was a real "morontia" shrub sent from Edentia, the celestial capital, and placed in the first Garden of Eden. Does the tree of life mentioned here mean something different? Isn't the tree of life also a designation for one's whole life when you stand before the heavenly judges?*

A: Yes, these are two different symbols. One stands for the literal tree; the other for the entire events of a life. [See also 2:7 in this connection.]

Q: If the leaves of the tree were used for the healing of nations, does that also mean that Adam and Eve and others who had access to the tree used it for the healing of nations?

A: You are correct in your analysis.

22:3 - And there shall be no more curse: but the throne of God and of the Lamb shall be in it; and his servants shall serve him:

Q: What is the meaning of, "there shall be no more curse"?

A: Once the "curse" of the animal nature is subdued, then shall all humanity come under the influence of God and his Son.

22:4 - And they shall see his face; and his name shall be in their foreheads.

A: God's "mark" will be on their foreheads.

God provides the light

22:5 - And there shall be no night there; and they need no candle, neither light of the sun; for the Lord God giveth them light: and they shall reign for ever and ever.

A: This provides further description of the light of the heavenly abodes. (See also 21:10-21.)

Last message of Jesus

22:6 - And he said unto me, These sayings are faithful and true: and the Lord God of the holy prophets sent his angel to shew unto his servants the things which must shortly be done.

22:7 - Behold, I come quickly: blessed is he that keepeth the sayings of the prophecy of this book.

Q: I interpret this to mean that Jesus says: "Blessed is he who understands the message of this book." Is this correct?

A: Yes, but there is additional import to this statement. Jesus is also indicating that future blessings will be assured to those who live a godly life.

22:8 - And I John saw these things, and heard them. And when I had heard and seen, I fell down to worship before the feet of the angel which shewed me these things.

A: John receives what is being revealed to him by hearing and by sight, and falls down to worship the angel.

22:9 - Then saith he unto me, See thou do it not: for I am thy fellowservant, and of thy brethren the prophets, and of them which keep the sayings of this book: worship God.

A: The angel says to not worship him, but to worship God only. Even Jesus states firmly that not he, but God the Father, should be worshipped.

22:10 - And he saith unto me, Seal not the sayings of the prophecy of this book: for the time is at hand.

A: The angel requires John to share the message of this prophecy.

22:11 - He that is unjust, let him be unjust still: and he which is filthy, let him be filthy still: and he that is righteous, let him be righteous still: and he that is holy, let him be holy still.

A: Delete entirely. Not John's writing.

22:12 - And, behold, I come quickly; and my reward is with me, to give every man according as his work shall be.

22:13 - I am Alpha and Omega, the beginning and the end, the first and the last.

A: Jesus, the Alpha and Omega, will give every man his due. (See also 1:8.)

22:14 - Blessed are they that do his commandments, that they may have right to the tree of life, and may enter in through the gates into the city.

22:15 - For without are dogs, and sorcerers, and whoremongers, and murderers, and idolaters, and whosoever loveth and maketh a lie.

A: Not really John's writings, but it is a symbol for those who live outside of a belief in God and who choose a mercenary life.

22:16 - I Jesus have sent mine angel to testify unto you these things in the churches. I am the root and the offspring of David, and the bright and morning star.

22:17 - And the Spirit and the bride say, Come. And let him that heareth say, Come. And let him that is athirst come. And whosoever will, let him take the water of life freely.

A: All those who listen may come and partake of the waters of eternal life.

22:18 - For I testify unto every man that heareth the words of the prophecy of this book, If any man shall add unto these things, God shall add unto him the plagues that are written in this book:

22:19 - And if any man shall take away from the words of the book of this prophecy, God shall take away his part out of the book of life, and out of the holy city, and from the things which are written in this book.

A: Delete these verses. Priests who wanted to control their people and to discourage critical thinking added them much later. These were never Jesus' or John's teachings.

22:20 - He which testifieth these things saith, Surely I come quickly. Amen. Even so, come, Lord Jesus.

22:21 - The grace of our Lord Jesus Christ be with you all. Amen.

A: These last two verses may be retained as written.

I, almost happily, had reached the end of decoding of the Book of Revelation.

As stated in the beginning of this book, revelation is not confined to a particular age. New revelations like *The Urantia Book*—and many others—will increasingly grace our world in the ages to come. The future is bright and filled with promise. Nothing will stop our path to a future Age of Light and Life. And indeed, there will be no Armageddon, no end-times, no mass destruction of the world and no anti-Christ.

Highlights from Chapter 22

— John is overwhelmed by the glory of what he sees and hears. He falls on his knees to worship the angel who accompanies him, but is told that only God should receive worship. Jesus also states that not he but the Father should be worshipped.

— John sees the river of the water of life, which is a steady stream of renewing and refreshing spiritual energy that is freely sent to all from God. This image also refers to the Spirit of Truth that Jesus sends to all.

— John is shown the tree of life in its original celestial abode; this is the same tree that once was literally here on the planet in the Garden of Eden and was used "for the healing of nations" by Adam and Eve.

— John is told to convey the good news of eternal life to all who would live a spiritual life.

— John is told to follow the edict of Jesus to go out to the world to prophesy.

— A variety of hopeful images for the future are presented to John.

— Even among these inspiring verses, priests and scribes inserted negative and fear-based passages (22:11, 22:15, 22:18 and 22:19) in an attempt to assert control over believers.

— There will be no Armageddon, end of time, mass destruction of the world and no anti-Christ. Nothing will stop our evolution to the future Age of Light and Life.

Epilogue: Concluding Messages

A Final Message from the Celestial Teachers

Q: Do you have a final message for readers of this book?

A: Yes, tell them that we are pleased with the growing interest in spiritual matters. There is a great renaissance taking place throughout the world, one that will eventually make a paradise of your planet—far different than what you see now. Such a future is in the making, and we hope to enlist all of you in creating it. But we cannot do this work alone. We need everyone of you to do what you can to help your fellow man, not only physically, but spiritually.

There are many souls who are hungry for spiritual truths, and many fine writers who are being contacted. Each person has a talent of his or her own. Use your talent in any way that is best for you. All working together will indeed make a better world, whether in agriculture, politics, religion, sociology—in every facet of your existence.

Know one thing, the greatest truth of all: Each one of you is loved beyond what you can comprehend. Your troubles and sorrows are relatively brief; in the afterlife you will have ample time to do what you failed to do, or could not do, because of circumstances beyond your control.

There is a just universe, and above all, a just God. Your pleas are not in vain but will eventually enable you to do that for which you were born. This may not necessarily happen in this lifetime, but time is endless.

There are many mansions in heaven, as our Lord

Jesus has said. These worlds are waiting for enlightened souls who will continue to work and play in a vast universe. You will have many future opportunities to serve, but use your time well on this earth; it is a rehearsal for far greater worlds to come. So be not discouraged with what you perceive as an unjust and cruel world. You have had many setbacks in the history of your planet. These were very unfortunate, but efforts are now underway to remedy these past defaults, for you all are greatly loved.

And as your Jesus, our Michael, says: *Be of good cheer!*

—Solonia, Corelli, and Aflana, with Meister Eckhart standing by

A Concluding Message From Jesus

On a sunny day in Whittier, California, I sat in the garden of my back yard wondering how I was going to get into my house. I had locked myself out. The day before, in thinking about my book, I thought it would be nice to have a letter from Christ as an epilogue, and then dismissed the thought as too improbable. But as I was sitting there, I heard a voice, different from the others, saying:

> **We have a message for you from Christ. We know you have been hoping for a message from him for an ending of your book. Here it is:**
>
> I commend you Stella for finishing your project. It is a message greatly needed by a suffering world. You do not know it yet, but your message will go far to allay the fears that Armageddon is coming. Rather than a war without, the battle will be within, in those humans who do not know which way to turn—towards the love of God and his teachings, or, back to the pressures of a secular world.
>
> There is no hell, but there is a heaven for all those who choose eternal life. There is much to do before the world enters into the Age of Light and Life, but I, as your Creator, know that this can be done by dedicated men and women who are working to make this a safe and beautiful world, one that is intent on doing God's will.
>
> I am not God, but one of God's sons who was sent here by my Creator to give the world another chance. You all have been greatly retarded by the unfortunate incidences of the Lucifer Rebellion and Adam and Eve's default. But despite these setbacks, most of you are on the path to Life and Light, the forerunners of a great movement which cannot be stopped. What my Father wills, will be.
>
> Be not impatient.

I, as your Creator, was honored to be given the task of creating your particular universe. I feel a special responsibility and love for this planet of my human birth, and will never allow it to be destroyed. There are many problems, I know, but the plan set into action so many centuries ago is coming about even more so than I had hoped. There are many of you now who are willing to do the Father's will to bring enlightenment to your world. This will take many centuries, but that is nothing in terms of cosmic time.

I know you are not interested in personal glory, but, nevertheless, you are one of many who will bring about a better world. As I have said before, be not dismayed at what seems a slow pace of change. It is not slow. In your century you have seen many changes, and this is minor in comparison with what is ahead.

Write your book, as we see you are doing. All will go well with it. John is very pleased with your endeavor and never really believed that anyone would take up such a courageous task. We are pleased. We love you and will guard you until that day when we stand face to face on the mansion worlds.

Please send my greetings to all those who may chance to read this. They are well loved, and we watch with great interest to see what is happening with the Teaching Mission. We are delighted with all of your progressions.

> Your Father-Son,
> Jesus Christ
> Michael of Nebadon

Appendix:

The Urantia Book, the Bible, and the New Celestial Teachings

A first glance through the table of contents of *The Urantia Book* can be shocking: It lists over fifty names and types of celestial personalities, few of whom have been heard of on the planet heretofore. The topics covered are all-embracing in scope. Its literary style is elevated and complex—often rather advanced. In addition, the jacket of this 2,096-page book describes it as an epochal revelation to our planet, which it purports is called "Urantia." Without a doubt, this text offers a formidable challenge to anyone approaching it for the first time! A key purpose of *The Secret Revelation* is to make the vast Urantia Revelation more accessible, by providing a general introduction to its teachings on theology, cosmology, planetary history, and the newly-revealed life and teachings of Jesus that it contains—to the end that Christians may come to a new and updated understanding of biblical prophecy. The author Stella Religa uses a novel method of celestial instruction that is explained below and in her Foreword.

THE TRANSMISSION OF WISDOM

The Urantia Book was authored and presented by celestial personalities and given to our world through a method that is not wholly understood. Popular lore recounts a twenty-year process in the 1920s and '30s in Chicago of direct interaction between a superhuman commission of celestial personalities and a "contact commission" of six humans. In addition, a group of several hundred people known as the Forum, which met once a week during these years in Chicago, was indirectly involved in the revelatory process, feeding (through the human contact commissioners) not only hundreds of questions to the revelators but even comments on early drafts of the papers. The finished version, a massive tome, was first published in 1955, and nearly 500,000 copies are now in print.

The Urantia Book is not a new "bible," but it does purport to be an epochal revelation to our planet. The so-called Teaching Mission (see Stella Religa's Foreword) is, by contrast, a grassroots phenomenon involving localized transmissions of celestial teachings based on the Urantia text to small groups and individuals—including "live" question and answer sessions such as those that appear in this book. It is not implausible that some version of the method of celestial contact that resulted in *The Secret Revelation* may have been used in biblical times when the prophets and teachers of old engaged in inspired contact with divine personalities.

Transcripts of Teaching Mission sessions are of variable quality and veracity, depending on the person transmitting; the Urantia text, on the other hand, is of uniformly superlative quality and carries an unmistakable flavor of revelatory excellence. The literary affinity of the Urantia text to the new celestial transcripts is comparable to that between a textbook and its oral explication. A good analogue might be the relationship between the transcribed lectures of a college professor and the authoritative textbook his course is based upon. Please bear this comparison in mind when you reflect upon the connection between the exegesis passages in this book based on responses of Stella's teachers, and those passages from *The Urantia Book* that were chosen to support her interpretations and commentary.

The first thing one notices when perusing this text is a huge volume of 196 chapters (actually known as "papers") that is divided into four sections:

I. The Central and Superuniverses, which presents the infinitely loving and merciful nature of the Universal Father and Eternal Mother-Son, the nature and activities of the Eternal Trinity and other high universe personalities, and the extent and structure of the far-flung cosmic domains of material creation.

II. The Local Universe, which details the nature and structure of the "local" sector of our galaxy containing ten million inhabited planets, including its administration and history.

III. The History of Urantia, which narrates the origin of our solar system, a chronological account of the history of the earth ("Urantia"), and the evolution of life on the planet, including a spiritual history of humankind.

IV. The Life and Teachings of Jesus, which contains a 700-page account of the life and teachings of Jesus-sometimes day-by-day and hour-by-hour—including a narration of the so-called "lost years" of Jesus' childhood, adolescence and young adulthood as well as an extensive and detailed account of his public ministry. The background data for this presentation is based chiefly on records supplied by the guardian angel who accompanied the Apostle Andrew.

This fourth section of the book is solidly rooted in the New Testament story. In one of five papers presented for a consultative panel on *The Urantia Book* held at the American Academy of Religion meeting in 1986, Dr. Meredith Sprunger wrote the following about the Jesus Papers:

> This superb presentation of the life of Jesus brings life to the sketchy New Testament picture and with it a new authenticity. It has a universal appeal even when it is viewed only as a historical novel for it is unsurpassed in theistic philosophical reasonableness, spiritual insight, and personality appeal. This life of Jesus not only fills in the "hidden years" from twelve to thirty but *The Urantia Book* gives a picture

of his pre-incarnation and post-incarnation experience. It is basically acceptable to all religions, emphasizing the religion of Jesus which is unifying rather than the religion about Jesus which tends to be divisive.

It is the mission of *The Secret Revelation* is to extend these new teachings of Jesus—contextualized within the Urantia Revelation—so that Christian believers may discover a more enlightened interpretation of the great vision of the Apostle John that now lies buried in the Book of Revelation.

—Byron Belitsos

Glossary

Adjudication (of the Lucifer Rebellion)—the case of Gabriel vs. Lucifer (the Lucifer rebellion of 200,000 years ago) is said to have been adjudicated circa 1985. As a result of this action by the celestial courts, Caligastia, Lucifer and Satan no longer exist. Other rebel adherents in the celestial hierarchy also met the same fate, while the majority chose rehabilitation. The completion of this case has also led to the ending of the quarantine of our planet, and the reconnection of the celestial circuits that link us to universe broadcasts and other spiritual energies and agencies, as well as to the special initiatives for planetary redemption known as the Correcting Time and the Teaching Mission. (See also Correcting Time, and Lucifer Rebellion.)

Adjuster—see Thought Adjuster

Caligastia—the "devil", the deposed former Planetary Prince of our planet Urantia. (See Planetary Prince.) Caligastia was a high universe administrator who was assigned to come to Urantia 500,000 years ago, with a staff of 100 assistants and the tree of life, to initiate and direct the progress of planetary evolution. Before going over to the catastrophic program of Lucifer, Caligatia's administration was effective for 300,000 years. Lucifer taught unbridled personal liberty as part of his scheme for planetary revolution. Caligastia recently met his fate in the adjudication of the Lucifer Rebellion. (See adjudication.)

Christ Michael (Michael, Jesus Christ)—our local universe father, creator, and sovereign, also known to us as Jesus Christ, who incarnated as Jesus of Nazareth on our planet. He is of the order of Michael—high beings with creator prerogatives who are also known as Creator Sons; they are directly of origin from God the Father and God the Son (see God the Father). In partnership with the Mother Spirits who are their equals (see "Mother Spirit"), Michaels create local universes and their myriad inhabitants, over which they rule with love and mercy. Their unending love for us is typified in the fact that they may incarnate in the likeness of their creatures on the worlds they have created, as our own Michael did on our planet Urantia.

Correcting Time—an umbrella term used by celestial teachers for the current period of celestially-inspired transformations occurring throughout the planet. The Correcting Time is a much more vast project than the Teaching Mission. The Teaching Mission is characterized by its explicit use of the Urantia revelation as a reference; the Correcting Time does not. The common element of the Correcting Time in all its features is a dramatic increase in celestial assistance for the purpose of fostering planetary evolution, both secular and spiritual. Technically speaking, the possibility for such celestial intervention had to await the reconnection of certain "spiritual circuits" made possible by the lifting of the quarantine that was placed on our planet because of its involvement in the Lucifer rebellion (see below).

The Eternal Son—the second person of the Trinity, also called the Eternal Mother-Son or God the Son, is described as the "first" personal and absolute concept of the Universal Father, is coequal with the Father, and is designated as the Second Source and Center. He is the "absolute personality"; he is the absolute expression of the personality of the Father. If we conceive of the Father as love, then the Eternal Son is mercy. His spirit bathes all creation, and he also bestows himself on all local universes through the so-called Michael Sons, who have the power of incarnation in the form of creatures for mercy ministry. *The Urantia Book* makes clear that the second person of the Trinity is not to be confused with Jesus; Jesus himself is a Michael Son, and is also often known as Christ Michael. (See Christ Michael.)

God the Father (also God, Father, Paradise Father)—God is love; as the universal Father, God is the first person of deity, the First Source and Center of all things and beings. According to the Urantia Revelation, the term God always denotes personality. God the Father is the infinite and eternal God of love, as well as Creator, Controller, and Upholder of the universe of all universes. The first person of deity—God the Father—loves us with an attitude analogous to that of a divine father; the love and mercy of God the Son, the second person of deity, can be considered akin to the love of a mother. God the Spirit is the third person of deity, also known as the Infinite Spirit.

Father fragment—see Thought Adjuster

First Garden (of Eden)—the original residence of Adam and Eve really existed, and was a long narrow peninsula projecting westward from the eastern shores of the Mediterranean Sea. Adam and Eve took up residence there 38,000 years ago. Much later this land mass submerged into the sea, due to volcanic activity. (See Second Garden.)

Jerusem—the headquarters sphere of the system of Satania, the local system of (up to) 1000 inhabited planets to which our planet belongs. Jerusem is a glorious sphere. It is 100 times the size of Urantia (our planet); rotating around it are 57 architectural spheres, among which are the seven mansion worlds, our first post-mortal residences. Lucifer was at one time resident on Jerusem as the System Sovereign, with Satan as his main assistant. (See mansion worlds.)

Light and Life (also Age of Light and Life)—the goal of all inhabited planets, the final evolutionary attainment of any world of time and space, is know as the Age of Light and Life. When a world has reached this utopian state of evolutionary consummation, its achievements along the way will have included the attainment of one world-wide language, one blended race, one unified world religion, universal peace, and a very advanced state of prosperity and happiness.

local universe—In Urantia Book cosmology, Paradise is a stationary body at the center of the space-time universe (see "Paradise"), which is surrounded by a central universe of inherently perfect worlds (not covered here), which is in turn encircled by seven discrete aggregations of galaxies (galaxy clusters) called superuniverses. Each superuniverse is comprised of 700,000 local universes. *The Urantia Book* indicates that a local universe is made up of approximately 10,000,000 inhabitable planets and is evolving toward perfection. Each local universe is ruled by one of the Creator Sons of God of the order of Michael. Our local universe, called Nebadon, is graced by the rulership of Christ Michael, who incarnated on our planet as Jesus of Nazereth.

Lucifer Rebellion—Lucifer was a high celestial being and brilliant administrator of a system of 607 inhabited planets, who with his first assistant Satan launched a rebellion against the local universe government of Christ Michael some 200,000 years ago. Lucifer's insurrection created pandemonium in the celestial hierarchy and on our planet—as well as in 36 other planets in our local system. Among other contentions, Lucifer claimed that the Universal Father does not really exist, and he attacked the right of Christ Michael to assume sovereignty of Nebadon in the name of the Father. The majority of celestial beings in the celestial hierarchy of our planet went over to the way of Lucifer, causing major distortions and aberrations ever since in the evolution and history of our planet. The planetwide era of conscious awakening known as the Correcting Time (of which the Teaching Mission is a part), was launched in the mid-1980's, we are told, after the final adjudication of the Lucifer rebellion in celestial courts.

Mansion worlds—in the afterlife, those mortals who survive the transition of death are repersonalized on these worlds; these seven heavenly planets are the first post-mortal residences for all survivors of life in the flesh. The mansion worlds are training worlds—the first two providing remedial training—whose purpose is to prepare us for the vast career ahead as we journey across the universe in our age-long ascent to God on Paradise. Some Teaching Mission lessons are based in part on the curriculum of the mansion worlds.

Michael—see Christ Michael

Mother Spirit—just as Michael is our local universe father, the Mother Spirit is our local universe mother. As Christ Michael is a personalization of the first and second persons of the Trinity, the Creative Mother Spirit is a personalization of the third person of deity. She is Christ Michael's consort in the administration and in the ministry of love and mercy to the myriad of planets in Nebadon (see "Nebadon"). Among the many powers and duties of Mother Spirits is the ability to give life; she supplies the essential factor of living plasm to all creatures high and low. She also loves and ministers to us through her vast retinue of angels and other ministering celestial beings.

Mystery Monitor—see Thought Adjuster

Nebadon—is the local universe in which our planet is located and presently contains approximately 3,800,000 inhabited planets. It is a relatively young universe and sits on the outer edges of Orvonton, the superuniverse in which it is located.

Nebadon is ruled by Christ Michael, also known as Jesus Christ, and his consort, the Mother Spirit.

Paradise—at the literal center of the cosmos, yet outside of space and time, is the only stationary body in all creation, and the Urantia revelation designates this as Paradise. God is personally present on Paradise, and from his infinite being flow the floodstreams of life, energy and personality to all universe. Paradise is a stupendously large island located at the geographical center of infinity. All physical energy and all cosmic-force circuits, including all forms of gravity, also have their origin at Paradise. It also has residential zones; all God-conscious mortals will someday attain and reside on Paradise.

Personality—is that part of a person by which we know them as unique, those personal qualities that endure and which are recognizable regardless of changes in age, status, behavior or other external qualities. We are told that personality is a high and divine gift to each person from God the Father—it is that changeless metaphysical quality (or entity) that confers upon them their unique identity in the cosmos. It could be called the "image of God" within us. Personality is absolutely unique and immutable; it does not in itself evolve, but its relationship with the indwelling spirit (Thought Adjuster) and the soul (see "soul") continually evolves. Functionally, personality also acts as the unifier and integrator of all aspects of an individual's relationship with his or her environment. Each individual's personality continues with them throughout the long ascent throught the local universe, the superuniverse and all the way to Paradise.

Planetary Prince—the ruler of an evolving inhabited world, who at the consummation of planetary evolution become the Planetary Sovereign. They are invisible to mortal beings. Caligastia was our original Planetary Prince. (See Caligastia.)

Salvington (see also Nebadon)—this wondrous sphere is the headquarters world of Nebadon, our local universe, and is surrounded by 490 architectural spheres. It is residence of Christ Michael and the Mother Spirit, who created it and the entire universe of Nebadon.

Second Garden—after Adam and Eve's expulsion from the first Garden of Eden, they and their party of Adamites fled to and established a new home situated between the Tigris and Euphrates Rivers. The progeny of Adam and Eve later migrated outward in all directions from this area, circa 25,000 B.C., mixing with most of the races of the planet and contributing greatly to planetary evolution.

Soul—the indwelling spirit is a perfect gift of God, but the soul is an experiential achievement. As we choose the divine will in our lives, the effect of this experience is that our soul grows in substance and quality. We are told in *The Urantia Book* that the indwelling spirit is the *father* of our soul, just as the material mind—as a result of its moral choice—is the *mother* of the emerging soul. In the afterlife (see "mansion worlds"), it is the soul that survives death and becomes the container of our actual identity, through the agency of our personality.

Spirit of Truth—is the unique spiritual endowment conferred on each person on this planet from our Creator Son, Christ Michael. This high and pure spiritual influence was first gifted to humankind on the day of Pentecost, just after Jesus' resurrection. The Spirit of Truth enhances each person's ability to recognize truth. Its effectiveness is limited by each person's free-will consecration of his or her will to doing the will of God, but its influence is universal. When actively sought, the Spirit of Truth purifies the human heart and leads the individual to formulate a life purpose based on the love of truth.

Thought Adjuster (indwelling spirit, Mystery Monitor, Adjuster, atman)—this is the specialized Urantia Book term for "God-within"—the indwelling spirit—and we are told that it is an actual fragment of God the Father that indwells every normal-minded and morally conscious human being. The TA is wholly subservient to our will, yet represents the actual will of God, resident in our own minds! Through the practice of stillness, meditative worship, and loving service to others, we can attune ourselves to the influence of this inner divinity, thereby discerning the will of God for us as individuals. Also known as the Father fragment or Mystery Monitor, the Adjuster is God's gift to each of us in addition to our personality, and its influence arouses our hunger for perfection, our quest for the divine. In addition, our Thought Adjuster and our material mind, working together, actually create our soul (see "soul"). According to *The Urantia Book*, the great goal of our spriritual evolution is to actually fuse with—i.e., come into complete union and identification with—the Thought Adjuster, the indwelling spirit of God, and by so doing achieve immortality.

Tree of life—an actual shrub imported from a celestial sphere for use on our planet, whose fruits were life-sustaining for Adam and Eve. It first came to this planet with the inauguration of the planetary administration 500,000 years ago. (See Caligastia.) The "tree of the knowledge of good and evil" referred to in Genesis is a symbolic reference to the tree of life.

Urantia ("you-ran-sha")—is planet earth; Urantia is the name by which our planet is known in our local universe, according to the celestial authors of *The Urantia Book*. Urantia is said to be a disturbed planet by virtue of its participation in the Lucifer rebellion (see "Lucifer rebellion"), and yet is a blessed planet because it was the site of the incarnation bestowal of Michael, as Jesus of Nazareth.

More About the Author

Ten or twenty years ago I would have scoffed at the idea of working with celestial helpers to write such a book as this. I would have looked at you in utter amazement and declared "no way!" Even five years ago it would have been the furthest thought from my mind. I certainly never would have believed myself capable of reinterpreting a scriptural text—let alone the Book of Revelation of which I knew absolutely nothing in 1996. But life these days has a funny way of turning something that once seemed incredible into a simple matter of fact.

Honesty requires that I first share with you the biases that I bring to this endeavor. As the work on this book progressed, I became increasingly aware of three religious issues which had concerned me all of my life, and which motivated me to undertake the decoding of the Apostle John's famous text.

The first was a wish to somehow refute the constant barrage of gloom and doom propounded by literal-minded Christians. Most of this, I came to discover, arises from their selective reading of prophecies of John, Daniel and Ezekiel, and other apocalyptical passages in the Bible.

My second wish was to better understand an intuition that goes back to my childhood: If there really was a God, I always felt that he could not be the wrathful and vengeful monarch often portrayed in the Bible. I also felt that the God I knew could not have given his blameless son to die for our sins—even though this is, of course, a basic tenet of Christianity.

And third, but not least, I have always resented the terrible injustices women have suffered through the ages that were supposedly sanctioned by God according to scripture. Long ago I founded a shelter for battered women and children, which is still in operation. Back then I was certainly aware of the discrimination and violence against women, but I did not fully understand how and why these prejudices developed until I researched the Bible and the Book of Revelation through my conversations with Corelli, my primary celestial contact for this book. It is she—and a small group of celestial helpers that include John himself—who guided me line-by-line through John's revelation, resulting in the book you now hold in your hands.

Strange to relate, my religious background is meager. I had no religious training from my Czech parents, who were former Catholics. As a child I did attend Sunday school of my own volition but only for a brief time. Later I read extensively and delved into various religions, but no real answers were forthcoming. The Bible was almost of no interest to me; I simply could not understand it. The one class in religion I had in college was in comparative religion, and that did not even mention the Book of Revelation.

As a child growing up in Illinois I would occasionally hear preachers on the radio—there was no television in those days. What I heard I didn't like. They said I was a sinner but I could not understand this. I hadn't even begun to live!

Still searching for answers, I grew up, married, and raised three children. I worked as a secretary for the telephone company for most of my business career. But finally, I began to find the answers I was seeking all my life. They came through *The Urantia Book*. My daughter Sharilyn had mentioned it to me earlier, but it was only after receiving the book as a gift from my son Robert back in 1972 that I paid any attention. I became a student of this tremendous revelation, and never looked back.

Fast forward to 1992.

My initial involvement with celestial teachers through what is called the Teaching Mission, or the Correcting Time, began on February 1, 1992, when I attended a special meeting of Urantia Book leaders at the Holiday Inn in Los Angeles. An unheard-of new phenomena was transpiring in Utah near Salt Lake City and was spreading to other locations. A young woman by the name of Rebecca, a dedicated Urantia Book student, was allegedly receiving important messages from beings on the other side. She and her cohorts had invited leading Urantians to an important announcement that was supposedly initiated by a celestial teacher named Ham. As resident of a Los Angeles suburb, it was easy for me to attend the event. I decided I might as well take down in shorthand as much as I could hear as I was sitting in the back of the room with about 100 people in attendance. The following is what I transcribed from my notes. Other transcriptions from other locations were soon to be emailed all over the world to Urantia Book readers.

Using terms known only to Urantia Book readers, the celestial being spoke through Rebecca as follows: [Please see the glossary for definitions of the new terms below.]

> The time has arrived for an expanded revelation of truth. We come not for ourselves, no indeed, rather in the service of Michael [Jesus]. This day marks the beginning of the Correcting Time. Machiventa Melchizedek [the priest of unknown origin who appeared to Abraham 4,000 years ago, as reported in Genesis] has arrived and has been duly inaugurated as Acting Planetary Prince of Urantia ["Urantia" is the name of our planet], an assignment he has accepted from Michael. Long years we have waited this day. The Lucifer Rebellion is officially ended in Nebadon [the name of our local universe]. The circuits that have isolated your world are being reopened. All these changes are occurring by and in accordance with the plan of Michael. Happy and joyous is this day. Blessed in the sight of our Lord. Gracious listeners I bid you welcome to change. Mark the beginning of the reign of Prince Machiventa on this day.

> Questions from the audience ensued.

One questioner wanted to know the purpose of the Teaching Mission. Ham replied that they were preparing a group of celestial teachers hailing from many planets who would bring spiritual enlightenment to individuals, groups and nations on economic, political, social, environmental and technical changes.

Another wanted to know what role Jesus would ask us to play. Ham said, "Love one another, love our Father, understand the gospel. Make your life a living testimony to the truth."

We learned from Ham that our celestial overseers were also preparing the way for a great world teacher, one who would guide the planet toward the era of "Light and Life" on our planet Urantia. Ham added that he could not adequately or accurately foresee and comment beyond that fact.

And there was much more in this announcement, notably the adjudication of the Lucifer Rebellion [see glossary], which as you will see as you read this book, was prophecied in Apostle John's revelation. Other main points are covered in the overview of the Teaching Mission earlier in this book.

As I left the auditorium I thought: maybe it's so, maybe it isn't. I really wasn't that interested in the odd phenomenon I had just witnessed, and I certainly wasn't interested in being a channel. I never dreamed I would become one and eventually take dictation from unseen celestials beings, of all things. My business background had not prepared me for such a contingency!

I put this transmission away for many years right up until the time that the idea of decoding the Book of Revelation occurred to me. When this idea hit me, I immediately thought I might receive some help through transmitting celestial beings in the manner I had witnessed in 1992. But I resisted this idea for a long time.

Then one Sunday in 1995 a friend of mine approached me and almost furtively whispered, "Do you know about the Teaching Mission?" I said not much (other than what I recounted above). She invited me to attend a Teaching

Mission session that met nearby in Arcadia, California.

By this time I had practically forgotten about Ham's message, but out of curiosity I accepted the invitation. The group met at the beautiful home of Hal and Lucille Ketell, with eight or ten people present, all devoted Urantia Book students. They gathered to pray, meditate and to partake of this new phenomena of receiving teachings from unseen celestial teachers.

It was nothing like a séance, table-tapping or psychic reading. We simply would quiet the mind—a key Teaching Mission practice that the celestials call "stillness"—and those able to transmit would wait for verbal contact. Before transmitting, one had to give permission to allow any contact to occur.

According to *The Urantia Book*, interaction with the dead is forbidden. But this is different. These contacts are with ascended human beings from other worlds, not this one, who have perfected themselves in the afterlife, and who were given a commission to contact humans throughout our troubled world. Potential contactees are not just Urantia Book students; people of the world's various religions and beliefs were also eligible. The messages offered structured lessons on how to live a spiritual life; methods of practicing truth, beauty and goodness in one's life; plus encouragement to be of service to humankind in any realm of endeavor.

A natural-born skeptic, I lurked in these Arcadia sessions for one solid year without saying a word. I listened and observed, just waiting to pounce on one false note. I was not going to be caught up in this questionable stuff—and besides, wasn't this merely the transmitter's own imagination? Neither did I approve of the idea of anyone taking over my mind—although I learned later that this is not what happens when you transmit. But after a while my suspicions began to abate, and in 1996 I began the celestial contact with Corelli, John, and the other teachers that you see presented in this book.

Not long after my first contact, I went into meditation while at a friend's house. A quiet voice in my mind said, "I am Michael of Nebadon, Jesus Christ." I shot back: "Oh, go away, I don't believe you." Somehow it felt like he looked back at me with puzzled amusement. Later on, I said to myself, "Oh, my God, what have I done? Was it really he?" I later discovered that, yes—the voice was indeed Jesus! He was contacting many transmitters in the Teaching Mission, and, he had forgiven me for denying him. I still shudder at this.

My concern and remorse regarding my rejection of Christ was somewhat allayed by a message I received from Corelli on February 28, 1996. It was: "Be of good cheer, from Christ Michael. He is happy you include him in your prayers to our Father." (I prayed to God but usually did not include Jesus.) The message went on to say: "Jesus doesn't mind that you bypass him ever so often. We understand your reluctance since you were not brought up with an understanding of him and his mission." There were innumerable messages after that, ranging across a variety of topics, some spiritual, some just answers to curiosity questions—most not included in this book.

After my curiosity about biblical prophecy was first stimulated in early 1996, many questions about the Book of Revelation stirred within me. I still could not help wondering if there was a way to uncover its secret meanings. As the saying goes, be careful what you ask for! It is my fervent hope and prayer that I have succeeded.

Give the gift of
The Secret Revelation
to your friends

☐ YES, I want ——— copies of

The Secret Revelation

at $21 each — please include
$4.50 shipping for the first book and
$1.00 for each additional book.
California residents add 7% sales tax.

Name _____

Company _____

City _____ State _____ Zip _____

Phone _____

Email _____

Total _____

☐ Check or money order   ☐ Visa   ☐ Mastercard

Card # _____ Exp. _____

Signature _____

Call our Toll Free order line: 1.888.267.4446
Fax your order to: 415.898.1434
Order online: www.**originpress/celestia**

Please make your check payable and return to:

Origin Press/Celestia
1122 Grant Avenue, Suite C, Novato, CA 94945

The Center Within
Lessons from the Heart of the Urantia Revelation

Edited by Fred Harris
and Byron Belitsos

☐ YES, I want ———— copies of
The Center Within
at $14.95 each — please include
$4.50 shipping for the first book and
$1.00 for each additional book.
California residents add 7% sales tax.

Name _____

Company _____

City _____ State _____ Zip _____

Phone _____

Email _____

Total _____

☐ Check or money order   ☐ Visa   ☐ Mastercard

Card # _____ Exp. _____

Signature _____

Call our Toll Free order line: 1.888.267.4446
Fax your order to: 415.898.1434
Order online: www.**originpress/celestia**

Please make your check payable and return to:

Origin Press
1122 Grant Avenue, Suite C, Novato, CA 94945

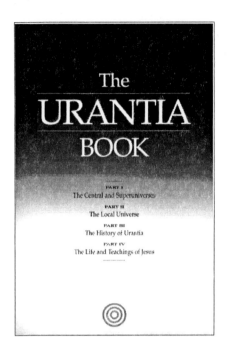

The
URANTIA
BOOK

PART I
The Central and Superuniverses
PART II
The Local Universe
PART III
The History of Urantia
PART IV
The Life and Teachings of Jesus

The Urantia Book

"The Fifth Epochal Revelation"

available online at:

www.ikosmos.com/TheUrantiaBook